"As they say in the North, I'm fixin' to pitch a fit that'll drive a preacher to drink a butter-covered biscuit at how funny Corey and Trae's book is. It really is. Their travelogue of the American South from the mouths American Southerners who are also comedians makes for a truly unique and first-time-ever accomplishment. Sure, it's not landing a piloted spacecraft to Mars, discovering a new element, or curing cancer (or anywhere close), but still it's the most fun you'll have reading or listening to a book this year, and fuckin' A—you'll learn something. Now go git it!"

—JOEL McHALE

COMEDIAN. ACTOR. AND TV HOST

ROUND HERE

AND

OVER YONDER

ROUND HERE

— AND —

OVER YONDER

A FRONT-PORCH
TRAVEL GUIDE BY
TWO PROGRESSIVE HILLBILLIES
(YES, THAT'S A THING)

TRAE CROWDER AND
COREY RYAN FORRESTER

HARPER
HORIZON

ISBN 978-1-4041-1755-6 (Ebook)
ISBN 978-1-4041-1754-9 (HC)

Library of Congress Control Number: 2023932915

Printed in the United States of America
23 24 25 26 27 LBC 5 4 3 2 1

From Trae: For Spook, who dreamed of such travels.

From Corey: To Danny Pye, for teaching me to treat everyone with kindness and to see things from a different point of view. If you were wrong and you're up there somewhere, I know you're smiling down and are proud of me. Go Dolphins.

CONTENTS

CONTENTS

INTRODUCTION

PONDERIN' THE YONDERIN'

We both grew up in small Southern towns. While we abhor a great many of the stereotypes and jokes thrown our way by people whose only claim at superiority is being born farther north, we can't deny all of them as being untrue. Granted, nothing is true for *all* people, but the notion that people in small towns never seem to leave said small towns is backed up by data, at least in our limited research on the subject. Now, it's stupid to assume that people choose not to travel just because they are content seeing the same cow store every day. As with most things in life, it's a financial thing. For example, Trae never took a single trip or vacation as a kid—but when he graduated high school, he and his buddies pooled all their money and set forth to the nicest place they could think of: Daytona Beach, Florida. How adorably white-trash is that? He certainly wanted to travel though. When you grow up in a place like Clay County, Tennessee, you tend to spend a lot of time daydreaming about a place like Somewhere Else.

Corey had traveled a bit more than Trae, but still, suffice it to say that before the two of us were fortunate enough to be able to sell tickets all across the country, we hadn't really seen much of the world. Sure, we'd been to a few beaches and various college football towns, and on occasion had been forced to travel to another, sometimes even smaller, Southern town to attend a family reunion or funeral.

Mark Twain wrote, "Travel is fatal to prejudice, bigotry and narrow-mindedness,"[1] and with that we could not agree more. We've found that doing stand-up, or being in the entertainment business in general, is a perfect way to experience new cultures and have your own childhood beliefs taken to task. Hell, when you first start doing stand-up, you don't even have to travel to other parts of the country to learn about their culture because if your home club is decent enough, people from all over the country will come to you! This was certainly our experience. To say it in the form of a joke: A Jewish feller, a purple-haired lesbian, an inner-city Black kid, and a redneck all walk into a bar. They heard there was an open mic.

Art brings people together; what can we say?

Trae grew up around a Black community, and while Corey's first cousins are Black, they didn't really live that close, so the first time Corey regularly hung out with people who didn't look exactly like him was in comedy clubs. Same goes for gay people, Asians of all types, drag queens, transgender women and men, you name it. The two of us have always considered ourselves a little more progressive than our accents may have you believe, but that line of thinking might've been stifled had we not been constantly challenged and had opportunities to hear other people's points of view.

We've also always been fascinated with stereotypes, perhaps because we belong to the group of people that is far and away the most fun to stereotype (no snark here—it's just objectively true). The ways people are different based on where they grew up (and the ways in which they are *not* different) have always been fascinating to us. And now, after the last few years spent on the road, we have a wealth of firsthand experience with it. Experience we felt was worth documenting in a fair way. The pages that follow are just our stories and opinions as we've lived and perceived them. We would never claim to be experts on any of the regions in these chapters. We are merely wandering jesters, chronicling for posterity the way of things, people, and places as we see it.

With that in mind, we've divided this guide into three parts. In "Part 1: Round Here," we introduce you to where we're from, the South. "Part 2:

---

1. Yes, we know. According to the internet, every quote is a Mark Twain quote, but this one actually is. It's from his book *The Innocents Abroad*. And yes, y'all, we read.

Over Yonder" features our thoughts on traveling around the rest of America. And "Part 3: Yonder Yonder" takes y'all with us as we go across the pond for the first time to visit England and Scotland.

This book is meant to be funny. It's meant to be entertaining. But at the end of the day, we hope you might take away more than just laughs. It is true that we are all different, and because of that, jokes can be made—and boy, are there plenty in the following pages. But we all have the same problems. Problems with money, disease, heartbreak, careers, family, our favorite sports team shitting the bed once again. We may at times react to these things in different ways, but *different* is not a synonym for *bad*, and we are both glad our families instilled that belief in us from a young age. Turns out our career choices, as crazy as they seem to some, have helped reinforce that belief too.

This book is not a history book. This book is told from the perspective of two Southern boys who got lucky and are able to see farther than Mammaw's front porch. There may be some things in this book that you don't agree with, and that's fine. I'm certain if we lived in your area longer, then we'd have a different perspective on it, but we are merely passing through—passing through on our never-ending journey not to prove how different we all are but instead to be reminded of how we are all the same. Everybody farts, y'all!

PART 1

ROUND HERE

THE SOUTH

Like most Southerners, we have a very complicated relationship with our homeland. The relationship is defined by the dichotomy at its center, the one every son or daughter of the South understands: pride and shame. We're not the first to point this out, nor is this the first time we've talked about it, but it's nearly impossible to discuss our feelings on the matter in any other framework. All Southerners exist somewhere on the pride/shame spectrum. Some of us live near the extremes. The gay intellectual who worked tirelessly to lose his accent and lives in perpetual fear of his fellow Brooklyn-based academics one day finding out that he grew up in—*gasp!*—Alabama? He's way down at the shame end of the spectrum. The fire-and-brimstone Tennessee preacher who named his children after Confederate generals, however, is plumb down at the other end: pure pride. Most of us, though, exist somewhere in the middle, and our position on the spectrum may not be absolute. Maybe it vacillates wildly depending on the circumstances. If the subject of conversation is Dolly Parton, we swing

1

multiple standard deviations back toward pride. If the subject of conversation is, on the other hand, pretty much any of our elected officials, we'll be dialing up the shame. That's just how it works.

We think (and hope) you'll find generous helpings of the two attributes applied fairly in the following section. There's a lot to be proud of about the South and some of its finer destinations, and we've tried to celebrate that fact. On the occasions when shame rears its ugly head, as it was always bound to do, we've endeavored to be honest. We don't know any other way to go about it.

A disclaimer (and really this applies to the entire book): All we can do is write about our own experiences with these places and the people in them. We know what it's like to be from the South in general, but despite what many would have you believe, Mississippi and Tennessee are not the same. New Orleans, Nashville, and Charleston are all lovely Southern cities, and while culturally they share some qualities, they are also exceedingly different from one another. Spending time in a given place is not the same thing as living there, let alone being from there. We are well aware of that, which is why, before conjuring the following pages, we made it a point to speak with friends of ours who are natives, lest we make a town out to be something it is not simply because we caught it on a bad trip (or got too drunk, or just did dumb things while we were there, both of which are distinct possibilities). Still, that's no guarantee that some of you won't reach the chapter devoted to your hometown and find yourself thinking, *Well, I don't know what in the world gave them* that *idea*. We understand that with a tome of this nature, that's likely inevitable. But two things we can promise you: First, we have made every effort to be as fair as possible, and second, this is all, every last bit of it, coming from a place of sincere love.

With all that said, we begin with the region closest to our hearts (which, by the way, you are free to bless as you see fit), the place we have and always will call home: the American South.

ATLANTA, GEORGIA

WHAT THEIR MOTTO SHOULD BE: We Promise We'll Figure Out the Interstate Soon!

WHAT TO PACK: Several audiobooks for the commute.

WHAT TO EAT AND DRINK AND WHERE: For our money on food or drink, it's hard to beat the tastes and the atmosphere of the Brick Store Pub in Decatur. Try the gussied-up crackers.

WHAT NOT TO MISS: The Ponce City Market is one of the best public markets our country has to offer with a food hall, bars, etc. And while we may be biased, it's hard to have a bad time at the Punchline Comedy Club—one of the oldest and most successful clubs in the world!

Atlanta is a classic example of a city we point to and say, "Does *this* not count as the South?" when people not from round here go on about how everything below the Mason-Dixon Line ain't nothing but dip-spittin', cousin-banging, truck-driving ne'er-do-wells. For what it's worth, it is possible to do all that anywhere, and our Atlanta people are certainly capable, but this city is just so much more! Atlanta's role in the civil rights movement has been invaluable, as have many of its cultural contributions, made possible largely by the diversity afforded to a place that acted as the terminus of a major railroad system. Of course, regardless of how much great hip-hop, food, or, for God's sake, Coca-Cola comes out of Atlanta, many currently only regard it as that place "where traffic is very bad" *or* "where that Yankee went full pyro during the war!"

I suppose I can imagine an outsider's perspective—someone whose only knowledge of the South comes from the show *COPS* or news footage of tornado survivors.[1] They see a place like Atlanta, full of vibrance and culture and pants that fit, and think to themselves, *How did this clearly Northern city get teleported into Possumville?* But once again, may we scream into the void: "Why doesn't this count as the South?!"

To us, it don't get much more Southern than wearing a Braves hat, sippin' a cold Coca-Cola[2] on your front porch, and reminiscing about the 1996 Olympics. All brought to you in part by Atlanta, Georgia, baby! During the nineties, the Atlanta Braves was America's team! You reckon that's why people don't wanna count it as the South? They don't want to reconcile with the fact that when they rooted for Larry "Chipper" Jones as he went yard over Josías Manzanillo in the ninth inning to beat the Mets (something he would make a habit out of), it made a bunch of Earnhardt-lovin', light-beer-chuggin' good ol' boys happy for the first time since Skynyrd's plane went down?

A quick aside from Corey: The city of Atlanta means a great deal to me because of the many folks in the area who helped me get a start in stand-up, but before that it was already branded in my heart forever due to my Granny Bain's love for the Atlanta Braves and the countless hours I spent sitting crisscross applesauce[3] on the floor watching games with her. I knew all the players and most of the stats, and between innings we would pass the time by tossing a pair of her rolled-up pantyhose back and forth.[4] Everyone knew Granny was the world's biggest Braves fan, but that didn't stop her sister-in-law, my aunt Pauline (pronounced *Aint* Pauline), from calling her on the phone soon as every game started. Aunt Pauline's husband, Herschell, being an elderly white man in the southeastern United States, was also a huge Braves fan, and Pauline would get bored during the games. I told Granny

---

1. They seem to only kill the pretty ones with teeth, based on who's left to talk to the news anyway.
2. Pronounced "Cocola."
3. Call me "woke" all you want, but you look me in the eye and tell me that ain't a more fun way to say it!
4. It was softer than a ball, and we couldn't risk knocking over the limited-edition John Smoltz Coke bottles.

4

many times she could just let it ring, but Granny was from the first generation to have phones and still adhered to the old ways of doing things, so not answering would be rude. Probably because back in her day, if you didn't answer the phone, people assumed you had been eaten by a wolf. Anyhoo, Pauline would call, and Granny would start in on her Southern Baptist style of cussing, which, if you aren't familiar, involved removing only the letter *i* from the word *shit* so you knew what she was saying, but it would still trick God. It'd go something like this.

Phone ringing.

"Ahhh shhhtt. You know that's Pauline! Dagnabbit, she always calls right when the Braves are coming on, and tonight's my favorite night! Greg Maddux is pitching, which means Eddie Pérez is catching, and you know I love to watch him squat!"[5] Granny would then proceed to listen to Aunt Pauline talk about Pond's Cold Cream or some shit for *four hours*!

Well, needless to say, Pauline died not too long after that (as old people are wont to do), and her funeral happened to fall on a day when the Braves had a doubleheader. So we had to hurry back home, natch. I will never forget this as long as I live. I'm sittin' there on the floor, crisscross applesauce, tossing pantyhose up in the air to myself when the phone rings. Granny goes to answer it, stops, laughs, and says, "Well, we know that ain't Pauline!"

RIP Pauline, and RIP Granny Bain. Hope y'all both watched 'em win the 2021 World Series together.

If you are reading this book from the future, you probably already know the truth of what we're about to say. If not, let us go on the record stating that Atlanta will one day be thought of as Hollywood Junior. Don't just take it from us. The state of Georgia has already been dubbed the Hollywood of the South for quite a while now, and Atlanta has pulled more than its fair share of the weight toward that achievement. Back in 2011, some itty-bitty zombie show you may have heard of called *The Walking Dead* was filming in the four-thousand-person town of Senoia, Georgia, and the Hollywood elites quickly realized, "Oh, wow, it ain't just no-teeth math-haters down here. There is also some quite beautiful and wondrous topography! Who would have ever guessed?" Thus a slew of studios started to crop up in the Atlanta area, and not just rinky-dink studios, mind you. We are talking

5. OK, I may have made that part up.

Tyler Perry's studio and some freakin' Marvel movies! Whattaya think about that, ya elite bastards?

Another quick aside from Corey: I was fortunate enough to have a small part in *Zombieland: Double Tap* because the director, Ruben Fleischer, had worked with us on another project. It was a supercool day, and I even got my makeup done with Jesse Eisenberg! I brought my dad with me because I like to take advantage of any opportunity to show off and prove I was *not* an idiot for doing all those free open mics and driving eighteen-hour round trips to make twenty bucks at the start of my career.[6]

Well, after I got my makeup done, I headed over to the tent that had been set up for us all to hang out in, and as I walked up, I heard the sound of my dad holding court while some unknown woman laughed hysterically. I threw the curtain open to reveal my dad and his new BFF Abigail Breslin watching stand-up comedy clips and bonding harder than he and I ever have. (I may sound dramatic here, but it was pretty intense.)

After that, Ruben told me he wanted to make the rounds and introduce me to everyone else. I was, of course, stoked. As we made our way out of the tent, we turned the corner, and I was immediately starstruck. There she was—the girl I fell in love with as a senior in high school during her break-out performance as Jules in the Judd Apatow classic *Superbad*. That's right: Emma freakin' Stone. I was very nervous but then remembered, *Dude, you're with the director. It's all good. You belong here.* She approached us with that trademark smile, and Ruben began the introduction.

"Hey, Emma, I'd like you to meet a friend of mine, Corey Forrester, a very funny comedian. We are actually working on a pilot together. He's going to be playing one of the hippies that get thrown off the roof today!"

I never felt cooler in my life.

That flame was extinguished, however, when Emma replied, "Oh, you must be Dale's son. Nice to meet you!" *Sigh.* No matter where we go, the man makes an impression!

Anyway, we went to the set where a bunch of extras were playing cornhole, and I got the final touches on my wig. About that time a helicopter very loudly approached and landed in a marked-off area to the side of the craft service table. Out walked Woody Harrelson, already in costume as his

---

6. Yes. Yes. I absolutely was an idiot.

character, Tallahassee. He made his way to the set, shaking everyone's hand as he went, stopped by the cornhole board, and single-handedly beat the shit out of one of the teams that was playing. Then he walked over to his mark, nailed his scene in one take, did another for safety, hopped back onto his helicopter, and was gone as quickly as he'd arrived. A Hollywood story I got to experience in Georgia because everyone has finally realized how badass Atlanta and the surrounding area are to film in.

Atlanta also has one of the best but low-key comedy communities in the entire world. Much like in the film industry, comedians no longer have to choose only between New York and Los Angeles when trying to decide how to further their comedy careers. Between a heavy rotation of wonderful independently run shows (Beer & Comedy Night at SweetWater Brewery, the 1AM Secret Show at Smith's Olde Bar, the great shows at the Star Community Bar, etc.) and the nationally recognized joints like the Laughing Skull Lounge and the Punchline Comedy Club, they have excellent options all over Atlanta.[7]

The Punchline Comedy Club opened in 1982, and two years later an unknown comic at the time by the name of Jeff Foxworthy would win the Great Southeastern Laugh-Off on his first night onstage. Jeff would go on to do pretty well in the industry, if you ask us. The Punchline has a sentimental history with us as well, as it was home to the first official show of the WellRED Comedy Tour.[8] No matter where our careers take us, we will always look back fondly on the night three nobodies[9] began a fruitful career in the business and were graced by the presence of first-ballot Hall of Fame comedian and Atlanta's own George Wallace.

Home to movie studios, a legendary comedy scene, and some of the most groundbreaking hip-hop acts in the country, it's safe to say that Atlanta backs up its claim as the capital of the South and should absolutely be taken into consideration when anyone starts jawing off about how there ain't nothing down here but backward politicians, deep-fried Twinkies, and toddlers sippin' Mountain Dew from jelly jars. Long live the A.

---

7. Arguably where comedy in the South started.
8. The stand-up comedy tour consisting of Trae Crowder, Drew Morgan, and Corey Ryan Forrester.
9. We'd already been doing stand-up well over a decade, but no one was really showing up then, so it barely counts.

HELEN, GEORGIA

WHAT THEIR MOTTO SHOULD BE: Overalls Meet Lederhosen

WHAT TO PACK: Boots and a bunch of shit you can throw away so you'll have more room in your suitcase for all the beer steins you accidentally take from the bars.

WHAT TO EAT AND DRINK AND WHERE: Go to the patio on the river at the Troll Tavern (best Reuben on earth) and King Ludwig's Biergarten in the center of town (for the pretzels). Then hit up the Heidelberg for schnitzel and half-liter pints overlooking the biergarten. Oh, and the littleneck clams at Hofbrauhaus . . . Damn, this place is tasty.

WHAT NOT TO MISS: Duh, Oktoberfest, baby!

We know that when a lot of you think of the South, you think of racism and a history of violent oppression toward a specific group of people—but don't you worry, because Helen, Georgia, has a ton of German culture, and the Germans have never done anything wrong! Located in the Blue Ridge Mountains, one of the most gorgeous areas on planet Earth, Helen hosts an annual Oktoberfest and has many Bavarian-style houses, bars, and restaurants, as well as tubing, hiking, and gold panning. It's like going to a lederhosen-laced fantasy camp while still being close enough to biscuits and gravy to feel safe. For everyone who has said, "It would be nice to visit the South while sorta feeling like we are somewhere different," Helen is the place for you!

Well, it's not the South as far as the food goes, but it still has plenty of the white-trash accoutrements to make the most NASCAR-loving of your brothers feel right at home, even if he is otherwise averse to change. Wanna get an airbrushed T-shirt to commemorate your family reunion? You can do that in Helen. Wanna spend a couple of mortgage payments on fudge that never quite makes it back to the people you bought it for? You can do that in Helen. Wanna get drunk and listen to a lady in all-black biker gear tell you how she fucked the fourth-most-wanted man in America? Yeah . . . you can do that in Helen.

Here's Corey with an anecdote that paints a pretty accurate picture of Helen. In early 2022, my wife, Amber (who is a second-grade teacher—that'll be important later), and I decided to take a trip to Helen to get away from the fast-paced life we live in Chickamauga, Georgia (watching paint dry from our porch while listening to the cicadas bone each other). Amber had been to Helen as a kid, but I was a newbie and was very excited to see the town my wife described as "Gatlinburg if Hitler was the mayor."

Heading to Helen from where we live, you drive through some of the most beautiful scenery imaginable: mountains, streams, homemade yard signs that speak of unprecedented election fraud.[1] God's tapestry on full display. One thing you will not find, however, is a cell signal,[2] so be sure to download a couple of Allman Brothers albums before you head out. Just before we got there, we passed a place called Babyland General Hospital—which, Amber informed me, is where Cabbage Patch Kids are born. It's nice to know that if we somehow can't have kids, we can just go right up the road to adopt.

We finally came up over the hill entering Helen proper, and I don't know what we expected, but it was absolute chaos. Bumper-to-bumper traffic and people runnin' around the streets drunker than Winston Churchill after the Siege of Sidney Street.[3] We later found out that we had decided

---

1. I promise I won't get any more political than this.
2. Or a copy of *Infinite Jest* by David Foster Wallace.
3. Bet you didn't expect this hillbilly book to hit you with Dennis Miller–style history references, did ya? Well, *we know stuff too.*

to visit Helen during the final days of Fasching, which is a sort of German Mardi Gras. Oh good. I've always said that what redneck tourists need is an officially sanctioned reason to get shit-faced and show their asses. We decided, "Well, if you can't beat 'em, join 'em. Here we go!"

We started off the first day trying to pace ourselves because, regardless of our maturity levels, our bodies ain't the same age we act. I thought to myself, *How 'bout instead of drinking, you just go overboard on food?* Well, as it turns out, nothing quite washes a Reuben down like seventeen German beers.[4]

"Maybe if we go schnitzel hopping, we can soak up some of this alcohol?" my wife said, coining the phrase "schnitzel hopping." After a full day being as American as we could in a German setting, my wife decided that no trip out of town was complete until I whipped her ass at mini golf (I'm paraphrasing), so we decided to walk to the course and have one last drink at the tent right across from it. I ordered some sort of fascist-sounding beer, and my wife, being both blond and from the South, fulfilled her duty of trying to drink every last berry-flavored seltzer in existence.[5] We sat down at a wooden table just as one of the locals was tuning his guitar, readying himself for a night of really sweet Drive-By Truckers covers. Hell, yeah.

'Bout then I noticed a woman, twenty years or so our senior, sitting at the table in front of us. She looked as though my wife had traveled back in time to visit us from the future. Then she opened her mouth.

"I tell you what, I'm 'bout to fucking quit teaching! It ain't the kids so much as it is the parents and all their bullshit!"

Oh my God. It *was* my wife from the future! I started laughing hysterically, and it caught her attention. My wife told her we were sorry but that she was also a teacher and knew how she felt. In case you don't know how teachers roll, this mutual commiseration was the foundation of what turned into an instant friendship between the two.

She came and sat down at our table, and it turned out that even though she was not from our area, her first job nearly thirty years before had actually been at the elementary school my wife and I both attended. She had not been back since. Before I could even process what a wild coincidence that

---

4. This particular meal shall henceforth be known as a blitzkrieg.
5. If you're a seltzer company looking for a new spokeswoman, call my wife. She'll answer once she wakes up from lying facedown on the beach.

was, her friend (another blond teacher who looked like my wife) stumbled over wearing a leather jacket, high-heeled leather boots, and, despite the sun having set, a pair of jewel-studded aviator sunglasses, and said, "When I first started teaching in Texas, my school was 82 percent white, and now it's 82 percent Indians!"[6]

No one really knew how to respond, but I took a stab at it by saying, "Well, I bet the cafeteria food is better now!"

She laughed and explained that she didn't mean anything bad by it; she was just stating facts. We then bonded over the shared knowledge that with our accents, almost *everything* we say sounds racist unless otherwise explained.

Of the many skills you must develop when doing comedy in a group, one of the hardest is knowing when to sit back and let the other person have the floor. Luckily I do have this skill now and could tell this lady was about to go on a heater!

She took another swig of her Crown and Sprite and started telling us that being a teacher was what finally gave her the stability to kick a meth addiction. "You can't be coming to school all geeked off your ass. They look down on that type of shit." And how!

She led us through the many sordid chapters of her life that had brought her to this moment. She introduced us to her new man, dressed head to toe like a *Sons of Anarchy* extra, whom I will not name for fear of repercussions.

The beers kept flowing, and so did the stories of growing up religious in Texas but never feeling like she truly fit in. "I did a complete one-eighty, I tell you what," she said, hiccupping. "I went from being a preacher's wife to being a Mexican cartel *whore*!"[7] Her words, not mine. She told us about the first time she quit a job: "I told my boss, 'You can fuck off, cuz me and these bull dykes are going to Señor Frog's!'" Her words, not—you get it.

Her man eventually realized that if he didn't get her back to the room soon, she might hold court all night or confess to myriad crimes they had most assuredly committed together. So we all took pictures, had a final shot of whiskey, and said our goodbyes.

We never got around to that game of mini golf.

---

6. Like the actually-from-India kind, not the we-just-call-'em-that-despite-knowing-full-well-for-hundreds-of-years-now-that-they're-not-actually-from-India kind.

7. A tale as old as time.

ROUND HERE AND OVER YONDER

If you are ever near the Blue Ridge Mountains and get an insatiable craving for German food, cheap screen-printed sweatshirts, and more pecan divinity than you can fit in the trunk of a Panzerkampfwagen, then we highly suggest checking out this little slice of lunacy they call Helen, Georgia!

NASHVILLE, TENNESSEE

WHAT THEIR MOTTO SHOULD BE: Be Your Best or Do Your Worst . . . Either Is Fine

WHAT TO PACK: Earplugs for the endless barrage of radio pop country that will be assaulting you while downtown . . . Unless you're into that sorta thing, in which case, go off, bayba.[1] Also the cowboy-est cowboy hat you can find. You know the deal.

WHAT TO EAT AND DRINK AND WHERE: Hot chicken, y'all! An absolutely unassailable way to render your arteries useless. The options are endless, but Hattie B's is probably the best known.

WHAT NOT TO MISS: The high-caliber comedy shows put on by Zanies, one of the best clubs in the business. Especially the weekend before Christmas. (That's when we're there.) Also the Opry or whatever, we guess, but mostly Zanies.

N ashville is one of the most "tale of two cities" types of towns in all of the South, and probably the country. Your experiences in Music City can and will vary wildly. You can soak up the rich cultural history of one

---

1. This is how we say *baby*. Sounds better this way.

of the South's chief artistic melting pots . . . *or* you can stay downtown honky-tonkin' and come away thinking the whole city is nothing more than a drunken, middle-aged Tammy wrecking a motor scooter into a party of vomiting Midwestern bachelorettes.[2] The choice is yours. Some of our very best artists and individuals have chosen to call Nashville their home, and some of our very worst dummies and drunkards have chosen to call it their toilet. So it goes.

First things first: Nashville is *awesome.* There's a reason it has become one of Those Cities in recent years, an It Town that people from all over tend to gravitate toward. But we'll get to the visitors in a minute. For now let's focus on the city itself and the people who live there. Nashville is a big city that doesn't *feel* like a big city. It features unlimited sights to see and things to do but without the crushing metropolis feel of New York or the endless megasprawl vibe of Los Angeles.[3] Nashville is vibrant and filled to the brim with *wildly* talented people. The easiest way to see this for yourself is to go to a karaoke bar in Nashville. Literally any karaoke bar. We guarantee you will be blown away. Some unassuming long-haired stoner-type dude will step to the mic and you'll think, *Oh, great, some guy mumbling through a Doors song. Just what the night was missing.* Until he absolutely *murders* "Midnight in Montgomery," and then you think, *Holy shit, is that George Jones's grandbaby? I think we just saw George Jones's grandbaby.*

But it's not just singers. With all the recording studios and labels in town, there must be more world-class musicians in Nashville per capita than anywhere else on earth. You can't throw a guitar pick in a dive bar without hitting some kind of damn virtuoso. That old beat-up feller in the corner with the shoe-leather face and threadbare denim jacket? Yeah, that sumbitch can probably set a Dobro *on fire,* boy. They don't call it Music City for nothin'.

Nashville is also a major producer of two of the greatest Southern commodities: charm and hospitality. Nashville has one of the most distinct vibes of any city in America. Pretty much anyone from anywhere in this country has an idea about Nashville: It's twangy, two-stepping, melodic, a little bit

---

2. We've really gotta stop talking about Corey's wife like that.
3. Same amount of spandex in recent years though.

brokenhearted, and more than a little bit drunk. As for the hospitality, y'all know how we are in the South. We pride ourselves on smiling at people and being kind and blessing people's hearts and sittin' a spell and all that type of stuff. Or at least we pride ourselves on doing all that *in public*, before talking all manner of shit behind your back. But we digress. People are nice in Nashville. There's a sense of community, and the locals are proud. But as we mentioned, Nashville has become a de rigueur destination city in recent years, which means two things: tourists and transplants. And as anyone from a place that attracts other people will tell you: Ain't nothin' can mess up a town quicker than tourists and transplants.

It seems like Nashville draws all different types of people. Or, at least . . . all different types of *white* people. We're not saying other ethnicities don't like Nashville; we're just saying white people loooooove Nashville. Drawn to it like arrhythmic moths to a farmer's market flame, they are. Seriously, it doesn't matter what type of white you are, there is something in Nashville for you. Mustachioed hipster? Come to East Nashville and play a board game in a coffee shop! White trash? Go to Kid Rock's bar and start a fight with your colostomy bag![4] Crypto bro? No state income tax, dawg! Masshole? Go to a hotel bar and assume everyone is cool with your racist jokes! Seriously, if you're white, you've either been to Nashville or you're planning to go. Why do you think they call 'em *honky*-tonks?

But we're not leaving you out, white women. Far from it. In truth no one, and we mean *no one*, loves Nashville more than white women. Honestly, if you've never attended a Nashville bachelorette weekend wearing matching boots and a custom-made shirt festooned with dicks and gotten so drunk you fell off the pedal pub on Broadway and then blacked out while crying before waking up for brunch at Biscuit Love and Instagramming it, can you really call yourself a white woman?[5] We think not.

Ah, Instagram and brunch. If there is a white-womanier way to spend a midmorning, we've yet to hear of it. And both are *huge* in Nashville. Hell, at this point, Nashville's economy is roughly 63 percent Instagram-and-brunch. And we get it: There is no better place on God's green earth to eat a gussied-up biscuit and get drunk before noon than Music City, USA, and

---

4. This really happened, by the way.
5. OK, for real, this is the *last time* we will mention Corey's wife.

if brunch occurs without a white woman there to Instagram it, did it even really happen?

At this point you may have picked up on the fact that we're not so much talking about Nashville the city as we are talking about the people who visit . . . so we're just going to keep doing that. We've established that people come to Nashville for a lot of reasons—but in our experience, the number one thing people come to Nashville *to do* is: cosplay as a Southerner.

Nashville is like Southerner Fantasy Camp. No matter where you're from, you can come on down to Nashville, buy some three-for-one boots and a pearl-button plaid, and go out there and yeehaw and bless hearts until the cows come home. Which is precisely what people do: get absolutely hammered on bushwhackers[6] and hoot and holler and scream along to a Luke Bryan song. And we're gonna be honest with you here, as Southerners and Tennesseans . . . that behavior is a little weird, and it's a little weird for us to go downtown and see an ocean of Yankees looking like they're auditioning for the role of someone's cousin Kenny Ray. But maybe we're wrong. After all, is it really any different from donning a lei when you land in Honolulu? Although honestly, when you *really* think about it, that's kinda jacked up too. Look, all we're saying is, you don't see either of us going to the Jersey Shore in a tank top and spray tan trying to arm wrestle a damn DJ, OK?

We know we're being a little pissy here, but this type of cartoonishly on-the-nose stereotyping has an effect on us. The last time Trae went honky-tonkin' was in Nashville back in early 2018 with a camera crew made up entirely of Californians, and on the last night of the trip, they all wanted to go downtown for the Full Nashville Experience. As someone who grew up going to Nashville, Trae was to be their guide, of course. Naturally, he tried to steer them away from Broadway and all its devilry, but they could not be deterred. So downtown they went. Here's what Trae has to say about that night.

We had already bounced around to a few different bars and heard a few different very talented cover bands doing their back-roads-and-blue-jeans thing, but we finally settled in at The Stage. By this point I was fairly drunk

---

6. If you don't know what a bushwhacker is, it's basically a milkshake that gets you drunk. Don't judge. It's hot, we're fat, and gettin' drunk hits.

and was spending most of my time seething over the Midwestern frat boys wearing farm clothes and butchering some Kenny Chesney songs. I wanted to grab the people I was with, shake them, and yell, "This is not Nashville! This is just what *they think* Nashville is! Please don't tell California!" or something equally well-adjusted. But I didn't do that. I just raged inward in quiet desperation, as is my custom. And then, the cover band launched into "Courtesy of the Red, White and Blue" by Toby Keith, as I believe all Nashville cover bands have been contractually required to do ever since 9/11. Everyone in the bar was singing "We'll put a boot in yer ass, it's the American way" at the top of their lungs while some ol' boy in full-length camo stood atop the bar, waving an American flag back and forth. (I assume the bar kept this dude on retainer.)

I couldn't take it anymore, so I started screaming, "TOBY KEITH IS A REGISTERED DEMOCRAT! TOBY KEITH IS A REGISTERED DEMOCRAT!"[7] until I was forcibly removed by a bouncer who looked like security for Florida Georgia Line. I asked him to name me two Billy Joe Shaver songs or go fuck himself. He declined both requests and hurled me into the street, at which point I realized my honky-tonkin' days were probably behind me. And while that may be true, I'll stop loving the city of Nashville on the day they place a wreath upon my door and carry me away, by God.

---

7. Before you ask, I know this *was* true at one point, but anyway it ain't really the point and I didn't go to Toby Keith school. All right?

MUSCLE SHOALS, ALABAMA

WHAT THEIR MOTTO SHOULD BE: Alabama Sounds Good! (No, seriously.)

WHAT TO PACK: You can wear any damn thing you want as long as you can make yourself say "Roll Tide."

WHAT TO EAT AND DRINK AND WHERE: Y'all, Alabama has made BBQ sauce out of mayonnaise. And the whole rest of the South went, "Damn, why didn't we think of that?"

WHAT NOT TO MISS: In Muscle Shoals proper, the studio tours are 'bout all there is. They're incredible though.

The thing most people know about Muscle Shoals, or at least the thing everyone damn well *should* know about it, is that it is a hotbed for sweet, sweet Southern sounds. The area is home to two world-renowned recording studios: FAME Studios and Muscle Shoals Sound Studio, which, combined, have produced recordings for Aretha Franklin, Otis Redding, the Rolling Stones, Bob Dylan, Paul Simon, Lynyrd Skynyrd, and many, *many* more. It could be argued that Muscle Shoals is the origin point for the "cross-pollination" of American musical styles—i.e., mixing white music and Black music. Sun Records founder Sam Phillips was from the area, and he credited the local radio station for playing both types of artists and inspiring him to meld the two in his future works with Elvis, among others.

The merging of these musical styles would come to define the "Muscle Shoals Sound," as well as much of America's musical tapestry. Some of the best music this country has ever made originated in the South, and some of the best music the South has ever made originated in Muscle Shoals, Alabama. That's a damn fine legacy.

Now, let's talk about the place itself. So this may be just an us thing, but we always *assumed* Muscle Shoals was on the Gulf of Mexico, along Alabama's southern coast. The name sounds super nautical, right? Sure, the word *mussel* is misspelled in this context, but this is Alabama we're talking about—not a place typically known for its aptitude for spelling or context[1]—so that doesn't really throw you off. Also, we should admit that we have absolutely no idea what a *shoal* is, but it sounds like some beach stuff. So you put the two words together and—*bam!*—a beach full of salty shell meat; that's Muscle Shoals.

So we always had this fairly well-defined image of Muscle Shoals in our minds growing up: a Southern beachfront music-topia. A place where down-home virtuosos sat barefoot in the sand, overlooking the ocean, Hemingway daiquiris in hand, dreaming up the songs that would define entire eras, regions, and ways of life. This was how we, and in particular Trae, always pictured the nigh-mythical place that was Muscle Shoals, Alabama. With this in mind, let's hear from Trae in his own words.

I married a lovely woman from Wayne County, Tennessee, which is an extremely rural part of Tennessee located right on the Alabama line. The closest town of any size to where she grew up is across the border—Florence, Alabama. For anybody who grew up in a truly tiny town, you know how y'all had a larger town you went to for stuff? Not regular stuff like groceries but bigger stuff like school clothes, braces, Cheddar Bay Biscuits, etc.? You know, the town with the movie theater and the Walmart Supercenter—i.e., Basically the City, Far As Y'all Knew? That Town? All us ultrarural folk had That Town. Well, in Wayne County, That Town is Florence, Alabama.

So shortly after meeting my wife, I was visiting her family with her, and we all took a big ol' Christmas shoppin' trip to Florence. (They got a Kohl's and everything, y'all. It's wild.) This was my first experience in Florence and . . . it was fine. Honestly, it reminded me of my own version of That

---

1. Calm down, Alabamians. Our states are super dumb too.

Town where I grew up.[2] I have a theory that every That Town is kind of the same: It has a struggling mall, a nice assortment of chain restaurants (though the ones that don't offer free bread are gonna have a rough go of it, bet), and probably a cow college.[3] You get the picture. Well, Florence fits that description to a T. And that T is a BURNING CROSS—no, I'm kidding. I kid, Alabama. Can't help myself.

Anyway, so I was in a prototypical Southern That Town, feeling right at home, wondering how much longer my future wife and mother-in-law were gonna be inside the Big Lots, and imagine my complete and utter astonishment when I spied a road sign that read "Muscle Shoals: 4 Miles." *What? That can't be right, can it? The Shangri-la of Southern musical culture is in* Florence? My brain refused to process it. I asked my would-be wife's uncle (the menfolk were waiting in the car, as is custom) in the manner of a kid who just saw a damn dinosaur-themed laser-tag billboard: "Muscle Shoals is here?! Can we go?!"

He flashed me a look of most sincere confusion and said, "Why would you want to go to Muscle Shoals? Nobody goes to Muscle Shoals."

"Uh, pretty sure the *Rolling Stones* go to Muscle Shoals."

"Muscle Shoals is trash."

And that was that. I spent the rest of the day trying to make sense of the absolute neutron bomb that had just been dropped on the very long-standing perception I had held for this place.

Let us make something clear: Muscle Shoals is *not* trash. Far from it. That's just Trae's trash in-laws doin' a little bit of good old-fashioned trash projection. Anyone of the whiskey-tango[4] persuasion will tell you that one of our people's favorite pastimes is talking about how trash some *other* group of trash people are. Think about it. If you're from a small town, I want you to imagine the small town next door. What are the people there like? They're trash, aren't they? Of course they are. Rich people do it, too, with each other's . . . paintings . . . and . . . stallions, or whatever. We assume. Anyway, that's not the point. The point is, Muscle Shoals is indeed one of the coolest places the South has to offer, and its juxtaposition to the larger area where it is located only amplifies that fact.

---

2. Cookeville, Tennessee, home of the nation's number one O'Charley's twenty-five years and counting.

3. Tennessee Tech class of 2008. Go Golden Eagles.

4. That means "white trash," and as a trailer baby, I'm allowed to say it.

Muscle Shoals is part of a larger region of North Alabama consisting of Muscle Shoals, Tuscumbia, Sheffield, and Florence, collectively known as the Shoals. And if you visit this area and look around without knowing any of the aforementioned history, you will absolutely think to yourself, *Yep. This sure is North Alabama.* Dollar stores, meat-and-threes, pro-life billboards, high school and college football paraphernalia, churches all over the damn place, and stunning, heart-stoppingly beautiful topography. The type of place where you expect to find exceptional BBQ and perhaps also a book burning (if there's time). No part of you would look around and think, *I bet this is one of American music's most historically significant places.*

In fact, according to locals, for a long time its significance probably wouldn't have been brought up. Up until relatively recently, the town's musical legacy was treated in much the same way that similar Southern towns might have treated the Resident Homosexual—i.e., sure, everyone is *aware* of it, but you just don't talk about that sort of thing. After all, rock-and-roll was of the devil, and North Alabama was a place for good, God-fearing Christian folks (and also racists). So what many would assume to be a badge of honor for any community was instead treated more like a dirty little secret. We know what you're thinking: Getting something bass-ackward? *Alabama?* Surely not. But it's true.

Thankfully this is no longer the case. Before we elaborate on that, we should first clarify that Trae's earlier assessment of Florence wasn't entirely fair. Much more than simply That Town, these days Florence, Alabama, is a burgeoning little It City, home to farm-to-table restaurants, art galleries, and fashion icon Billy Reid. Reid himself has played a large role in the cultural rejuvenation of the area, and many of his efforts have centered around highlighting the status and importance of Muscle Shoals's musical legacy. Between this and the popularity of the 2013 documentary *Muscle Shoals*, the area now wears its musical pride on its sleeve. Or, since this is Alabama, perhaps on the bare arm where a sleeve would otherwise be.

A final note on the Shoals. The area was the birthplace of both the "Father of the Blues" W. C. Handy and author, activist, and *hard-core socialist* Helen Keller. So next time you hear some hipster deride the Deep South as naught but a cultural wasteland, point to North Alabama as you tell them to kiss your ass.

OXFORD, MISSISSIPPI

WHAT THEIR MOTTO SHOULD BE: Get Drunk and Talk Like Foghorn Leghorn!

WHAT TO PACK: Seersucker. Just seersucker. Head to toe.

WHAT TO EAT AND DRINK AND WHERE: Can't go wrong with anything brown! Fried food and iced whiskey—what's not to love? For the fried food we recommend Mama Jo's.

WHAT NOT TO MISS: One of the best bookstores in the South—Square Books in downtown Oxford. Also in the fall you can dress up like an antebellum frat boy and prep for an Ole Miss loss by getting blind drunk in the Grove!

L isten, we want to make something clear: With many Southern stereotypes, we totally get it. Hell, we oftentimes feel the same way. It's easy to rely on stereotypes when you don't have much else to go on. As was the case for us when our travels first took us to Oxford, Mississippi.

Let's start with the state of Mississippi. The old joke in the South is that anytime an unfortunate statistic is thrown around,[1] all the other Southern states say to themselves, "Thank God for Mississippi." Which is to say, in

---

1. Poverty, literacy, heart disease, cornholin', etc.

many seemingly objective ways, Mississippi makes the rest of the South look like . . . uh, Norway? Somewhere nice, we're sayin'. Of course, we would point out that both the culinary and musical tapestry of this country would be *immeasurably* worse off if not for the Magnolia State, not to mention many other arguments we could make regarding Mississippi's merits. But this joke about Mississippi always being first for the bad stuff and last for the good stuff is undoubtedly *the perception*.

And then there's Oxford. The home of Ole Miss and William Faulkner. Sure, it's in Mississippi, but Oxford kind of has its own reputation, and that reputation is . . . pretty Foghorn Leghorn-y. Right? I mean, what do you picture when you think of Oxford? A bunch of white-haired professorial gentlemen in seersucker, walking around just *declaring* shit all the time,[2] probably about the Civil War or sweet potato pies or some such. The women all wear floppy hats and talk about horses a bunch. The sheriff knows everyone's name and is super friendly and/or sort of OK with certain murders probably. Everything feels a little more old-fashioned in Oxford.[3] Truly, this is a place where time stands still . . . at gunpoint, else they'll string time's ass up. That's Oxford, right?

That's definitely what we expected the first time we visited. But the reality is that Oxford is a certain breed of American city that happens to be among our very favorites: the Southern college town, or SCT. God, we love SCTs. They're essentially like other typical American college towns: There's art and culture and ideas and youth and thought and debate and progress . . . but in SCTs, all that stuff is metaphorically covered in gravy. SCTs are quintessentially Southern, but at the same time they fly right in the face of many of the South's worst stereotypes. And Oxford is a *great* Southern college town.

So when those regressive, old money–types of influence do crop up in Oxford, they are met with pushback. A few years ago, the Oxford school board had an innovative new proposal. They basically said, "What if the school districts were segregated based on family income? You see, that way children can be surrounded entirely by their equals and won't have to feel any discomfort based on how much money their parents make. Wouldn't

---

2. You know, like, "Well, I do declare! The silent obedience of this young debutante is mighty fine!"
3. Which is to say the racists are more smiley.

that be ideal? And no, this has nothing to do with *race*; it's about *income*. There's a difference!" Yeah. Pretty outrageous.

Personally, we have no idea how a sane person could fail to see the issues inherent in such a proposal. That'd be like the Oxford-Lafayette County Chamber of Commerce coming out and saying, "Hey, did y'all know that if you simply force people to work for you with zero compensation, you can make, like, *way* more money?!" And then someone says, "You mean like slavery?" and the chamber of commerce responds indignantly, "What?! No, nothing like slavery! We're just talkin' about *free labor*! Totally different things!" That's how patently absurd this school board proposal was. *But*, the point of the story is the Oxford community was outraged by it, shot the notion down with extreme resolve, and shamed the school board for their shortsightedness.

Oxford was also the first city in Mississippi to cease flying the former state flag because it included the Stars and Bars. And we know what you're thinking: *Wow, you want us to throw a parade for this place just because they stopped flying a Confederate flag?* That's not what we're saying. All we're saying is that Oxford, like most SCTs, has a history of being ahead of the curve, however skewed the curve might be in a state like Mississippi.

Oxford is also arguably the epicenter of Southern literature,[4] and there's a wonderful independent bookstore called Square Books on the . . . well, it's on the town square, and the inside of this place smells and feels the way an old Southern folk ballad sounds.[5] The Lyric Oxford, where we were lucky enough (and they were silly enough to allow us) to perform a comedy show, was originally Faulkner's stables and once housed one of the first motion picture theaters in the Southeast. Oxford is just one of those places with history dripping from every corner.[6]

We had a wonderful show in Oxford in front of a large crowd of progressive Southerners. However, we should probably point out that after said show, a drunk woman tried to punch Trae for giving the wrong answer to a Drive-By Truckers trivia question she had asked him.[7] And afterward,

---

4. The one creative arena wherein the South actually gets some credit.
5. The shared ingredient is murder.
6. Much of which is bloody and truly unfortunate, of course. Which, if you think about it, is sort of history's whole deal.
7. After all, it is still Mississippi.

some of Oxford's finest hosted us at their home for drinks and fried snacks. These people were pillars of the Oxford community—doctors and lawyers and professors and writers—and they treated us like kings. However, Trae is white trash, and they had a nice house with books in it, so he kept referring to the hosts as the "landed gentry" to their faces all night, which they weren't altogether fond of. Why did he do that? Because of stereotypes. He had it in his head that any fancy house in Oxford, Mississippi, must be some sort of haunted plantation presided over by an Old Money Blood Cult.[8] In Trae's defense, he was so drunk he cried himself to sleep listening to Conway Twitty that night.[9]

The point is this: We all give in to geographical stereotypes. That's totally fine, so long as you allow those perceptions to be altered by the actual experiences you have along the way.

---

8. A common mistake.
9. AGAIN.

SOUTHERN
TRAVEL BINGO

Look for an object, and the first one to five in a row/column/diagonal wins a Moon Pie.

SNAKE FLAG	ROADKILL	SPOT WHERE ROADKILL USED TO BE	ABANDONED VEHICLE WITH GRASS GROWING THROUGH IT	RESTAURANT SIGN WITH BIBLE VERSE ON IT
SKULL FLAG	MISSPELLED YARD SALE SIGN	LOCAL AMBULANCE-CHASING LAWYER'S CATCHPHRASE	BUMPER STICKER WITH A GUN ON IT	CHURCH SIGN THAT MAKES YOU FEEL LIKE YOU'RE GOING TO HELL
AMERICAN FLAG	PRO-LIFE BILLBOARD FEATURING A PRECIOUS BABY	BLESS YOUR HEART	BOX OF PUPPIES	BOILED PEANUTS FOR SALE
CONFEDERATE FLAG	GIGANTIC TRUCK DRIVEN BY A SMALL BLOND WOMAN	ELECTION AD FOR A CANDIDATE WITH THREE NAMES (E.G., BOBBY LEE BUFORD)	ROAD OR SCHOOL NAMED AFTER A FAMOUS SLAVE OWNER	SOMEBODY SELLIN' 'MATERS OUT OF A TRUCK
UNIVERSITY FLAG*	WELCOME SIGN FEATURING THE WORD *UNINCORPORATED*	SOMEBODY DRIVING A LAWN MOWER BUT NOT MOWING A LAWN**	T-SHIRT THAT SEEMS MAD AT YOU	GROUP OF MAMMAWS IN CHURCH CLOTHES

* Only counts if it's clearly there for football reasons and not stupid college reasons.
** A tractor is acceptable, so long as it's not farming.

NEW ORLEANS, LOUISIANA

WHAT THEIR MOTTO SHOULD BE: Experience the World's Only Boobs-and-Beads-Based Economy! *or* Parades Just Sorta Happen Here! *or* We're Cool with Stuff Soundin' French!

WHAT TO PACK: Gold Bond. *Lots* of Gold Bond!

WHAT TO EAT AND DRINK AND WHERE: From the tourist traps that are way too crowded to the hidden gems that only locals seem to know about, every meal in New Orleans has been great in our experience. Our advice would be to go everywhere and try everything . . . so pace yourself.

WHAT NOT TO MISS: We're sure the locals get tired of it, but every day seems like Mardi Gras! Let your freak flag fly, dance in the street, drink a frozen daiquiri, buy a stupid T-shirt, eat everything.

One thing New Orleans has in common with Texas is that, though it is Southern, it also feels very much like its own country. It may sound cliché, but New Orleans isn't so much a place as it is an experience. A feeling. It is borderline mystical. New Orleans is the type of place you can't imagine living in, because how would you survive? Yet at trip's end, you can't imagine leaving, because having to go back to the harsh reality that everywhere else *isn't* New Orleans is sometimes too much to bear.

While in New Orleans one does not move; rather, one *is moved*. A symbiotic relationship between man and city is formed, and like most symbiotic relationships you see in the superhero movies, intervention will be necessary lest the connection grow dangerous and out of hand. The city has a rhythm all its own, and one would do well to simply let it lead and try not to step on its feet. New Orleans is not just mountains of oysters and fried po'boys. It is not just tall fruity drinks and the smell of freshly baked beignets. It is not just the chorus line of young artists making a paint bucket sound every bit as good as Neil Peart on the drums. New Orleans is about knowing all of that will be there tomorrow, and the next day, and the next day, and . . . you get the idea. But just in case, here's a story from Trae on the subject.

So first off, let the record show that New Orleans is my favorite city on the planet. In the interest of fairness, I should probably offer the following disclaimer: I have not been to most of this planet. I hear much of it is lovely. My travels so far have been limited to North America (at least until the third part of this book!), but New Orleans is easily my favorite city on this continent.

This is going to come up a few times in this book, but I simply *adore* places that know how to be two particular things: fat and drunk. From Chicago to Ybor City and everywhere in between, verily do I love a Fat Drunk Town. And no, you don't have to actually be fat to enjoy an FDT; you just have to be willing to get your fat on. And, dear readers, I put it to you that there is *no* finer city in which to get your fat on than NOLA. Incredible food is literally everywhere. And the booze. Lawdamercy, the booze. The only downside is that if you're not careful, you'll black out and slip into a food coma, only to come to later having forgotten many of the sweeter, fatter details of the experience, which of course is a shame. No one wants to wake up thinking, *I'm pretty sure I ate a crab that changed my life last night, but I can't remember.*

But as much as I love all things gluttonous and besotted, none of that explains why New Orleans is my favorite city. There's more to it than that. New Orleans is just *special*, man. When I think about the city, one experience in particular stands out in my mind.

Early on in our relationship, my then girlfriend (now wife) and I took our first trip as a couple to the Big Easy. I was beside myself with excitement. At that point in my life, I was a twenty-three-year-old recovering trailer baby whose only travel experiences had been a weekend in Daytona Beach after graduation and a Carnival Cruise with a girl who later cheated on me with a bartender. (Did I mention that I'm white trash?)

The first day was great, even though my then girlfriend made me walk like nine miles around the Garden District bouncing in and out of boutiques she openly had no interest in actually patronizing. Apparently simply looking at the price tag of a designer dress counts as an activity? I mean, I've heard of window-shopping, but we were *inside* the shop, like on the whole other side of the window. I guess I just don't understand why you would want to peruse an entire retail district if you already know you're not going to be spending any money there. But it doesn't matter. I guess what I'm really trying to say is this: Sometimes, when you least expect it . . . women *don't* be shoppin'.[1]

That night she wasn't feeling too well. We had gotten in really early and then walked around all damn day, so she was worn smooth out. She just wanted to take it easy and recharge for the next day. I, on the other hand, was under the impression that since we had gotten all that boring shop-goin' and dress-lookin' out of the way, it was now time to truly start the day and *throw down*. At this very point we first discovered what would become a defining dichotomy of our relationship: She's an early bird, and I'm a night owl. It was also at this point that we discovered the key to making a relationship work despite such a fundamental difference—a little technique we like to call "Just Leave They Ass in the Bed." Are you an early bird who wants to go on a hike or see the sunrise but can't get your partner to stir? Just Leave They Ass in the Bed. Are you a night owl who wants to go do something that actually hits? Is your partner already snoring? Just Leave They Ass in the Bed. It's worked for us for years.

And it worked for me this night as well. She gave me her blessing to go forth and do well (get mugged) and turned in for the night. This was before smartphones were ubiquitous, and we didn't have a computer or Wi-Fi, so I just straight-up walked out of the hotel, which was on a street near the edge of the quarter called Esplanade, without any semblance of a plan.[2]

Before long I came to a street that seemed to be more active than the

---

1. If you would like a written apology for this paragraph, feel free to DM me on Instagram.
2. While I think this is often the best way to go about life, I don't know if I would fully endorse employing this strategy in New Orleans at midnight. For crime-y reasons. But that's what I did.

others. I could see neon lights and hear jazz notes and smell étouffée (and maybe also pee a little bit, on account of all the drunk). The street sign said Frenchmen Street. What I now know is that Frenchmen is a legendary Crescent City avenue, renowned far and wide for its jazz clubs, dive bars, and Cajun fare.[3] But I didn't know any of that at the time. I had no idea where I was.

I wandered into a bar. (It was either Blue Nile or the Spotted Cat. I wish I could remember for sure, but I can't . . . well, on account of all the drunk.) A jazz band was setting up, and I somehow struck up a conversation with a bunch of people who had just joined the Peace Corps and were shipping out the next day to some far-flung part of the world to try to save it, I suppose. Did y'all know that was a real thing? That some people in their twenties actually cast themselves into the grand unknown to try to do some actual good in the world, instead of just partying and playing a shitload of *Halo*? I didn't know that was a real thing outside of movies, but it is, evidently.

Just as I was figuring out these people on their way to Azerbaijan might not be all that interested in my third consecutive fantasy football league championship victory,[4] the band started up. And you'll never believe this, but that New Orleans jazz band? They were pretty darn good. Now I'll be the first to admit I'm not a jazz aficionado—far from it—but by God I know what makes my head bob, and on this night it was bobbin' up a damn storm. Bobbin' like a fat kid at a fall festival apple tub, baby.

All of a sudden, the crowd parted, and a springy young white dude in suspenders and one of those flat-brimmed sailor hats (he looked like he was in a Portland-style barbershop quartet) jumped to the front of the stage and started tap-dancing his *ass off*.[5] I mean, he was burnin'. It. *Up*, y'all. He flowed perfectly with the music. The band would play him on, then he would do an elaborate tap solo, and in perfect time, the band would rejoin. Then they would do (I really wish I was smarter about music, by the way) these sort of musical volleys, where they would go back and forth. He would tap for a bit, they would play for a bit, the whole thing would build, and

---

3. Shout-out to Adolfo's and their ocean sauce, which is so good you'll wanna slap at least three different mamas.
4. That is a true story, though, just so everyone knows.
5. I'm sorry I don't have more technical terms for these things, but hell, this ain't a jazz and tap dance book.

then they all joined together for a truly epic crescendo that blew everybody in that place completely away, even someone as truly jazz-dumb as I am.

Standing ovation. Uproarious applause. Smoke everywhere. Roses in the air. All that. They could not possibly have smashed any harder than they did. As they went on a break to grab cigarettes and a bucket of mudbugs, I glimpsed the tap dancer hanging out by the bar. Not able to help myself, I walked up, gushing, and said, "Hey, buddy, that was incredible!"

He smiled and nodded as if to say thanks.

"So how long have you been at it? You work with these guys a lot?"

Nothing. He just looked kind of confused. I couldn't tell if I had offended him or what. So I tried to express myself a different way, until finally I realized what was going on.

Turns out he was Israeli. He didn't speak any English. He'd never been to New Orleans, set foot in that bar, or spoken a single word to any of the band members before the performance I saw. And as far as I could tell, none of them talked about it afterward either. It wasn't a big deal to them, but it was literally the coolest thing I had ever seen in my life. What was an otherworldly experience for everyone else in the bar was just another Thursday for those musicians, and a night like literally any other in the city of New Orleans.

OK, now that the love letter has been written, *yes*—New Orleans can *also* be an absolute drunken mess that can put the infield at Talladega to shame on its worst day, but that is 100 percent the tourists' fault, so it feels wrong to dump on New Orleans for being so awesome that bags of shit the world over flock there to get a piece. But since this is a comedy book, the late, great comedian Tim Wilson once said, "Louisiana was purchased for four cents an acre. I bet if we sold it today we could triple our money!"

LEXINGTON, KENTUCKY

WHAT THEIR MOTTO SHOULD BE: Southern Enough to Be Home, but You Should Still Double-Check Your Sweet Tea

WHAT TO PACK: All blue EVERYTHING!

WHAT TO EAT AND DRINK AND WHERE: Tony's of Lexington for some steaks and Blue Heron for some dranks!

WHAT NOT TO MISS: Keeneland's April and October race meets.

I f Kentucky has one thing in common with Florida, it's that neither place has a shortage of unhinged lunatics on trucker crank with shotguns. If it has *two* things in common with Florida, it's also that many people debate whether the state actually counts as "the South." The obvious reason most people give is, well . . . Kentucky's location. If it *is* the South, then it is certainly close to the cutoff because Kentucky sits geographically in the middle of the country. It isn't far enough over to be considered Midwest, and for some reason, that's the only "Mid" we really have in the US. I truly wish this was not the case, though, because it would be hilarious if Mitch McConnell had to say he was from the Middle East.

The Mason-Dixon Line, which most people use to divvy up the states into either "dumb, dirty rednecks" or "out-of-touch Yankee buttholes," helps Kentucky's case, as they are very firmly south of it. It's a shame though . . . would've made for some very interesting "This House Divided" license plates for families of Civil War reenactors. Speaking of which, during the Civil War, Kentucky started out as a neutral state that would eventually side with the Union. We know several people who, for that reason alone, would automatically claim it as a blood traitor, and therefore 100 percent the Yankee North. *Buuuuuut* despite siding with the Union, Kentucky was also a slave state, which for the other half of the country puts it firmly back on the side of the South. Yikes.

They also put cinnamon and shit in their chili and then stick all that on top of spaghetti,[1] and while we would never disparage any type of food-related debauchery, ain't no rollin'-pin-wieldin' redneck mammaw with dough on her ankles we could see condoning that mess. However, they also make gravy out of chocolate and put it on biscuits, and while that is still inferior to the white sawmill gravy that most people think of when they hear B and G, you can't sit here and tell us that adding *more* sugar to something ain't a Southern thang, baby!

You know what though? Kentucky is the home of bluegrass, they drink whiskey[2] like they're drinking Gatorade after a jog in the hot sun, and by God they are in the only football conference that matters, which is the SEC. So damn it, we are claiming them . . . KENTUCKY IS THE SOUTH!

Though not the capital, Lexington is the largest city in the Commonwealth of Kentucky and one of our personal favorites in the country. Sure, that may be because Comedy Off Broadway is one of the absolute finest stand-up comedy clubs around, and it always gives us five packed houses a weekend. We can see why you would think that, but it's also simply a great place filled with great people, all of whom we could just 'bout guaran-damn-tee would say they are Southern and proud.

We mentioned that you should pack "All blue EVERYTHING!" when visiting Lexington, and for the non–sports fans reading this (or the ones who for some reason don't pay attention to the nation's greatest collegiate conference), that is because blue is the official color of the pride of Lexington: the University of Kentucky Wildcats. Now sure, the University of Kentucky hasn't traditionally been great at God's favorite sport and the one that matters

---

1. Many will recognize this culinary abomination as belonging to Cincinnati, but they've corrupted northern Kentucky as well.
2. We know it's *bourbon*, Kentucky. Just trying to rile y'all up. Read on.

most,[3] but they have a storied basketball legacy and are considered a collegiate blue blood in that regard. If you want to see people absolutely losing their shit, we encourage you to visit any damn sports bar in the Lexington area during a University of Kentucky versus Louisville basketball game. And God help you if you are wearing a Cardinals jersey. Only the Bloods and the Crips have a more violent history concerning people in blue or red clothing, and we wouldn't want to be on the wrong side of either of them!

While watching said game at a bar, the insanity is upped even more because Lexington, Kentucky, has some of the biggest bourbon drinkers in this solar system. The Kentucky Bourbon Trail goes right smack-dab through there, and they have at least fifteen distilleries within fifty miles of downtown. Also, just so you know, bourbon and whiskey are not the same thing, and you'd better not mistake one for the other when talking to one of the many mustachioed distillers, or they'll give you a look that could turn a black cat's hair white. In short, all bourbon is whiskey, but not all whiskey is bourbon. Bourbon has to be made with at least 51 percent corn. Whiskey/bourbon is sorta like the ice cream / gelato of the drunken lunatics world. Regardless of what you call it, it'll getcha where you need to be, and there aren't many that do it better than good ol' Lexington, Kentucky!

OK, so you're drunk and there isn't a college basketball game to watch. What do you do? Well, have you considered the possibility of losing a mortgage payment by placing a bet on a horse named some shit like *The Hoof, the Hoof, the Hoof Is on Fire*? You can certainly do that in Lexington, Kentucky, and while we aren't sure that is an actual racehorse's name, it certainly could be, considering all the ridiculous ones you will hear if you're at the Red Mile, Ellis Park, or the previously mentioned Keeneland horse track. These folks take their horsing around pretty damn serious, and with good reason.

Horse racing toes that line between fancy-people shit and redneck-people shit just perfectly. Sure, you may see plenty of seersucker suits and fancy floral dresses with matching ridiculous hats worn by Scarlett O'Hara and Rhett Butler types who are six mint juleps deep and doing some serious insider trading—but you're just as likely to see Joe Dirt and Brandy look-alikes suckin' down a twelve-pack of Milwaukee's Best, rolling their own cigarettes, and hanging their child's college fund in the balance as a

---

3. Which is football. Duh.

homunculus whips the back of a noble steed around the final turn. The duality of the South on full display!

Horse racing is much like Formula 1 driving and all those fancy winter sports that kids named Braylen and McKinley get real good at. That is, to buy, raise, and train horses costs a shit ton of money and very much excludes a certain class of people. And as everyone knows, that is super intentional and just the way they like it . . . but by God, gambling on them glue factories is an all-inclusive activity. So move over, Ms. Kardashian. Billy Bob is 'bout to ride this five-dollar scratcher money all the way to the bank . . . *skeeew!*

People can debate 'til they are blue in the face about whether or not Lexington, Kentucky, is the South. Everyone is entitled to their opinion, no matter how wrong it is. But as for us, we will take the whiskey-drinkin', bluegrass-pickin' horse lovers in the first round every single time. For the love of God, Bill Monroe is from there! Go Wildcats![4]

---

4. Only said that to pander, LOL. Go Dawgs and Vols!

ASHEVILLE, NORTH CAROLINA

WHAT THEIR MOTTO SHOULD BE: Come for the Beer, Stay 'Cause You Can't Drive

WHAT TO PACK: Don't pack anything. Just pick up a shirt from every brew pub you stop in and completely transform your wardrobe from bland to hipster chic!

WHAT TO EAT AND DRINK AND WHERE: It's easier to tell you what *not* to eat or drink . . . So don't go to a chain, and don't have no damn regular-ass domestic beer!

WHAT NOT TO MISS: Catch a show at the Orange Peel, no matter who is there. The atmosphere is pure rock-and-roll paradise!

L et's say you consider yourself an intellectual, yeah?[1] You spend your nights reading Kurt Vonnegut books by the light of a fire through your thick, black-rimmed glasses. You wouldn't be caught dead taking a sip of that watered-down, carbonated piss-juice middle America calls beer, and you prefer your music in the form of vinyl, not only for the quality of sound purists understand, but also because reading the liner notes is a pastime of yours and something you require in order to appreciate the artist's true

---

1. We know, we know: "As if an intellectual would read this book."

intent. You may be thinking to yourself, *There's no chance my way of life could be pursued south of the Mason-Dixon! Why, I must relegate myself to the Pacific Northwest or perhaps a more gentrified neighborhood of Brooklyn.* Well, not so fast, my friend. Asheville, North Carolina, is right up your alley.

Oh yeah, you heard me loud and clear, baby! Right smack-dab in the heart of Dixie is a hipster's paradise that will make any skinny-jeans-wearing, kombucha-drinking Rotten Tomatoes critic feel right at home. We don't mean to disparage, of course. Asheville is one of our absolute favorite cities. It's earned its place among the ranks of contenders for the Mount Rushmore of Crunchy-Friendly Cities—namely, Portland, Bushwick, Seattle, and San Francisco. Matter of fact, if you ask us, when it comes to liberal cities, the ones in the South actually kick more ass because that sense of elitism that normally plagues such places is usually overshadowed by the innate Southern hospitality required to function properly in a region such as ours.

Much like the South itself, which is a complicated and confusing place, Asheville has a duality of its own that further flavors the town's unique pizzazz. As described thus far, Asheville is a hipster's paradise where one can find a variety of good local beers, grub, and live entertainment. Though we already advised against ordering some non-hoppy domestic beer, it should be said that Asheville is full of PBR bars for people trying to save a buck on their drunk—and there ain't a damn thing wrong with that! However, Asheville is also home to something that could not be further from the townie-gastropub scene, and that is the Biltmore—perhaps its most famous landmark.

If you've seen *Downton Abbey*,[2] then you are familiar with grandiose houses that required numerous staff and whose yearly expenditures could've easily fed an entire country's poverty-stricken population. Well, that's the Biltmore! You may not have heard of the Biltmore, but we'd be willing to bet you know its namesakes, the Vanderbilts. Built by George Vanderbilt toward the end of the Gilded Age, the Biltmore was, is, and shall forever be *the* example of luxury. But don't just take our word for it. You absolutely must check it out when you are in the Asheville area. They offer guided tours, and when we tell you it's an all-day affair . . . well, buddy, make sure to eat before you go, ya hear? This damn place has toilets more impressive

---

2. Our favorite show. No, seriously.

than our entire houses. There's a full gymnasium, which at the turn of the century meant old leather balls to toss back and forth to help you look super muscular when you rode your horse that was trained to walk fancy. There are bedrooms coated with paint that cost more than your stupid wedding, and it even has one of the first domestic elevators because having to walk down the stairs to fire a chambermaid for making your bed wrong is gross and for the poor!

All kidding aside, the Biltmore is quite the spectacle, and I'd argue it's one of the seven man-made wonders of North America. Add that to all the wonderful antique stores, boutiques, and (of course) breweries, pubs, and rock halls, and Asheville is a place that no matter what type of weekend you are trying to have, you almost can't have it in a better place.

CHARLESTON, SOUTH CAROLINA

WHAT THEIR MOTTO SHOULD BE: ~~Heritage, Not Hate~~ (TBD)

WHAT TO PACK: Some Kentucky Derby–adjacent types of stuff.

WHAT TO EAT AND DRINK AND WHERE: It's a bit of a cliché in Charleston by now, but Hyman's Seafood lives up to the hype and has maybe the best damn Bloody Mary we've ever had.

WHAT NOT TO MISS: Y'all, they got this tree there called the Angel Oak, and its primordial majesty must be seen to be believed. You feel like a wood elf is gonna show up and give you a side quest at any minute.

H ere's the thing about Charleston. It's a beautiful city with boundless character and a vibe all its own; however, it is also a bit . . . *slavery-y*.[1] We know we shouldn't be so glib about it, but it's definitely a thing. There's just a serious Old South type of feel to many parts of Charleston. You feel like you could still find people who talk like plantation owners there. Hell, you can still find plantation owners there! (More on those a little later.) We're

---

1. Which is actually the theme some people request at their wedding.

not generally the paranormal types, but the city feels haunted somehow. Maybe it's the way Spanish moss seems to float above a cobblestone street in a heavy fog. Or maybe it's the objectively horrific centuries-long history. A little of column A, and a little of column B, probably. But either way, if there are ghosts in Charleston, you know damn well they're Civil War ghosts, which is one of the more unfortunate types of ghosts to have around.[2]

The ghost of the Confederacy itself seems to be haunting Charleston. The Civil War is *everywhere*. And look, don't get us wrong; we understand that a massive part of Charleston's history is wrapped up in the Civil War, and it would be horrible to ignore it or pretend it didn't happen. It's just that they seem a *skosh* too proud about the whole damn thing. Now, we know what you're thinking: *The South has a misplaced sense of pride regarding a war they fought and ultimately lost over their crimes against humanity? Surely not!* But it's true. It's a long-standing problem where we're from, and though things are getting better on that front, we're ashamed to say the mythical Lost Cause of the Confederacy lives on in the South. And in Charleston. And now a related anecdote from Trae.

My wife and I honeymooned in Charleston. This turned out to be a *terrible* idea, but only because we did so in June. If you are thinking of going to Charleston, you should. But not in June. It was triple digits and humid *as hell* every damn day we were there. And keep in mind we're from Tennessee. We've been hot. We've been humid. This was a whole other level. The air was just hot water masquerading as oxygen. You ever breathe hot water for a week? Ain't it.

But I digress. Weather aside, we *loved* Charleston. We really did. But even while loving it, we felt something weird about it too. It's like this: We all know that most of America doesn't feel old *at all*. Tour guides in American cities will say, "And this clock tower was built almost *eighty years* ago!" And we'll all go, "Oooh, ahhh, eighty years. Can you believe it?" Meanwhile Europeans are like, "Last night I threw up in a pub built by Vikings," and it's nothing of note. Well, Charleston is one of the few cities we have that actually feels old, which is wonderful. But the *full context of that* is . . . well, less so.

In Charleston, you can get hammered drunk and nearly murder

---

2. Asylum-fire ghosts are rough, too, but at least slavery's not involved.

yourself with shrimp (Charleston is a *fantastic* Fat Drunk Town). Then you can wander out onto an old cobblestone street lined with those incredible droopy-ass trees, climb into a goddamn *horse carriage,* and think to yourself, *Look at me! I'm a colonial governor! Somebody bring me a powdered wig and a blunderbuss!* But then you remember you're in Charleston, so you think, *Oh no! That means I have slaves! But I don't want slaves! No, Charleston, why?!* That's how Charleston is. You know, to be honest, I'm only just now realizing that this experience may have a lot to do with me being a Southern white man and the shame inherent therein, but either way, that's how Charleston was *for me,* at least.

Here's another example, but let me first say that this anecdote comes with a very important postscript. OK, so my wife and I did one of the more popular plantation tours while we were there.[3] We felt weird about it in the first place and debated going, but we ultimately had a morbid curiosity. Besides, the tour came highly recommended . . . which kinda reflects my overall point about Charleston here. If you ask someone for a recommendation in a particular city, and the immediate answer is "The plantations are lovely," that's something of a red flag, in my opinion. A red flag consisting of two diagonal blue lines containing thirteen stars, to be precise. And it isn't just the plantations. You can be walking in downtown Charleston and overhear white tourists jovially discussing how incredible the slave market is. And then perhaps some white locals will chime in and say, "Actually, I'll have you know that slaves were never actually sold here!" And then they'll take a beat before pointing a couple of blocks away. "They were sold over there!" Shit like that. It's pretty wild, y'all.

Now look, I know I'm being a little unfair to Charleston here. After all, what are they supposed to do? The plantations *are* historically important. We can't change the past, and we shouldn't bury it either. The Civil War and slavery are objectively massive pieces of Charleston's history that should be acknowledged. It's just that, in my personal experience, that acknowledgment comes across as some reeeeaaal *Gone with the Wind*–type shit. To wit, when we were touring the plantation, we passed by the old slave quarters, and the (white) tour guide said—cheery and pleasant as can be, like she was describing her favorite true crime podcast or a dessert made in a Mason

---

3. I'm not naming the specific one because I'm 'bout to talk some shit about it.

jar, or some other thing white people get really excited about—"And here we have the slave quarters. The primary unit on the end was home to the overseer, who directed the daily work of the slaves. Fun fact: The building has been updated over the years, and that man's direct descendants have continued living there and working the grounds to this very day!"

All the other white people on the tour murmured, "Neat," "How interesting," and other similar white-isms, while my wife and I cringed at each other like one of our mammaws had said something racist in front of company. Because if you ask me, the subtext of that fun fact was a variation of one of the most popular lies told about slavery by the "War of Northern Aggression" types among us: i.e., that "the slaves really didn't have it all that bad."

"In a lot of ways, they were better off," these people will say, or "You know, some slaves even chose to remain with their masters!" Talk about complete and total horseshit rationalizations—some of which were, in fact, parroted by our tour guide. Feel free to say I'm overreacting or reading too much into that if you want, but it left a bad taste in my mouth. Which was a real shame because, for the most part, my mouth and its taste buds had a *wonderful* time in Charleston.

Three more things I'd like to say about the plantation tour: First, it ended in the plantation house itself, with a history lesson on the family that founded and operated the plantation. Their portraits hung on the wall, from the first duke or earl or viscount or whatever the hell he was (the one who was given the plantation by a king as a reward for having the right grandpa) all the way down to the modern-day descendants who still own the plantation today. It's very possible this is just my poor-white-trash DNA and upbringing (and the requisite discomfort with all-things-aristocratic that comes with it) talking here, but the whole thing just felt a bit too damn celebratory for my liking. Which summed up my issues with the experience. The atrocities were acknowledged, sure, but everyone was still smiling. Still taking selfies. Still having a big ol' time. The tone of the tour was just . . . off. And wrong.[4]

The penultimate thing I'll say about the plantation tour is that it was, without a doubt and unequivocally, one of the most breathtaking, nigh-unbelievable aesthetic experiences of my entire life. That shit was *purdy*, y'all. After all, with a background that ugly, it kinda has to be.

---

4. Said the guy who attended after brunch on his honeymoon.

And finally, the last thing I have to say about my experience is this: It was over ten years ago. A lot has happened in Charleston, the South, and this entire country in that intervening decade. While I haven't myself revisited the plantation tours, I have it on good authority that they have evolved since then, making it a point to better acknowledge the brutal reality of slavery and the bloody legacy with which they must forever grapple. Which, in a way, makes them metaphors for the South as a whole. Getting and doing better is all we can ask from ourselves.

We bet some South Carolinians reading this book are probably feeling a little defensive right now, so we would like to emphasize something: Charleston is full of people, and a large majority of them are likely not down with all that "states' rights" bullshit. For example, and unsurprisingly, the area's Black community, without which Charleston would not, *could not* exist. As in the rest of the South, the food, the art, the music, the way they talk in Charleston—should be credited to Black people. All of it. Other cultural influences have intermingled throughout the years, but the foundation is Black. One of the largest blocks in that foundation is the Gullah Geechee people, a distinctive community of African Americans who have preserved a culture of strong African influence and whose impact can be felt throughout the Lowcountry.

Our point here is that Charleston, like any American city, is not defined by only one aspect of its history or by one segment of its population. Sure, the United Daughters of the Confederacy are all about Charleston. But the city belongs to the Gullah, too, whether the UDC like it or not. On a related note, since the horrific Emanuel AME Church massacre in 2015, there has been a growing push to appropriately reckon with the city's blood-soaked past, and not just on the plantations. If progress is made, the history won't be quite so whitewashed, the tour guides quite so chipper, the tours quite so . . . Pinterest-y. And with that progress, the views won't be any less spellbinding, the food any less mouthwatering, the city any less captivating. Charleston can continue to evolve *and* remain what it has always been: a crown jewel of the American South.

WHERE WE FROM

CHICKAMAUGA, GEORGIA

COREY'S HOMETOWN

WHAT THEIR MOTTO SHOULD BE: "It Was About States' Rights!"

WHAT TO PACK: Chewing tobacco, a Civil War uniform in case a reenactment breaks out, and a bumper sticker memorializing a dead loved one (angel wings optional).

WHAT TO EAT AND DRINK AND WHERE: Choo Choo BBQ, home of the finest Brunswick stew in the land.

WHAT NOT TO MISS: The Chickamauga Battlefield not only is gorgeous but also boasts tons of Civil War history and many landmarks that give you a great idea of how one of the bloodiest battles in American history was fought.

What can be said about my hometown that hasn't already been said about an Al Jolson performance in the 1920s? Sure, it's a little racist at times . . . but there's also some nuance to it!

Chickamauga, Georgia, is home to the bloodiest two-day battle in the entire Civil War, and that is what people from here are most proud of. *By. A. Lot.* I mean, you can't walk down the street in Chickamauga without some bearded, overalls-wearing, potbellied sumbitch[1] jumping out at you from behind a bush and screaming, "MORE SUMBITCHES DIED HERE IN TWO DAYS . . . GET YOU SOME OF THAT, YOU YANKEE LIBERAL PANSY!" then farting loudly and whisking himself back into a Jack Daniel's bottle like a Confederate genie.

Chickamauga is *also*, however, close enough to the big city[2] that at least a few people with money live there. "Not that you can tell by the way they dress," my momma would say.[3] Those moneyed few, however, are scattered among those who were left completely impoverished once the factory left town (same as in Trae's hometown—one of many things he and I have in common). If you wanna get shit-faced with folks who look like extras from *Deliverance* while shooting old paint cans with shotguns and smoking the butts of some of Mammaw's cigarettes, then you can certainly do that in Chickamauga. You can also go two houses over and hear someone who looks and sounds like Delta Burke talk[4] about people from across the tracks who wouldn't have to live that way if their sorry-ass daddy had just done something else with his bootstraps. Chickamauga is a beautiful place at times. Chickamauga is a dark and ugly place at times. Chickamauga is, well . . . America, and despite how it may sound to some, I love it.

You always hear the older generations talking about how much simpler life was "back in the good ol' days." It never made much sense to me, because from where I was sittin', my life didn't seem much different from what they were describing. When we were kids in Chickamauga, we'd get up every morning and set out on our bicycles for an all-day affair. Sometimes we'd go down to "the big hill" and try our damnedest to paralyze ourselves from the waist down by jumping our Mongoose bikes off that big ol' dirt mound while someone's little brother held on for dear life with his feet on the pegs. Never did it occur to us that what we were doing was dangerous, I don't think; and if it ever did, then that's probably why we enjoyed it so much.

As kids in Chickamauga, we didn't lie around watching TV all day long like we were accused of doing by all the gray-hairs at the beauty shop

---

1. Sorry, Bill. Didn't mean to out you.
2. Chattanooga, that is. Which I found out later in life is not actually that big.
3. One day I think I'll write a book of just Momma quotes.
4. I'm not saying Delta Burke is like this. She just sounds like she is.

and the VFW.[5] Sometimes I think they had to make up stuff like that so they could feel tougher than they actually were—hell, I don't know. We'd ride down to our baseball field and have home run derbies with tennis balls when we weren't actually having sanctioned practices, and lucky for us, the recycling center was located directly behind it.

Now, I know what you are thinking: *Southern* adults *don't get excited about recycling, so what the hell did you kids like it so much for?* Well, I am so glad you asked! The recycling center in Chickamauga was a glorious paradise for elementary-aged kids. It truly had it all. It sat directly behind the press box for the nine- and ten-year-olds' baseball field and was divided up into sections. Plastic bottles and milk jugs were in one section, and we didn't have much use for those, but directly beside them was the glass bottles— and *hoooo-weee*, were those fun! You know, it's funny to think back on what I clearly remember as a plethora of brown beer bottles spilling out of that bin—because whenever it came time for the town to vote on alcohol sales regulations, it seemed that almost no one drank. Quite the mystery.

Me and all my buddies, whose names I shan't mention in case the statute of limitations on vandalism exceeds thirty years, would toss one of us up into that bin. Then he'd start handing us beer bottles one by one. We'd then strategically place said bottles on all the abandoned railroad ties that sat in front of Smith Garage and take turns chucking rocks at them until we had shattered each one and won the war. And that was just how the day started.

After that it was time to take advantage of the *real* hidden gem a small-town recycling center provides: the magazine bin. I am not kidding when I tell you that my buddies and I spent literal hours digging through a recycling bin like Scrooge McDuck jumping into his pool of gold coins. The bin was mostly full of old car magazines, but the effort was all made worth it when just before sundown one of us would find that elusive *Playboy*. And the only thing better than getting to see boobies as a fifth grader was checking the mailing address on the front to see whose daddy it belonged to. Then we'd know where the best sleepovers were held.

In Chickamauga you can expect to eat pretty good, so long as what you are craving is BBQ or Mexican. Seems those are the only two genres we can get to stick down here. You'll have an ol' boy screaming "Build that wall!"

---

5. I could've also gone with the library or Hardee's.

with lettuce from a fifty-cent taco hanging out of his mouth, unaware he's rooting against his Tuesday night date spot. The only one he could afford.

We usually have two BBQ restaurants at any given time: Choo Choo BBQ (a long-standing staple) and then whatever flavor of the month thinks they are going to come in and take a shot at the champ. They never succeed.

Growing up in Chickamauga, I was unaware of the reputation the town had as uppity—or "preppy," as it was called in high schools. Turns out, this notion stemmed from our school having a stricter dress code than most schools in the area, meaning we had to tuck our shirts in and—God forbid—wear collared shirts sometimes. The horror. I guess it always confused me because we were still drinking and snorting as many pills as we could get our hands on while wearing those tucked-in shirts, and most everyone I knew would untuck the damn things right after school to go shoot turkeys.

Yeah, snorting pills was a way of life when I was younger. I grew up right in that sweet spot when you could get a ton of pills but no one knew how bad they were for you yet. Boy, we sure do now. While my town wasn't ripped completely to shreds by NAFTA like Trae's was, I do take particular issue with the pharmaceutical companies for picking up the slack. When we were in high school, we'd take 'em for pains gained on the football field, but that quickly turned into mixing 'em with our Natty Lights to make the party that much better. Pills turned into more pills, and for some kids, pills turned into heroin, which then turned into a coffin. So it goes.

I have a complicated relationship with my hometown. I am accused by some of being a blood traitor, as I know Trae is in his, because of some particular views I hold that seem to buck up against "the way we do things round here!" That's all well and good. I can take the heat. I can handle the notion that I don't belong because I'm just a sissified Hollywood type who done got too big for his britches. If I'm being honest, it sorta gives me life. I love being looked at funny at the grocery store on occasion. Round here, hatin' something often means being scared of it, so I'll pretend it's that for a second and feel tough for once in my life. Then I'll grab that ice cream I tried to convince myself I didn't need and mosey on to the register where I hope my ninth-grade English teacher doesn't recognize me. If she does, I bet she has some notes on our first book that I'd rather not hear today. One thing they can't say to me, however, is that I done gone and ran off. 'Cause my ass is still here, five minutes from my momma's house and a stone's throw from all the BBQ I can handle.

CELINA, TENNESSEE

TRAE'S HOMETOWN

WHAT THEIR MOTTO SHOULD BE: They Still Haven't Taken the Lake from Us—Yet

WHAT TO PACK: Anything metropolitan you can't do without, 'cause you ain't gonna find it here.

WHAT TO EAT AND DRINK AND WHERE: Dale Hollow 1 Stop BBQ is head-to-toe legit, as is soul-food joint Ollie's Place. As for drinks, ya ever had moonshine made in a radiator?

WHAT NOT TO MISS: Your Tennessee Tech Interstate 40 exit, else you run the risk of accidentally ending up in Celina. But in all sincerity, Dale Hollow Lake is unassailable.

I've thought for years that if you wanted to understand the plight of rural America writ large, you could do worse than to start with my home-town of Celina, Tennessee.[1] When I was ten years old, in 1996, it was like any other quaint and cozy small Southern town: a tight-knit, Rockwellian community of friendly, middle-class, salt-of-the-earth folks . . . and also racists. Matter of fact, many of the former were indeed also the latter.[2]

---

1. Pronounced "Sa-LY-na."
2. But, ya know, they were the super smiley type of racist, so it wasn't as bad.

At that time, my dad owned a video store, his brother owned a deli, their dad owned a car lot, and my maternal grandmother owned a restaurant—a real bootstrappin' bunch of small-business owners, right? Well, that year the only factory in town, an OshKosh B'gosh plant, moved its operations to Mexico, taking all three hundred jobs with it (along with the whole community's will to live). Fast-forward ten short years, and by the time I was twenty, every single one of those businesses had shuttered and half of those people were dead. Also, my mama was in prison for pills. I know, I know . . . pretty damn folk song-y. But true.[3] So that's fun.

Now, twenty-five years later, Celina has never come close to recovering. That town literally died the day the factory left, and it has been shambling along in an undead state ever since. So if you ever look at people from places like that and wonder, *Gee, what are they so upset about?* Oh, I dunno, maybe it's that they've clearly been forgotten by both Time and God? Through no fault of their own? Also maybe the world is a very different place now, and that which is different both frightens and enrages them? There are lotsa reasons, gang!

If you know anything about my career outside the confines of this book, it will not surprise you to hear that I'm not exactly the most popular person in my hometown these days. We don't have to get into the gory details, but suffice it to say that I am, in the words of the older rednecks at my high school, a bit of a queer. To be clear: I'm not gay; I'm a queer. You may be confused by that distinction, but if you're from a town like mine, you get it. Back then I was a queer because I liked to read and wore glasses and made good grades and didn't go to church and had a gay uncle—that type of thing. Nowadays, I'm still a queer back home, but it's because of . . . well, everything about me, really.

Perhaps because of this history, I've been known to make fun of my hometown a lot. Further, I've been accompanied to Celina by various camera crews, either for a documentary I produced or for a segment on ABC's *Nightline*. As a result, I have been accused of "making the town look bad." Personally I would argue that the *cameras* made the town look bad, by virtue of capturing the way the town looks. But maybe that's just me. Either way,

---

3. I've always thought OshKosh B'gosh had to be the most whimsically named company to ever RUIN COUNTLESS LIVES.

my point is, sometimes I come across—to people from Celina and to people in general—as if I hate where I'm from, or at least have a large amount of disdain for it. So in order to avoid adding to that reputation with this section of the book, I'd like to take the opportunity to clarify and emphasize some things right quick.

The first is something I didn't appreciate about Celina until years after I left, and until I gained said appreciation, my perception of the South was kinda messed up for years. As a young adult, I used to get positively *indignant* on the subject of Southern stereotypes. "All that racism stuff is overblown!" I would say. "I've never even *seen* a Klansman!"—as if that fact alone disproves the existence of racism. (Twenty-year-olds are really stupid, guys.) As a result, I would downplay the accusations of bigotry or regressiveness until I was blue in the face. But then I would meet someone from a different small town in the South, and the stories they told would blow my mind (in a bad way). For example: "We had one Black kid in the whole school, and they used to put a noose in his locker." That's a real story I heard from the town *one county over*. When I first went to my wife's hometown, which is in a different, equally rural part of Tennessee, my mother-in-law told me, very matter-of-factly, that there were literally no gay people there because, I quote, "You can't be that here." You get the idea.

Yeah, well, things like that didn't happen in Celina. Not when I was growing up, at least. We had multiple openly gay men in town, three of whom, including my uncle, owned successful businesses (until the damn factory moved, anyway). A Black community also resides in Celina, the Free Hills, so it wasn't a "we had one Black kid in the whole school" type of situation for us. When I was in school, saying the N-word was a good way to get your ass whipped. I saw it happen on more than one occasion. (Cedric didn't play that shit, y'all.)

Listen, *please* don't get me wrong: Celina was not and is not some progressive utopia. You'll still find plenty of Confederate flags, plenty of racist jokes . . . and I believe I've mentioned how I was called a queer. It was still pretty redneck, to be sure. And I know it may seem like I'm talking out of both sides of my mouth right now, but what I'm trying to say is that I have since come to the realization that, when it comes to hateful bassackwardness in the deep rural South, you can do a whole lot worse than my hometown.

The last thing I want to make clear is this: I love Celina dearly. I wouldn't be the person I am had I not been forged in those fires. And Celina in the nineties and early aughts was absolutely a trial by fire. If the first three paragraphs of this section didn't make it clear enough, I fully understand what happened there because I lived it too. It breaks my heart, the fate of that place. The factory left forever, but the pills showed up for good; the resulting fallout has been apocalyptic, and we didn't deserve any of it. This country and the people who run it have long since left towns like mine for dead, and it's a goddamn shame.

Now that you've got the full context for my hometown, I'd like to share one final anecdote. My dad passed away from pancreatic cancer in 2013.[4] After he died, as the oldest child, I was in charge of . . . well, everything. At this time, I had a pretty solid day job, but I also had two babies in diapers and a mountain of debt from putting myself through college. And my little sister had even less in the way of resources, so we were pinching pennies with regard to the funeral service. And despite having him cremated and skimping everywhere possible, we were still looking at a final bill of over $3,000. It's pretty wild how expensive it is to die in this country.[5] Anyway, I didn't know how I was going to pay that, but the funeral home had already told me beforehand that I could set up a payment plan (which was convenient because I had just been thinking to myself how I needed another bill added to the pile).

After the service was over and everyone had cleared out, I went into the office to get the official word on what the damage was. The man told me I didn't owe them anything because the full balance had been paid. I said that couldn't be right, as I had yet to pay him anything. "Everybody in town pitched in and covered it," he said. The whole bill had been paid by these people, most of whom I assure you were dealing with their own never-ending debt piles at home. None of them said a word to me about it before, during, after, or since. I still think about that all the time, and damned if I don't get teary-eyed over it, even now.[6] So to anyone from Celina reading this: Whether you believe it or not, I promise you . . . I'm on your side. Always have been, always will be. Go Bulldogs.

---

4. I know, I know. Finally, something funny in this comedy book.
5. Please play "Ain't That America" by John Cougar Mellencamp in your head right now. Thank you.
6. Classic queer.

ROUND HERE
Travel Ad-Lib

Fill in the words below and have yourself a homegrown Southern story!

While traveling through _____, Mississippi, we met
                                (ANIMAL) + (BODY PART)

a man named _____. He invited us in for some
              (YOUR CHILDHOOD DOG'S NAME + A COLOR BOOTS COME IN)

_____. We obliged, and he introduced us to his wife,
(WOODLAND CREATURE) + (TYPE OF PASTRY)

_____,
(CHOOSE ONE: WANDA/BEULAH/BESSIE/DARLA/RUBY/BETTY/MINNIE/PATTY) + (CHOOSE ONE: FAYE/ANN/JO)

who was wearing an airbrushed _____ shirt down to her
                                (LOONEY TOONS CHARACTER)

_____, which made us feel _____.
(LOWER BODY PART)   (NEGATIVE EMOTION)

Still, they were _____ people. At least until
                  (ADJECTIVE ONE MIGHT USE TO DESCRIBE A COW)

_____ came up. We tried to leave
(ADHERENTS OF A RELIGION BESIDES CHRISTIANITY [PROBABLY JEWS])

but _____ insisted on showing us his collection of
      (MAN'S NAME FROM LINE 2)

_____ and _____ first. Though we briefly feared
(PROJECTILE WEAPON, PLURAL)   (NATIVE AMERICAN ARTIFACT, PLURAL)

for our _____, after the tour they let us be on our way, and we headed
          (SENSITIVE BODY PART, PLURAL)

toward _____.
       (NAME OF FAMOUS EUROPEAN CITY BUT MISPRONOUNCE IT TERRIBLY IN YOUR HEAD) + (SOUTHERN STATE)

IS IT THE SOUTH? FLORIDA EDITION

Is Florida the South? An oft-debated question, to be sure. And at the end of the day, anyone who knows anything about Florida knows that more than anything else, Florida is just Florida. Ain't no other Floridas out there. Can't be, because if anywhere else tried, Florida would do bath salts and murder them, as Florida works the same way the Highlander does.

Around Florida, the saying goes, "In Florida, the farther north you go, the farther South you get," and in our experience, that's pretty damn accurate. The northern part of Florida is every bit as Southern as any other part of Dixie. Maybe more so. I mean, people turn lizards into boots there, for God's sake. The region also gifted the world with both Tom Petty and Lynyrd Skynyrd, so damn right it's the South.

KEY WEST, FLORIDA

WHAT THEIR MOTTO SHOULD BE: More Than Meets the Pie

WHAT TO PACK: A white fedora, a white shirt, white pants, white shoes, white belt, and a Tide pen.

WHAT TO EAT AND DRINK AND WHERE: Obviously you're gonna wanna eat the namesake pie, but don't sleep on the pink shrimp! Something 'bout the water round there makes the shrimp pink.[1] Also there are Cuban sandwiches all up Duval Street that will soak up them margaritas real nice!

WHAT NOT TO MISS: It's touristy, but snagging a picture at mile zero is something you gotta do when you are there. Hurry before it becomes some sort of Elián González–themed boat chute . . . You know how America be.

Do you like pie? How 'bout staring off into a faraway and forbidden land filled with old-timey cars, white leisure suits, and cigars that are still illegal for some reason? If so, then Key West is the place for you! Ninety miles north of Cuba, the southernmost town in the continental United States is a stunning four miles long and one mile wide.[2] If Panama City

---

1. Is that why Pappaw called Cubans *pinkos*?
2. Do we sound to anyone else but us like the announcer from *The Price Is Right* describing a showcase?

Beach is a sandy flea market filled with dry-rotted water hoses, then Key West is the quaint little antique shop off the beaten path where you can get an old sewing machine and a Raggedy Andy lunch box at the same time. While some may associate it now with drunken lunatics in Hawaiian shirts filling the streets to catch an impromptu performance from their lord and savior Jimmy Buffett,[3] it was also once residence to some of America's fancier literary heroes, such as Tennessee Williams and Ernest Hemingway. Hemingway loved it so much that he famously decided to shoot himself somewhere else!

Someone not from round here would probably find it confusing that we don't consider Key West the South seeing as how it quite literally does not get more southern than Key West. But as we've said, Florida is so very much its own thing, and frankly, Key West is its own thing even by Florida standards. A few things, though, may qualify it as being Southern in our opinion:

1. **There are a *shit ton* of chickens running around, y'all.**
    I'm talking a wholllle lot of loose chickens just struttin' their little asses up and down Duval Street and anywhere else a chicken can strut its ass. Apparently these chickens are descendants of some Caribbean chickens from way back, and since no one has bothered to tell 'em otherwise, they act like they own the damn place. Back during one of the Cuban wars, a whole bunch of people migrated to Key West, brought their roosters with them, and trained 'em how to fight. Cockfightin' and chickens on the loose. I've known a Tennessee man or two with a shed that boasted the same amenities.

2. **They eat fried food and pie like it's goin' out of style!**
    Now maybe it's just what they give to us fat, stinky, no-account tourists, but hot damn, y'all. You can eat like you're back at the county fair down here! You remember them big ol' conch shells— how people blow into them like sea trumpets or hold them up to their ears trying to hear the ghosts of pirates past? Well, turns out, critters live in them things, and when you fry those bastards up, it makes for a helluva meal! Of course, no good, fat meal is complete without dessert, and Key West is known for one of the best. While

---

3. Not that there's anything wrong with that—fins up, bitches!

you'll never catch anyone where we're from turning up their nose at one from the freezer section at Publix, a key lime pie enjoyed where it got its name is just a touch better. Hell, it may've been the first time I realized that key limes weren't naturally green! Fried fish and pie . . . sounds like we are back at Meemaw's house, y'all!

3. **These sumbitches seceded from the Union!**
   OK, it was only a brief secession, and it didn't have anything to do with the Civil War—but yes, for a short period of time, Key West declared their independence from the federal government and became the Conch Republic, and they still jokingly refer to themselves as such to this day. They've got their own flags and everything!

So to recap: They got chickens and fighting roosters running around everywhere, deep-fried fish and pie as far as the eye can see, and a genuine distaste for the federal government that led to the creation of a microeconomy of treasonous flags . . . Yeah, I think our pappaws would like it here!

Once you get past all that, though, it ain't nothing like the South we're from. Quite frankly, Key West seems more like if Casablanca and Margaritaville had a baby and slapped it right smack-dab between the Atlantic and the Gulf. The pastel britches and gold jewelry worn by the locals shimmer against the crystal-clear waters of Key West, and the nightlife moves to the beat of a salsa band, entrancing you like a snake charmer until you're too full of margaritas and Cuban sandwiches to realize you've been put under a spell.

Not that it gets—to quote our meemaws—"colder than a witch's titty" anywhere in the South save for a few days in February, but the temps stay in the seventies damn near year-round in Key West, which makes for some pleasant fishing, snorkeling, scuba diving, and all that stuff skinny active people seem to enjoy. And the weather had better be good if I'm gonna justify driving over that damn 106-mile bridge again! "Shoo-ee, son . . . lotta stray puppies been chucked over that thing, I bet!" Pappaw would say. Reckon we oughta take him next time!

PANAMA CITY BEACH, FLORIDA

WHAT THEIR MOTTO SHOULD BE: Ya Know, They Can Cure Hepatitis Now!

WHAT TO PACK: Any kind of shirts you want, as long as the sleeves are cut out and they're covered in cartoon characters, preferably either driving a cartoon truck or shooting a cartoon gun. Or you can get 'em airbrushed in town.

WHAT TO EAT AND DRINK AND WHERE: They genuinely do have some great places in town, but if you're doing it right, you'll be so hammered it'll all taste the same. Just go for it, dawg.

WHAT NOT TO MISS: The beautiful springtime migration of the Southeastern American College Trash, who flock en masse every year to PCB to perform their mating rituals and punch each other.

Ah, PCB. The Redneck Riviera. Where every year trash from all around this great nation make their yearly pilgrimage like devout followers to a holy shrine. If you wanna eat a shitload of happy-hour oysters and maybe get a divorce (the order is entirely up to you), then seek ye no further than Panama City Beach. Also, just for the record, both of us have taken countless trips to PCB because everything about it hits very hard for us (as we are trash).

Panama City Beach is a true testament to mankind's capacity for wrecking this beautiful, sweet earth of ours. We bet the first settlers who arrived in Panama City Beach, overwhelmed as they were by the idyllic setting and boundless oceanfront vistas, *probably* did not think to themselves, *One day, on this very land, frat boys from far and wide shall gather to engage in rum-fueled feats of bluster and shame. Verily, this fair settlement shall be known as a place where all people are afforded the God-given opportunity to contract a venereal disease and puke into a crab bucket.* We don't know exactly what PCB did to deserve becoming the official spring break destination for the entire American South, but surely the cosmic punishment has by this point far outweighed the crime.

Have you ever thought about what it would be like to hail from or live in a place like PCB? Imagine if every year, Alabama, Mississippi, Tennessee, et al. sent their drunkest and horniest twentysomethings to *your* hometown.[1] As on the nose as it may be, genuinely all we can think to say is . . . bless their hearts. Anyone who has ever worked in the service industry understands the rigors and frustrations that accompany working with the public. This is true for any public, anywhere, but just *imagine* doing it in PCB. No wonder they're always in the news for smoking meth and throwing alligators at people.

Listen, we're having some fun with PCB here, but the truth is, it wouldn't be so popular if it wasn't a *hell* of a good time. However, at least in our experience, the particular brand of good time offered there is a young person's game. We've heard some say that PCB isn't the same debauched college party place it used to be, but we can't speak to that and, frankly, would find that somewhat disappointing.[2] The idea that the Sandpiper Beacon Beach Resort might be filled with nice suburban families and well-to-do working professionals as opposed to sentient cans of Monster Energy drink? Not our PCB. No, our PCB is a singular place with a singular vibe.

Anyone can appreciate the appeal of walking barefoot on those sugary beaches in the warm embrace of a salt-scented breeze . . . it's just that in

---

1. "Do they have money?! We'll take 'em!"—Trae's hometown.
2. That'd be like finding out Portland outlawed tattoos and white-guy dreadlocks.

PCB, moments like these are punctuated with the sounds of Sig Eps starting an impromptu blowjob-themed chant (just as one example). And if you're the right age and sensibility for that sort of thing, then you absolutely, 100 percent, should go to Panama City.

IS IT THE SOUTH? TEXAS EDITION

I s it the South? Is it its own country? Is it going to come alive, turn Mexico into a pistol, and shoot California for allowing *Brokeback Mountain*? No one really knows, but regardless, we sure do love our friends in the Lone Star State. Some of the greatest country music, food, sports, and Yosemite Sam truck decals have come from Texas, and from Austin to San Antonio, it's also about as diverse a state as you can get without having a movie studio in it. They say everything is bigger in Texas, and that goes double for the personalities you will find there. Plus, I mean, Hank Hill, son. You can't get no better!

AUSTIN, TEXAS

Austin is one of our favorite cities in America, full stop. Arguably the liberal-redneck, gay-cowboy capital of the world, there's something in Austin for every type of white person. We kid, we kid. You don't have to be white; *obviously* there's all kinds of Mexican stuff goin' on in Austin as well. But still, when most people think of Austin, they think of one of two things: rootin'-tootin' Texas Ranger types and Portland-barista-but-in-Texas-somehow types. (On that note, we're sorry, but it's hilarious how applicable the classic "Steers and Queers" doctrine is here.) At the end of the day, though, Austin is very much its own thing while also feeling unequivocally Texan. That's a hard line dance to pull off, but Austin does so better than a recently divorced county fair pageant queen. Which is to say . . . pretty damn well.

When we are on tour, we do not always have our shit together. To say we do would be a lie because that is just not the case.[1] There are, however, towns where—no matter how healthy we've been back home, no matter how hard we've been going, and no matter how much we ought to stop for spiritual and medical reasons—we just know taking it easy will not be in the cards. Austin is one such city. The absolute *second* we hit the city limits, our stomachs grow like the Grinch's heart on Christmas, and the only thing that can fill that void is BBQ, Shiner Bock, and, more often than not, a trash bag's worth of psychedelic mushrooms.

One time we had just sold out Austin City Limits Live, and seeing as how we still very much consider ourselves . . . oh, what's the phrase? Stupid, small-town pieces of shit who deserve nothing? That's a big damn deal, y'all. After the show, of course, one of Austin's local trippin' cowboy mammaws[2] gave us a truckload of shrooms and sent us on our way. Only problem was she sent them with Corey's buddy Josh, who was acting as our de facto road manager for the weekend. Not thinking, Josh went back to the hotel to catch up on some paperwork while we went to the Continental to get drunk as shit and see whatever band was playing there. Corey called Josh to inquire whenabouts he might be bringing said bag of drugs down to us, and he said he was very busy and it would be a while. With his thinking cap already on, Corey hailed a taxi, sent it to the hotel, and had Josh toss the backpack in it before sending it right back downtown to us. Passengerless . . . sack of mushrooms only.

We're not saying Austin is the only place where a cab driver wouldn't even think twice about doing this, but it's probably the only place in the state. We ended up climbing on top of a hotel roof later that night wearing nothing but bathrobes. God bless Texas.

---

1. Hell, we've debased ourselves in Salt Lake City.
2. I know it's cliché, but that's a sweet band name.

SAN ANTONIO, TEXAS

WHAT THEIR MOTTO SHOULD BE: Remember the à la Mode

WHAT TO PACK: A good pair of walking shoes and some of them hangover pills, baby, *because it's about to go down*!

WHAT TO EAT AND DRINK AND WHERE: Go to the River Walk, have a margarita, get on the boat taxi, get off at the next stop, have a margarita, get on the boat taxi. (You see where this is going? Eat a bunch of tacos for strength.)

WHAT NOT TO MISS: Of course you have to see the Alamo. And then, for Christ's sake, don't you dare forget about it!

C harles Barkley once famously said of San Antonio, "There's some big ol' women down there!" Now, while that is horribly offensive and a sweeping generalization, it is also very hilarious. All jokes aside, though, if people in San Antonio *were* bigger than anywhere else in the country (they are not), you almost couldn't blame them because the food down there is just *so* freaking good.

Being from the southeastern part of the United States, we've only really ever gotten the type of Mexican food that Mexican people think stupid, fat rednecks can handle. You know, mushed-up stuff covered in cheese—and hell yeah, that stuff rules. But because of that, when you actually get the real deal, it will damn near blow your Richard Petty socks smooth up a wildcat's ass.[1] From tacos to churros to all the salsas and guac in between, you owe it to yourself to check out the River Walk. Take your cholesterol medicine with you.

We aren't going to sit here and act like the River Walk ain't eat up with tourists, 'cause it sure is. Hell, we ain't sure anyone in San Antonio is actually from San Antonio anymore, but with certain tourist traps, you can't help but understand. The River Walk has a commercial vibe and a bit of an Epcot feel to it, but that isn't necessarily a bad thing. I mean, you can drink margaritas the size of your head and eat table-side guacamole on chips that look like dinner plates made out of corn, and after all that go hop on a damn boat whose only job is to get you to another place where you can do it all again. What tourist in their right mind wouldn't want to flood an area like that? And, brother, don't even get us started on them damn puffy tacos! If you ain't ever had a puffy taco, I guess the best way to explain it would be that it's like a regular taco, but they have replaced the shell with one that resembles something more like an orthopedic pillow than something related to corn.

Of course, every up has its natural down, we reckon, and as good as the food is down there in beautiful San Antone, one thing we can't abide is the abundance of slippery, slimy critters. I guess they get used to 'em down there, but we ain't never gonna be the ones to just shake off a run-in with a doggone rattlesnake! Also, did you know they got scorpions down there same as we got like . . . roaches here? Maybe not in *that* great of infestations, but sometimes you'll just see a damn scorpion in your hotel room acting as if it don't look like a damn prehistoric monster! That ain't something you're prepared for on a Tuesday before you've even had your breakfast burrito. And we believe we'll have a robot president before they ever get done with their road construction.

The Alamo is supercool and also one of those things that feels like a tent pole to the fabric of our nation. You've heard "Remember the Alamo" so many times that the whole thing can almost feel like a joke until you actually get there and see it in person. This country is still a baby in the eyes of the rest of the developed world, and because of that, nothing here is really

---

1. Yes, that's totally a real saying . . . but don't look it up.

old.[2] Seeing the Alamo and being reminded of the gritty struggles this country faced in its early days puts a lot of things into perspective, and if you're a so-called man like we are, the sight can make you feel like a pussy, pardon the phrase! It's wild to think that nearly two hundred years ago, eight hundred men defended the Alamo from an army nearly twice that size, and all these years later we can stand where they bled, making duck lips for selfies on Instagram and crying tyranny when told to put on a mask so our grandmothers can make it through Christmas. LOL. We really suck sometimes.

Something that don't suck, however, is San Antonio, Texas, and the good and diverse people from there. We hope to return as soon as we can—and get so drunk we forget all about the scorpions again!

---

2. Not counting members of Congress. *Hey-oh!*

PART 2

OVER YONDER

THE REST OF AMERICA

We're not going to lie to y'all: Growing up down South, one is not given the best impression of . . . well, pretty much any other part of America. Sure, the cursed North gets the brunt of the abuse, but people back home weren't overly fond or trusting of the various other regions of the country either (especially the wretched hive of scum and villainy known as California). We don't think it's so much that the South hates everywhere else; it's more like the South is *convinced* that everywhere else hates *them*, and by God if that's how they wanna play it, then we'll surely oblige in kind. At a certain age, though, you start to think things like, *Ya know, Pappaw's never even* been *to Michigan. How does he know they all need their asses whooped?* And you become curious about these other mythical lands and their inhabitants; you want to know the truth of the matter. Is everyone in San Francisco really naked and high all the time? Does every trip to the grocery store in New York truly bring with it the threat of being stabbed with a heroin needle? Does Wyoming actually exist? You want to know these things.

Well, after years spent telling jokes nationwide, we've gleaned some manner of insight into the Rest of Y'all. And as it turns out, yuns are pretty all right. Yes, a place like Portland can seem fairly alien to a couple of hayseeds, but (hopefully) one comes to realize that "different" doesn't have to mean "bad." Also, if you drive a couple of hours out of the city, you're basically in Arkansas but with different trees, so that's comforting too.

In fact, that's probably the most striking revelation we've had about this great country: Yes, her various regions and peoples are remarkably diverse and profoundly different from one another, but a whole damn lot of it is the same too. People call America a melting pot, but it's really more like a salad (one of the big-ass kinds with bacon and cheese and fried chicken on it). Each of the ingredients is present and bringing its own flavor to the party, but we're all in the same bowl and contributing to one big dynamic and fulfilling dish. We suppose that metaphor is at least somewhat contingent upon how you feel about salads though. Our pappaws, for example, would probably say that America cannot be a salad, as America is not a gay waste of time. Still, you know what we mean.

After many privileged years spent traversing it, we can say that this country is vast and unique and divergent and undefinable, but it *is* one nation. (We're not going to do it, but feel free to say "under God" here if you are so inclined—we won't be dicks about it.) And it is beautiful. *Insert sound of eagle screeching here.* It was with these thoughts in mind that we wrote the following pages.

WEST COAST

LOS ANGELES, CALIFORNIA

Growing up in the South, we thought California was synonymous with many things, and none of them our grandmothers cared too much for. Where we are from, California isn't necessarily considered a beautiful and culturally diverse state that boasts the largest national subeconomy *in the world*, and aside from our propensity to cheer on the excavation of our world's natural resources and bastardize what God gave us for the progress of man, we don't much think of the gold rush when thinking of California either. Naw. Where we come from, when you say California, usually all you'll hear is "Oh . . . you mean Hollyweird, where the queers live? Yeah, I know where that is!"

California was barely even real to us growing up, and it certainly was not a place one would just go! No, California was not a place for good, red-blooded Christian Americans.[1] It was one big amusement park full of weirdos who every now and then took a break from licking each other to make a sweet-ass war movie so we'd let them keep living.

Most of the above generally applies to all of California, as far as the South is aware. But also in most Southern people's eyes, California only really has two parts: the north part, with that fancy bridge you see all over the TV, and the south part, i.e., Hollyweird. For now, let's focus on the latter: the ironically termed City of Angels (since to any Southern meemaw's eyes, it is very much the Sodom to San Fran's Gomorrah), Los Angeles.

We've always maintained that LA has more in common with the South than people realize. Think about it: The people have similar stances on shirtsleeves, they're all really nice but in a way that seems like it might be bullshit, and a huge chunk of the population is irrationally devoted to the belief that someday they will be chosen by a higher power for eternal glory. *Bam!* Got 'em! But seriously, Los Angeles is another multifaceted town. Both beautiful and soul-sucking, inspiring and depressing, authentic and made of plastic, the bright lights and dark shadows of La-La Land will show you who you are, whether you like it or not.

As comedians, we've obviously spent a lot of time in Los Angeles. In fact, Trae has lived there since January 2017. And he's *just* about done. No, it's not as bad as all that. Or is it? Honestly, it varies week to week. He, presumably, like many people who live in LA, vacillates wildly between disbelief at the benevolence and favor of a universe that has seen fit to bring him and his life to this incredible city . . . and loading his entire family up and driving twenty-five hundred miles nonstop down I-40 with his middle finger facing west out the window the whole goddamn way. With that said, let's allow him to expand on the experience in his own words.

As mentioned elsewhere in these pages, I grew up in my dad's video

---

1. It's far too much fun for them.

store—a converted single-wide trailer called Crowder's Video in Celina, Tennessee. As such, I cannot remember ever wanting to do anything else with my life except for . . . *that*. Whatever *that* was that they were doing in those VHS tapes. Well, that's not entirely true. For a few months after *Jurassic Park* I wanted to be a paleontologist, but I had yet to realize that the actual profession was less about fending off velociraptors and more about dusting off bones in Utah. Once I figured that out, I got over it pretty quickly. And other than that brief dalliance, it was show business or bust for ya boy.

I could write pages and pages, probably an entire book, on how that whole thing played out for me as a kid. Most people around me, especially my grandfather (a patriarch if ever there was one), were not *overly* thrilled with the idea. I had always made very good grades in school, which to them meant "He can do anything he wants": a small-town phrase that loosely translates to "He can be a doctor or a lawyer." When I would say I wanted to be a comedian, they reacted like Charlie's friends might have if Charlie had found the golden ticket but opted to tell inappropriate jokes in front of strangers for a living instead of touring the famed chocolate factory. They weren't crazy about the idea, is what I'm saying. And honestly, they weren't entirely wrong. But this isn't the book for all that. So suffice it to say, up until I moved here five years ago, I had been dreaming of moving to Los Angeles for literally my entire life.

And now I'm here! And it's . . . fine. It's the fine-est[2] experience a man could ask for, given that "fine" is the mathematical average of "incredible" and "soul-crushing." The reality is that most of the experience is one or the other of those two extremes—or even both at the same time. Everyone knows about the bright lights, but there's real darkness here too. All these big shots live out here, but there ain't a single star in the sky. It's that kind of place. I suppose we should first focus on the "incredible" aspects.

Pretty. Everything. Everybody. All of it is just so pretty. Well, except for the tent cities and the urban sprawl and the heroin and the violence and the smog and the—sorry, we're focusing on the positive right now. I don't know if it's because of the constant immaculate lighting or what, but everything just seems *brighter* in Los Angeles: smiles, dispositions, Lamborghini paint

---

2. Not *finest* . . . fine-est.

jobs, etc. Much as flowers generally do better with exposure to sunlight, so do human beings, it seems. Of course, on the other hand, skin cancer. Sorry! I can't help myself. Constant sunshine is nice, y'all.

It is a cliché, but LA weather is top-shelf pretty much 100 percent of the time. Living out here, I swear to God I sometimes forget "winter" is a thing. I have literally flown to Wisconsin in late October to do stand-up without packing anything with long sleeves. That fact, coupled with my hillbilly accent, pretty much cemented for those wonderful cheese people in Wisconsin that I am just about the dumbest sumbitch who ever lived. But you just don't think about things like "cold" or "snow" or "the least degree of physical discomfort" when you live in Los Angeles. Some adoptive Angelenos like to lament this. "Oh, I miss the *seasons*," they'll say in between sips of the mimosa they are drinking on an outdoor patio in January because they live in freakin' paradise. I've never cottoned to that line of thinking myself. Keep the damn cold; I been done with it. LA weather is amazing.

I will say, though, that one downside of living in a land in which winter dare not tread is that you become *massively* ill-equipped to handle even the slightest bit of chill. The first night I was in LA after driving across the country, it was January in Santa Monica. The temperature was exceedingly mild, yet everywhere I looked people were bundled up in fleeces and winter coats. I thought to myself, *Ha, these white people are just dying for any excuse to break out the North Face, huh?* Fast-forward five years, and I'm outside on the porch screaming at my kids not to forget their jackets because "the high today is sixty-four!" It's insane how quickly your tolerance for cold dissipates (not that I had much to begin with as a native Tennessean).

This next thing may just be another Me Thing, but one thing I love about LA is that it's a big city that doesn't really feel like it, depending on where you are. The sprawl is so great that LA is a massive collection of neighborhoods and suburbs masquerading as a city, and none of it has the same type of intimidation factor that, say, New York can have. You look up and can see the damn sky. And as a hayseed-American, I appreciate that. My meemaw, bless her heart, does not at all understand this aspect of LA. She's more like the people we talked about in the opening paragraphs of this section. In her mind, I'm living in a hedonistic metropolis, something out of an eighties John Carpenter movie. She thinks I'm in literal danger of being stabbed every time I go to the grocery store. But I live in Burbank. My kids walk down the street every day to attend *Walt Disney Elementary School*.[3] It's all very idyllic and picket fence-y and Rockwellian. But good luck getting Meemaw to believe that. Either way, while some people might consider this a knock against LA, I absolutely love it.

Next up, and I swear I'm not just being a pandering progressive, the diversity of this city is amazing. You wouldn't believe how many Mexicans and Chinese they got out here, y'all! Black people too! Eat up with 'em! And it's *wonderful*. There's something for everybody here. I couldn't even begin to guess the number of heritages represented in my son's elementary school classes, but it's a lot. And I, for one, am thrilled that he has a bunch of friends with wild names, as opposed to Brayden / Asheleigh / Foenix / all them super-white names like that.

I know there's lots of mammaws and pappaws out there who would be terrified by all of that, but I love it. Hell, where I grew up, there was a small Black community and two types of white people: regular and trash (I was the latter). That was it. Do you have any idea how ignorant that made me, despite my intentions? Y'all, I literally met my first Jewish person when I was twenty-two years old. *I still remember it!* I don't give a damn what anybody says: That type of thing isn't good for a kid, and you don't have to worry about it if you live or grow up in LA. Also that level of diversity means the city's food game is just off the charts.

Let's see, what else . . . There's a crazy amount of stuff to do, if you're the doin'-stuff type. Mickey Mouse is from here. There's an ocean, which is pretty neat. We also have mountains on the other side. We got caught in a literal blizzard once about an hour outside of downtown Los Angeles. Did you know that was possible? It is, and it was terrible. It's a city of dreamers, which gives it an aura, but on the statistical flip side, almost all of those dreams fail to come true (which, honestly, is kind of LA in a nutshell). Regardless, whatever you're looking for in life, you can probably find it in Los Angeles.

All right, now on to the bad stuff. First of all, and you already know what I'm going to say . . . *the traffic*. I won't belabor the point because everyone on earth already knows this about LA, but let me just say this:

---

3. My friends back home think I'm messing with 'em when I tell 'em that. "Bullshit; that ain't real." But it is.

However bad you imagine the traffic in Los Angeles to be based on what you've heard about it, I assure you—it is worse in reality. And there's not much rhyme or reason to it.

Yes, rush hour is a thing, but I swear to God I have sat in standstill traffic on the 5 at eleven thirty on a Thursday night.[4] It's unreal. I live on the other side of town from LAX, about sixteen miles away. Which means it takes me anywhere from forty minutes to, I shit you not, two hours to make that trip. If you have to move around town for work reasons, like I often do (meetings and the like), 70 percent of your day will be spent sitting in traffic. If you have something to do in the middle of the day on the other side of town, don't even bother making additional plans for at least a couple of hours on either side of the actual meeting time. You will be sitting in traffic then. Matter of fact, just try to make as few plans as possible in life, generally. If you live in Los Angeles, you will be sitting in traffic for most of them.

Next up on the Shit List, and once again you already know what I'm going to say: It is insanely, stupidly, *offensively* expensive to live here. Granted, that's largely because of all the naive goobers from places like Clay County who keep moving here and dumbing up the works year after year. True story: At the first bar I ever went to after moving to LA, I was sitting on the patio waiting on a friend and wearing a Titans shirt. Someone else on the patio noticed it and asked if I was from Tennessee. I responded in the affirmative, and she said, "Oh, me too!" Someone at the next table overheard this and chimed in that they were *also* from the Volunteer State. The bartender handing out drinks nearby interjected: "Really? I'm from Chattanooga!" And then another couple. I know this sounds made-up, but I swear it turned out every single person who happened to be on that bar patio in Los Angeles at that moment was a Tennessean. As a general rule, if you meet someone new in LA and ask them where they're from, odds are the answer will not be one of the neighborhoods in the greater metropolitan area but rather some "flyover" state.[5] And more arrive every single day. So yeah, it's expensive. If everyone grew up dreaming of living in Toledo, then it'd probably be pretty damn costly too.

Still, though, it's one thing to understand a phenomenon and another to

---

4. You gotta put the word *the* before highway numbers out here or they deport you back to regular America.
5. I hate the term *flyover*, too, but I'm a flyover-American, so I'm allowed to use it.

experience it. It is *shocking*. I live in a cozy little two-bedroom house, about nine hundred square feet, and if my landlord decided to sell it, it would easily go for around a million dollars. *A million dollars.* It's not just the housing. If you live in Middle America, next time you're upset at the numbers staring back at you from the gas pump display, take solace in the knowledge that it is *at least* 60 percent higher in California. Groceries too. And utilities. And don't even get me started on *taxes*. But again, the reason it's so expensive is because in most people's estimation, it's worth it. So the question really is: Would you rather look at your bank account and smile in Ohio? Or do the same and cry on the beach? The choice is yours.[6]

You've probably heard people describe Los Angeles as being "plastic." In my experience, that's a fairly apt description—and not just because of all the fake lips and butts and stuff (though those are legion). I don't know if it's because this is the land of make-believe or what, but a lot of the smiley, sunshiny aspects of LA oftentimes feel superficial. Hollow. Like none of this is real. Like we're all lying to ourselves. Or maybe that's just the coke wearing off.[7] There's a thing in LA where no one ever really talks about who they *are*, but rather who they're *trying to be*. Everyone's got a thing they're working on. Something that might happen. Some shit they might do or a story they might write. A guy they know who knows some guy you need to know because that guy knows *everybody*. Everyone grins and laughs and congratulates each other, but you can just kind of tell that they would all hurl their grandmothers from the Griffith Observatory if it meant getting what they want. I've been at many a Hollywood after-party and longed instead to be transported to my buddy Colby's garage back in Celina—where I'd be surrounded by deer heads and inflatable Busch Light decorations and NASCAR posters and innumerable empty cans and cigarette butts. Most importantly, I'd be with people who really are being themselves instead of doing their best impression of the person they think they're *supposed* to be. Holy shit, I should get back in therapy.

All right, time for another disclaimer.[8] The preceding paragraph is 100 percent more about *show business* than it is about the city of Los

---

6. Of course, some of the people in Ohio still have to cry, whether for bank account reasons or just general Ohio reasons. So it goes.
7. I'm kidding. Nobody does coke in Hollywood anymore. Strictly Adderall, thank you very much.
8. This damn book is chock-full of those, isn't it?

Angeles. It's just that the two are inexorably linked in my mind and the minds of many. It is entirely possible that most Angelenos—those living and working in regular human-being fields like medicine or construction—are not *at all* fake and full of shit. So your mileage may vary.

At the end of the day, Los Angeles is objectively one of the best and most exciting cities this country—and probably the world—has to offer. I know I've just been on a bit of a tirade about it, but if I could go back in time, I'd still pack up that U-Haul (and my family) and hit the road. There's nowhere else quite like it, and if you're the type with wanderlust or big dreams or a sense of adventure or a world to take by storm, and if you think you can handle it (and *afford* it), then I say to hell with it . . . Go West, young man.[9]

---

9. Or woman. Not trying to be exclusive. Look, the quote says "man," and I was doing a thing, OK?

NAPA, CALIFORNIA

WHAT THEIR MOTTO SHOULD BE: My Other Car Is a
Sailboat Filled with Duck Fat

WHAT TO PACK: Your wallet and an extra liver.

WHAT TO EAT AND DRINK AND WHERE: The French
Laundry if you can afford it. If not, just sample all the cheeses
and get drunk. Calories are calories!

WHAT NOT TO MISS: The Buena Vista Winery feels like
touring something medieval.

A handful of places we've been to could best be categorized as "postcard
towns." If you make your index fingers and thumbs into a rectangle
like them old-timey directors used to, then look at everything around you
through that frame, then you would be hard-pressed to find an image that
doesn't look exactly like something they would print and stick in a rotating
stand at the local Stuckey's. Napa, California, is without question a postcard
town. You won't believe this, but in a place like Napa, where there are more
vineyards than there are cavities, a couple of ice-in-their-boxed-red-wine
sons of bitches like us stick out like thumbs sorer than a grape stomper's
big toe.

Napa, California, could not be more different from the only Napa we
knew growing up, which was an auto parts store with a really catchy if

annoying slogan. The first time we were offered a gig in Napa, California, was pretty terrifying from a performer standpoint. Don't get me wrong—it ain't like we had exclusively done shows in the South. We tour the whole country, and while, yes, some of it plays better in the South, we still sell shitloads of tickets everywhere from New York City to Portland, Oregon. Napa was a little more intimidating, though, because big ol' liberal cities like Portland and NYC are well-known for having all types of different people, which usually includes some redneck expats who flock to our shows. Napa isn't really known for that. Napa is known for being like the fucking France of America or some such, and it didn't help that the venue we were booked to play was not at all a comedy club but rather a jazz club. And jazz can go one of two ways.

Jazz was, as most should know, invented by Black people and is one of two universally recognized American arts (the other, coincidentally, being stand-up comedy). When you go to a Black jazz club in, let's say, New Orleans or the Mississippi Delta, you are in for a really cool, laid-back environment, where people are drinking and maybe going out back to have a smoke and generally just having a good time. But this is Napa, California . . . this is *white*-people jazz, LOL. I mean, if I remember correctly, the act that was there the week before us was fucking Kenny G. And hey, I have all the respect in the world for Kenny G and wish I was as good at what I do as he is at what he does, but let's face it: The Kenny G jazz audience is far from our usual crowd. White-people jazz is stuffy, pretentious, up its own ass, high on its own supply, and usually more interested in pithy discourse than it is in having fun. Not even a little bit what you want from a crowd coming to see you talk about your meemaw and her walkin' farts.

Let's also add the fact that this place is known for its wine. I'm not going to sit here and disparage wine drinkers, for I am one. However, I have never even come close to *identifying* as a wine drinker. Does that make sense? We drink wine for one reason and one reason only: to get drunker than we could on beer. End of story. As we alluded to earlier, we also pour our red wine over ice, which I'm pretty sure in Napa would force the mayor to bring out the gallows, or at the very least the stocks and pillory so passersby could throw tomatoes and wilted lettuce at the uncultured swine before them. Wine is not a drink in Napa. It is a religion, a way of life, an attitude, and obviously the whole goddamn economy! There are over four hundred wineries in Napa alone, which is more than the number of people who attended my damn high school! Hell, you could take both of our tiny towns combined, split them up among the various wineries in Napa, and still have enough room left to set up a pull-behind trailer for Lynyrd Skynyrd[1] to play a full set on. "Gimme Three Steps" and a bottle of your cheapest blend, monsieur!

Here's a little bit about Corey's experience in Napa: My momma was raised by her grandmother, who had grown up dirt-poor in the Great Depression. Granny worked hard, and while they still barely had anything, she spent all her money making sure my momma had a chance to get out. Momma went to nursing school and met my dad, who had grown up fairly middle-class and who would later go on to do pretty well for the family because my momma supported him when he was starting out. My mom's upbringing being what it was, she spent a lot of time fantasizing about what life could be like if she ever did have money. Fancy dinners with white tablecloths. Seven courses and a butler or some shit who would replace your fork between 'em. One of the places she had put on her bucket list later in life was the French Laundry in Napa.

The French Laundry is a Thomas Keller joint, and the Michelin Guides have given it three stars. The highest you can receive. BTW, holy shit, did you know that those are the same Michelins that make the tires and stuff? Ain't that wild? Anyways, I digress. When I found out that we had sold out our shows in Napa and that I would be making a pretty sweet paycheck, I decided to do what all good Southern boys do and take care of my momma. I flew her out to meet me in Napa and, through the diligence of my manager, Nat, was able to procure a reservation at the French Laundry. My mother was so excited—for the obvious reason that she had always wanted to go, but also because her baby boy was now past the point of telling dick jokes in dingy bars and being paid in Percocets.

We toured the facility, and, y'all, it looked more like a damn laboratory than it did a kitchen. A whole sous vide station kept steaks and other meats I couldn't wait to eat at just the right temperature, and the chefs were clad in white outfits that may as well have been lab coats because of all the

---

1. The original lineup. Don't even get us started on what they have become.

experiments they seemed to be doing with glazes, foams, sauces, different-sized plates, you name it.

We sat down to lunch, and for the first time in probably ten years, I was wearing a button-up shirt that wasn't made out of denim and smelling of Camel full-flavor cigarettes.[2] My mother looked like her normal Audrey Hepburn little self. We were both so excited, though I was probably more proud than anything. We blazed through the courses, and it truly was a magical experience. I wish I could describe all of the tastes, but as those who follow my work probably know by now, I'm not *that* good of a writer. We had chicken and fish. Pork and bison. Little medallions of some sort of Yankee vegetable I'm not sure I'd ever seen, charred, glazed, and placed atop a bed of greens. It was delicious, but I was too embarrassed to ask once again what it was, and I'm pretty sure the servers couldn't understand me anyway. Then came the dish that would ultimately be my favorite but that definitely surprised me . . . rabbit! Now, I've had rabbit before, but in a stew and made by a man named Tommy Two-Fingers. This rabbit was different, and if I think back real hard, I can still taste it ever so slightly. It was just 'bout the purdy-est thing anyone ever did to a poor little woodland creature.

We had our desserts, which were chocolate truffles with them real color-ful designs on top, some of which looked like black holes in space. They, along with the various dessert wines, were wonderful. Then I got the bill . . . 350 dollars. Not total—per person. And, oh, I forgot to mention I was paying for four people because my aunt and her friend had come along for the trip, and I of course had to prove to them that slacking off in class had not led me to ditch-digging in the end (not that there's anything wrong with that!). Truly, it was delicious. But next time I think I'll have ol' Tommy find me a rabbit.

We may have been a little hard on Napa here, and that really ain't fair. It's just intimidating for a couple of boys who prefer to cut the sleeves out of their shirts and prefer pontoons over sailboats to uncork bottles worth more than our childhood homes. There are mighty fine people there, and while everything is very expensive and you will undoubtedly run into your fair share of pretentious snobs and fart-sniffing intellectuals, the scenery is absolutely breathtaking, and you can get some pretty damn good food as well. And hell, white-people jazz ain't half bad!

---

2. I have since quit smoking, so please stop writing your letters right now!

PORTLAND, OREGON

WHAT THEIR MOTTO SHOULD BE: You Can Literally Just Do Whatever

WHAT TO PACK: Pretty much anything will fly in Portland. You wanna bring some maracas? A banana costume? And a *shitload* of sage? Sure, knock yourself out.

WHAT TO EAT AND DRINK AND WHERE: Portland's great because they got all that crunchy vegan-type stuff but also Voodoo Doughnuts, one of our nation's finest monuments to sugary excess.

WHAT NOT TO MISS: There is no city on planet Earth that can hope to compete with Portland, Oregon, in the time-honored tradition of people watching. If you're in Portland and there's people around, just watch 'em for a while. You won't wanna miss it.

People think of Portland and picture an emaciated white barista with a handlebar mustache. But this is unfair. The truth is, Portland is inhabited by an eclectic, diverse collection of mustaches. We kid, we kid. But Portland is absolutely one of the most heavily stereotyped cities in this country. Generally outsiders associate two things with Portland: hipsters and antifa. People think Portlanders get dressed up like Victorian-era haberdashers to go set city hall on fire, then act as though this is a point of ridicule. But if you, amid a full-scale riot, saw a chimney-sweep-lookin' sumbitch emerging from the smoke-bomb haze atop a damn penny far-thing,[1] you'd be wise to take him seriously. Unless you're looking to get choked out with a pocket-watch chain, that is.

The antifa element of Portland's reputation is a more recent phenom-enon, arising mostly from the extended news coverage of the protests that erupted in the city in the wake of George Floyd's murder. The rest of us were watching the stories coming out of Portland at the time, doing double takes like, "Did I just see a soccer mom throw a brick through a bank window?" It was wild. But some people took this to mean that Portland was now basically Somalia. Hell, people in our hometowns literally thought Portland had started *exporting* hippie terrorists, so great were their numbers. They believed platoons of women's studies majors armed with weaponized vegan-ism were being loaded onto VW buses and deployed to Middle America to . . . turn farm boys pansexual, we guess? We're still not really clear on what the endgame was supposed to be, but for a while there, small towns lived in fear of the Great Rose City Scourge.

The reality is this: Yes, Portland is one of the most progressive cities in the country (though it falls outside the top ten, according to most rankings online), and yes, people in Portland have a predilection for activism—*but* it's not like they distribute gas masks at the community center or anything. In most respects and in most neighborhoods, Portland is a regular city filled with regular people living regular lives. Though to be fair, in Portland a "regular person living a regular life" could mean a "dude wearing a Pikachu onesie at 2:00 p.m. on a Tuesday." And that's fine!

While the militancy stereotypes are more recent in origin, Portland has been considered the Hipster Capital of the World[2] for a minute now. The perception exploded with the popularity of the wonderful sketch-comedy show *Portlandia*, and we feel like if you ask most locals how accurate that show was, they would say, "Around 70 percent." And they would say it in a way that implied, "Which isn't so bad, eh?" Meanwhile, you're sitting there thinking, *Oh, OK, so y'all wild as hell then.*

---

1. You know, them old bicycles with the comically oversized front wheel.
2. Or at least the US. We're not really up-to-date on global hipster trends.

In our experience, that element of Portland is very real. In fact, we still remember the first person from Portland either of us ever met, due to how well he fit this particular stereotype. A Portland comic was in Knoxville for a comedy festival, and he asked us where to find some weird and hard-to-spell drink. In this particular case, the drink in question was yerba maté, but this was East Tennessee in, like, 2011. We wouldn't have yerba maté for at least five more years. Hell, we probably didn't even have kombucha yet. Either way, they love weird and hard-to-spell drinks in Portland, and usually before the rest of white America even knows about them. And before you ask, the answer is yes: The guy had full-sleeve tattoos and smelled like beard oil.

That was just one dude, of course, but in the intervening years we've taken multiple trips to Portland that have done very little to dampen the reality of the city's hipster stereotypes for us. *But*—and we feel this is extremely important to note—it's endearing, not insufferable. Portlanders march to the beat of their own weird bongo, but what's wrong with that? They're not boring, and they're not assholes. They're supportive. It's not like you have to conform to their particular brand of weirdness or anything. You can be any kind of weird you wanna be in Portland—so long as you're not hurting anybody else—and that's beautiful.

Portland is very inclusive, if not *all* that diverse. The running joke is that there are more BLM signs than Black people in Portland. Though in fairness to them, they do really like signs. They're some sign-makin' SOBs in Portland, now. Hell, there's probably more protest signs in Portland than there are Black people in some whole states (lookin' at you, *Wyoming*). But still, like a lot of other cities in this book/country, it *is* pretty damn white. But what they lack in racial diversity, they make up for in the diversity of lifestyles. Sure, they got a bunch of white people, but some of those white people identify as foxes. And some of those foxes are in polyamorous relationships with sapiosexual dispensary workers and also, like, account-ants named Todd. And that's all just fine, thank you very much. That's what makes Portland wonderful. It's maybe the best city in this country to go and *be yourself*, no matter what the hell kind of self you're trying to be. Unless yourself is a Nazi. In which case the city demands that you fuck off. Never change, Portland.

SEATTLE, WASHINGTON

WHAT THEIR MOTTO SHOULD BE: We're Real Smart but Also, Like, Sad, Ya Know? So It's Cool.

WHAT TO PACK: Rain jacket. Rain boots. Sleeping pills to offset the caffeine. Shirt from a band that *isn't* Nirvana. Nirvana shirt.

WHAT TO EAT AND DRINK AND WHERE: You've heard it before, but you absolutely must go to Pike Place Market. Spend a few hours walking around, and then stand in the long-ass line to sample every single chowder. It is the best chowder in the world. I'm sorry, Boston.

WHAT NOT TO MISS: Go to a dive bar and see a shitty band trying their best. It may not be the nineties, but the heart and soul of grunge is still alive in some of these kids, and you never know who you'll be able to say that you saw. And hey, at the very least, you'll probably get to watch a breakup or see someone get punched!

H ey baby, I hear the blues a-callin', tossed salads and scrambled eggs! Mercy!" Now to quote the judge in one of his many divorce hearings, "I have no idea what the fuck Kelsey Grammer is talking about right now," but we do love it. More than that, we love the city our favorite fictional psychiatrist lives in! Seattle is known for many things—be it the birthplace of grunge, one of the country's most gorgeous skylines, or cool-ass Chinese dudes chucking fish at each other in a crowded market. It is certainly not just that "place where it rains a lot" (even though, trust us, it does that too).

You know how even if you didn't know what day it was, if you woke up on a Sunday you could just tell it was a Sunday? In our opinion, Seattle is the exact same way. If you woke up facedown and butt naked on a hotel floor (which we have done) and had absolutely no idea where you were, once you took the first step out of the lobby and into the streets of Seattle, you'd know it right away. And I don't mean because you could see the Space Needle, or because you'd see nineteen coffee shops within spitting distance, and not even because you'd see a man in a fedora playing Soundgarden on an accordion. You would just know because Seattle has a vibe that permeates the misty air the Emerald City is known for.

Yes, every time we've been to Seattle, it has been raining. They always say, "Well, technically, it doesn't even get as much rain here as in other major cities 'cause it only rains a little every time it rains." OK, that's great, but we'd prefer a few torrential downpours a year over living every day like we're walking through a Woody Allen[1] movie on our way to the suicide store. Obviously, that is no one's fault but God's,[2] so it isn't an indictment of the city or its fine Seattleites, but the stereotype about Seattle's weather is *very real*. It's also interesting, too, because you don't really see as many people with umbrellas as you'd think. People sorta just soldier through, getting drenched with an "ugh, this may as well happen to me" attitude that we really respect. We guess you can truly get used to just about anything. It's kind of like how in the South we don't notice the dip spit drizzling off our meemaws' whiskery chins as much as maybe a tourist would.

If the rain and overall dreariness of the almost permanently cloudy days has got you down, you can always go to one of the umpteen-bajillion coffee shops the city boasts. Seattleites like their coffee shops the way James Bond likes his women: a whole lot of 'em all over the fuckin' place. You can't throw a rock without hittin' three baristas and then hearing someone yell, "Hey, that redneck is throwing rocks again!" You can get 'em with

---

1. Look, his old movies were great, but we haven't watched them in a while for . . . reasons.
2. Don't get us started on that guy.

foam, no foam, oat milk, coconut milk, almond milk, soy milk, caf, decaf, half-caf, hot brewed, cold brewed, iced, blended, shrimp kebab, shrimp creole, shrimp gumbo, panfried, deep-fried, stir-fried—shit, never mind. We're thinking of something else. And definitely don't expect your barista to be named Bubba.

We would like to see that though. A misplaced Bubba in the rainy city of Seattle trying to make it as the bass player in a Pearl Jam cover band forced to work day shifts at some coffee place called Espresso Your Opinion. He's a great barista, but no one can understand a goddamn thing he is saying. One of many ways he relates to the song "Yellow Ledbetter." We think that would play out something like this:

> **BUBBA THE BARISTA:** Welcome to Espresso Your Opinion, buddy. What can I do ya for?
>
> **CONFUSED SEATTLE PATRON:** Um, what do you recommend?
>
> **BUBBA THE BARISTA:** I recommend changing ya oil by yaself to save thirty-five dollars—skeeew! I'm just bullshittin', friend. Hell, I don't know. You want hot or cold?
>
> **CONFUSED SEATTLE PATRON:** It's July. I'll take cold.
>
> **BUBBA THE BARISTA:** Boy, I tell you what, if my pappaw had lived to see the day they served coffee cold, he'd be irate! 'Course Pappaw was in the war and came back sayin' a lot of stuff he ourt notta said. And to be fair, he drunk warm Dr Pepper that'd been sittin' in his floorboard since he went to the grocery store a week back, so I don't exactly know if his opinion on beverage temperature is one to be respected.
>
> **CONFUSED SEATTLE PATRON:** Are . . . are you having a stroke?
>
> **BUBBA THE BARISTA:** Sorry, buddy. One iced coffee coming right up. Tell ya mom and them I said hey!

Since we've already done the ole cliché of "Seattle has a lot of coffee," let's go ahead and up the ante by stating the obvious: Seattle's seafood is fucking amazing. If you are planning a trip to Seattle but also are vain and worried about your waistline, might we suggest you cut five to eight pounds in the weeks preceding your trip? Because you will gain that much on clam chowder alone. You can get fresh fish and do it yourself by visiting one of the many fishmongers in their various fisheries (we think that's a word), or you can always go down to the world-famous Pike Place and feel the fish whipping past your head as you stroll toward that stupid gum wall. Oh, you didn't know about the gum wall? OK, how do we explain this? It's an alley where people go to stick gum on the wall, as if Diagon Alley in Harry Potter was managed exclusively by fifth graders. It smells like nothing but old gum and is on our short list of places where we think COVID-19 may have started. That said, it is a quirky and fun little addition to the already supercool Pike Place Market, which, as we said, is a great place if you want some of Seattle's best seafood, ice cream, art, stupid T-shirts, custom-made wallets for some reason, and crowds that will make your anxiety spike if you haven't taken some of your mammaw's nerve pills that day. Oh, and coffee. The first Starbucks is there, but you will wait in a line longer than Ichiro Suzuki's contract extension.

Seattle is just about the most fun you can have in the rain. The city is very diverse, and because of a large Asian population, you can also get some pretty tremendous noodles. We know it isn't good to boil an entire group of people down to just their culinary contributions, but as we are two chubby rednecks who love food, you'll have that from time to time. Looking at the Seattle skyline with its shiny buildings and the Space Needle, you would almost think you were getting ready to experience something from *The Jetsons*, but then you get in the city and are met with the grungy attitude that was made so famous on MTV in the nineties. Then you look up and see Mount Rainier and realize that while you are in the big city, you are not far from natural beauty. Seattle is one of the most outdoor-friendly cities in the country because of this, which is good because finding a place to park is harder than trying to convince Corey's uncle that the Clintons didn't kill Kurt Cobain too.

WEST COAST
TRAVEL BINGO

Look for an object, and the first one to five in a row/column/diagonal wins a coffee drink made with one of them fake milks.

INDIAN CASINO	CLEAN-CUT TWENTYSOMETHING WHO TURNS OUT TO BE A HOBO	CAFÉ WITH CATS IN IT	SUBARU WITH BICYCLES STRAPPED TO IT	THAT GUY FROM THAT THING YOU SAW THAT TIME
BEACH WHERE NO ONE IS IN THE WATER (BECAUSE IT'S COLD AS SHIT)	STRANGER WHO TRIES TO SELL YOU SOMETHING	THREE OR MORE PSYCHICS WITHIN WALKING DISTANCE OF EACH OTHER	BUMPER STICKER ABOUT THE EARTH BEING COOL	SMOKE FROM A RAGING FIRE SOMEWHERE
BEING CUT OFF BY AN ASSHOLE IN A CONVERTIBLE	BIG-ASS TREES		DUDE WITH REAL PRETTY HAIR	BLACK LIVES MATTER SIGN IN THE WHITEST NEIGHBORHOOD YOU'VE EVER SEEN
SOMEBODY NEKKID IN PUBLIC	PERSON SCREAMING INTO THE ABYSS ON A BEAUTIFUL DAY	SHOP DEDICATED ENTIRELY TO CRYSTALS	SOMEONE TAKING A PICTURE OF THEIR BUTT FOR INSTAGRAM	A PLACE YOU'RE PRETTY SURE USED TO BE A START-UP
BUNCH OF TENTS ON THE SIDE OF THE ROAD	MOTORCYCLIST WEAVING THROUGH STANDSTILL TRAFFIC	BILLBOARD OFFERING PET PSYCHIATRY	SOMETHING VEGAN THAT SHOULDN'T BE VEGAN (LIKE A BURRITO)	CRYPTO STUFF

A NOTE ON HAWAII AND ALASKA

Here's the deal: Both Hawaii and Alaska deserve more than we are able to give them in these pages. While we have done stand-up shows in Honolulu,[1] our travels have not yet taken us to the vast and wild country of Alaska. Alaska, by all reports, has not missed us. But as a result, we can only speak in stereotypes and expectations where Alaska is concerned. With that in mind, we'll lay out how we *imagine* Alaska to be in hopes that in the future we can go there and find out firsthand just how insultingly off base we were in this section.

First of all, moose. Just lousy with 'em. Bears too. Seals. All kinds of wild animals, really, as thus far inexorable industry has not yet blighted Alaska to the extent it has the rest of the country. So that's nice. Although they do have a lot of resources up there, like trees and oil and fish and stuff,[2] which we have to assume corporations will sooner or later commence exploiting to the land's extreme detriment. Guess we'll see.

The sun is weird there. It either vanishes for weeks like a drunken stepdad or it just *will not leave*, no matter how much you want it to, like a . . . well, like a drunken stepdad. Let's see, what else . . . Sarah Palin's up there somewhere, not reading. It's harsh country, as evidenced by the shortsighted ne'er-do-well from *Into the Wild* who apparently thought it'd be a good idea to just hobo his ass out into the Alaskan wilderness.[3] Some of the hardiest people on planet Earth are the natives of the area.

On that note, we have no idea if igloos are real or not, and we're kind of afraid to ask. Anyway. Working on a boat up there is pretty hard, as we

---

1. Thank you for that, internet.
2. Verily this is a scholarly tome.
3. Turns out, it was a bad idea.

understand it, annnnnd . . . that's about it. Sorry, Alaska. We promise one day we will darken your proverbial doorstep (for which we apologize) and see for ourselves the surely awe-inspiring truth of the matter.

As for Hawaii, we, like all self-respecting middle-class white Americans, have gotten drunk off coconut drinks while wearing unbuttoned shirts with flowers on them in Honolulu. And it was *lovely*, thank you very much. Here's the thing with Hawaii though: You have to be internet-Karen levels of oblivious—or just an asshole—not to realize how tragic the history is there. What was done to Hawaii was jacked up, even by American standards. It was like a world-record speedrun for colonialism. All in the name of pineapples. And look, we love pineapples. All pineapples, not just the ones that come on top of ham. Regardless, we ourt notta done what we did to Hawaii.

Really, it would be more accurate to say that what was done to Hawaii was done in the name of sugar (as well as pineapples), but is that any better? Fun fact: Beginning in 1861, the Confederacy stopped selling sugar to the Union states, who had to turn elsewhere for sweet-tooth appeasement. And "elsewhere" ended up being Hawaii. This led to JUST SO MUCH blood-thirsty capitalism-type stuff on the islands, which in turn led to the royal family being overthrown so (white) captains of industry could take over.

So yeah, you may not have known it, but even the atrocities on the other side of the planet were the South's fault too! We just couldn't do shit right back then, huh?[4] So . . . we're sorry, Hawaii. But all that aside, it is a mind-numbingly beautiful place and you should visit.

---

4. Unlike today, of course, when the American South is a shining beacon of utopian progress.

NORTHEAST

NEW YORK CITY, NEW YORK

WHAT THEIR MOTTO SHOULD BE: Welcome to New Yawk. Now Go Fawk Yaself.

WHAT TO PACK: Walking shoes! With all the walking and public transportation, you'd almost think New Yorkers were European (except for every single other thing about them, that is).

WHAT TO EAT AND DRINK AND WHERE: Just walk down the street until you realize you're hungry and then buy the closest thing to you. Odds are it will be the best bagel/dog/kebab/slice/you-name-it that you've ever had in your life. Do this drunk at 2:00 a.m. for maximum efficacy.

WHAT NOT TO MISS: Trae went to New York prolly ten times before he ever laid eyes on the Statue of Liberty. He was too busy gettin' hammered in Queens with a buncha different dudes all named Mike (and it was wonderful). But yeah, they got all kinds of shit like that there if you're into it.

We don't know if y'all have seen any movie from the 1970s or any procedural cop show from the . . . well, from anytime, but if ya have, then you have a pretty good idea of how New York City is perceived where we come from. That was our only exposure to the place, and why the hell wouldn't we believe Executive Producer Dick Wolf? When has that guy ever lied to us? Point being, if you told one of our grandmothers you were headed to the Big Apple, hell—she'd probably go ahead and start planning your funeral on account of you're definitely gonna get stabbed in a subway station, murdered by the mob, or be found dead in the bushes by some jogger in teeny-tiny neon shorts. And this, of course, is if you are a man. God forbid you be a *woman* in a *city*. I mean, my God, can you imagine?

Like LA, New York City almost didn't seem like a real place when we were kids. It may as well have been Mos Eisley, Tatooine, or Agrabah, because from the perspective of a young Southerner, it seemed as mystical as any of them movie towns on-screen. Every shot of New York in a TV show or movie was just people jaywalking through gridlocked traffic while a sea of yellow cabs laid on the horn to create a demonic score of rage-inducing cacophony. How could anyone live in a place like that? Furthermore, it appeared (again, from our perspective as kids watching TV) that it snowed without ceasing, was covered in garbage, was always dealing with a burning building, and: HOW IS THE FIRE TRUCK SUPPOSED TO GET TO IT THROUGH ALL THE TRAFFIC? What else? Oh yeah . . . everyone is a criminal, you have to walk up thirty-eight flights of stairs while moving furniture, you only have pizza to eat (that part seemed rad), everyone is yelling at each other for seemingly no reason, you have nowhere to park but even if you find a place it costs a million dollars, alleyways are full of stabbers, and grown adults can all just skip work to have coffee with each other in the middle of the day.

Granted, some of that is actually true! But New York City, it turns out, is a way less scary place than we were led to believe about the home of the Yankees. You don't need us to tell you how diverse New York City is because the people who live there and write blogs are happy enough to tell you that multiple times a day,[1] but it really is wonderful. As a couple of chubby fellers,[2] we cannot express how fucking amazing it is that no matter what you are craving—and we do mean *no matter what*—you're only a train ride away from it in the Big Apple. You wanna get some spaghetti and then cut up some Polish sausage on top of it? Wanna mix all that together in a

---

1. Plus, Trae already did that once in the LA section. He really should start a blog, huh?
2. We've both lost some weight recently, but you can do that and still be chubby so long as you start out "real fat" like we did.

bowl with some Mongolian beef and wash it down with a Mexican soda? Of course you do, you sack of shit. This is America! Certain lawmakers love to paint flyover states and the heartland as "the real America," claiming that places like New York City are out of touch and elitist. But how much more "American" does it get than stumbling around a city with a culinary Epcot brewing in your stomach, puking it up in an alley, waltzing into a bar that is still open at 4:00 a.m., and hearing the Irish guy pouring drinks call you what you think might be a slur—that is, if you could understand him? New York is American as apple pie, baby, and we'll have two slices, thank you very much. All you fake-ass country politicians pandering for a vote can fawkin' fuggeddaboutit!

Did we mention how great a place New York City is to get drunk? Sure, it's pricey, but let's just put that aside for a second and assume that if you do the type of drinking we tend to do, you budget accordingly. Not only are there so many cool-ass Irish bars just like you see in the movies, but you also don't have to worry about getting a DUI because unless you are one of them mysterious people we only hear tell of in movies, your ass ain't gonna be driving anywhere! We really don't know what all the traffic is about because every single sumbitch we know from New York, or who just lives in New York now, ain't set foot nor ass behind a damn wheel the whole time they've been there. They also don't hop in taxis left and right like you see in the movies 'cause that shit is expensive. If you do get in a taxi, though, hold on for dear life—because even though traffic is normally at a standstill, if the driver sees an opportunity, or just sees an empty sidewalk, they will haul ass to your destination in order to squeeze in as many rides as they can that night. But you don't need to worry 'bout that because you can just get your MetroCard and pray to God you hop on the right train, lest you be heading in the wrong direction with no way of knowing because you forgot to bring your power bank and your phone has been dead for three hours! Thank God there are apps that tell you exactly where to get on and get off, 'cause without them, our direction-dumb country asses would probably still be in Coney Island trying to figure out how to get back home.

Coney Island actually leads us to another point. New York City is *huge*! If you pass out on the train and ride that sucker all the way to the end of the line, then you have just lost damn near your entire day.

Manhattan is all they usually show you in the movies unless the characters are visiting their working-class parents in Queens, but each borough is big enough on its own that when you put it all together, to quote our meemaws: "It just beats all you have ever seen." Doing shows and living in New York, we have mainly stuck to Queens and Manhattan and Brooklyn on occasion, but between those, Staten Island, and the Bronx, they all have their own unique flavor that makes New York City a melting pot in and of itself. I don't really know how things used to be back before all the subway graffiti got cleaned up and the crime rates went way down, but nowadays the stereotypes for NYC's boroughs are as follows: Manhattan is for the rich people, Brooklyn is for the hipsters, Queens is for working-class Mets fans, Staten Island is where New York's rednecks are, and the Bronx is where J.Lo is from.[3]

Our main reason for visiting New York City so frequently—and of course our favorite thing about it—is because it is arguably the home of stand-up comedy. When you hear the phrase *stand-up comedy*, your mind probably envisions someone wearing a suit or dressed in all black, standing in front of a brick wall, holding a mic stand—and you just inherently know they are performing in one of the many wonderful NYC clubs because that image has been burned in our brains through television and film. New York's gritty, artsy feel lends itself to performance, not just of stand-up comedy but of all types. Of course, it was also known for its folk scene during the Greenwich Village era when Bob Dylan was freewheelin', and it ain't short on jazz clubs, rock halls, and live karaoke joints. The hip-hop scene should go without saying, but where on earth would we be without Jay-Z, Biggie, and the Wu-Tang Clan?

For a couple of Southern boys who move slower than molasses and weren't raised to walk everywhere, NYC was a huge culture shock—but it felt more like a jolt of energy than an electrocution. Are the people there as rude as they say? In our experience, we've found dickheads pretty much everywhere, but people in New York have always treated us more than fine. Matter of fact, if you've got our accents, you probably won't have to pay for all of your beers when you are hanging out at Donovan's Pub in Woodside, Queens, because all the potbellied Yanks sittin' at the bar are more than

---

3. Look, we know there is more to all of them, but we have a page limit!

willing to buy you a couple rounds so you'll keep talking in that funny voice about all the times Chipper Jones came to Shea Stadium and beat the absolute shit out of the Mets. They'll forgive you because even they respect ol' Larry!

THE REST OF NEW YORK

WHAT THEIR MOTTO SHOULD BE: Yes, We Are Also New York

WHAT TO PACK: Hockey jerseys and shit like that.

WHAT TO EAT AND DRINK AND WHERE: Buffalo is an underrated food city and not just for wing reasons. Come to think of it, Buffalo's an underrated city in general. Oh, and get a garbage plate in Rochester.

WHAT NOT TO MISS: The summer. What we're saying is, having done shows in Buffalo in December, there is just no reason on planet Earth to be there in wintertime unless you're from the area. You may think you like lakes, and you may think you like snow, but put 'em together, and you have a Southerner's nightmare.

People love to tell us when they have any kind of connection to redneckery. We call it their "red cred." They always say things like, "I'm not from the South, but I'm from *somewhere-such*, and believe me, it's redneck as *hell* there." And of all the different places to name, absolutely far and away the most common is Upstate New York. People don't tend to think "redneck" when they hear *any* variation of "New York," but believe us: The Upstate part is redneck-adjacent. It's blue-collar as hell, it boasts a lot of farmland and agriculture, and the people there "tell it like it is"—i.e., they are sometimes vocally racist! So you can see the parallels. (For the record, we don't think Upstate New York is any more racist than any other part of this lovely and dysfunctional nation, the South included.)

Now, if you're not from the area, you may not have known that about Upstate New York. We didn't, either, and we realized the reason we didn't know that was because . . . well, we didn't know much of anything about Upstate New York. And it seems this is not an uncommon sentiment. Hell, we didn't even realize what "Upstate" meant. In our minds, if you take the state and split it roughly in two, horizontally, then below that imaginary dividing line is the "Downstate" part and above it is the "Upstate" part. Stands to reason, right? Of course not! These are intricacies of regional identity we're talking about here, and such things are not bound by reason. No, the reality is that while the state of New York *is* divided into two parts, those two parts are "the city part" and . . . the rest of it. So "Upstate" basically refers to any part of New York that *isn't* the Big Apple. Side note: That's a somewhat ironic nickname for the city considering apples are a big damn deal in Upstate New York. They grow more varieties there than anywhere else in the country. They *love* pickin' them shits, and fourteen consecutive World Bobbing for Apples champions have hailed from Upstate.[1] Yet the city gets the name?! Seems unfair to us. More like the Big Asshole—are we right, Upstaters?![2]

The whole "What is Upstate?" thing doesn't stop there though. It's more complicated still and seems to depend largely on who you ask. To Manhattanites, Yonkers and Westchester might as well be Upstate, but to somebody in Rochester, those places are solidly city-slicker-fied. It's a whole thing. That is, given that the Manhattanites in question deign to consider Upstate at all. Over the years, we've met people in other parts of the country who said, "I'm from New York," and, being the ignorant outlanders that we are, we've asked them, "Yeah? The city or Upstate?" And in our experience you can always tell they are from the city before they actually answer the question, because they will look at you like you just asked them if they wipe

---

1. This last part is entirely made up. They really do love apples though.
2. We know we are not right.

their ass from the front or the side. "Did you not hear us say New York?! The city, *of course*; we're not *farmers*."

And you wanna go, "Well, I mean, there's a whole other part of the state called New York. Hell, the capital of the state is up there!"

And they'll say, "Is it though? Maybe, but we're the capital of *the world*, so . . ." And then they walk out in front of a taxicab on their way to start a fight on a train.

The point is, where the rest of the Empire State is concerned, we have a knowledge gap—and Upstaters are very aware that many people only think of New York as its biggest city. While touring Upstate, we'll ask people what they think the rest of the country thinks about Upstate New York, and often their answer will be some variation of: "Wait . . . they think about us?!" And we have to say they have a point. For the record, though, it's not like they're bothered by this or anything. Upstate New Yorkers, like their downstate city cousins, do not seem overly concerned with what outsiders may or may not think of them. Still, the fact remains that, for most of us, the region is shrouded in mystery.

So what *is* Upstate New York like? Well, in a word, *lovely*. As long as you follow our advice (only visiting in the summertime). Them winters are no joke. People Upstate keep those ice scraper / snow-brush thingies[3] in their vehicles at all times, *just in case*. If you visit in the summer, though, we promise you will be stricken by how pretty and green and hilly the place is. And the cities there are very charming, too, each having this down-to-earth working-class feel to them. Except for uppity-ass *Saratoga*, anyway. What is it with places that race horses?[4] People in Upstate New York are a little more rough around the edges, a little less refined—which is exactly what we're about. You can keep the Ivy League–educated museum curator types; give us somebody with some regrettable tattoos and a sailor's vocabulary any day. A quick anecdote on that point, from Trae.

So the last time I was in Syracuse, I was sitting at a bar after the show (as I am wont to do), presumably fretting internally over something vitally important like whether or not the new bit about an emotional support horse in a hospice ward is funnier than it is weird. At any rate, as sometimes happens, I

---

3. We're from the South. We snow-dumb.
4. We kid, Saratoga. Horses are cool.

got into a conversation with the bartender—a fortyish woman with just the right amount of a whiskey-tango vibe named Darlene. Immediately thinking of any number of drunken country aunts I have known over the years, I knew this was a person with whom I should converse. So we started talking, I started laughing, and it went on that way for a while.

"Yeah, I been here for about two years now. Used to be at the Fridays in the mall, but they fired my ass. Can't remember why, exactly. Prolly stealin' shit. They hate it when you do that. You ever steal shit? It's the best. Yeah, I used to steal shit all the time. Not no more though. Nope. Put all that behind me. I mean, I did find a purse on the ground the other day, but I only took forty dollars out of it before I turned it in. Way I see it, that was my finder's fee, ya know? It's only fair. Hell, to me, if you lose your purse and then get it back with only forty dollars missin', that's an absolute win! There was pills in there too!" Stuff like that.

She went on to tell me how she had met another comedian while bartending one night—this time a very well-known, nigh-legendary guy (ya boy was *quite* the letdown in comparison) who thought she was so funny that he asked her to open for him the next night. By this point I'd begun to suspect that I might be dealing with somewhat of a professional bullshitter. I've been a comic for twelve years; you don't hear about bartenders being hired to open very often. But she had pictures to prove it.

Now, listen: I'm not about to start a jerk-off session here, but stand-up comedy, especially in the beginning, is sort of terrifying. I don't think I slept for forty-eight hours leading up to my first open mic. Meanwhile, this gal went onstage for the first and only time in her life in a packed comedy club filled with a certifiable Hall of Famer's rowdy and unforgiving fans, *on a whim*. Her words were "Ah, I thought . . . fuck it, why not? It'll make for a good story. Plus, he gave me, like, fifty bucks." Most people ain't built like that, y'all. And I'm not saying that *all* Upstate New Yorkers are like Darlene, but if you ask me, she's a damn fine representative.

Another shining beacon of Upstate New York sensibility is a motley crew of lunatics that call themselves the Bills Mafia. These are fans of the NFL's Buffalo Bills, and they are, put simply, wildern shit. Every team in every city has its fans, but there's only one Bills Mafia. These crazy sumbitches willingly hurl themselves through flaming folding tables at the tailgate, fling gigantic dildos onto the field during games, bring signs that say things like

"Tom Brady sits when he pees," and just generally act plumb damn fools all the livelong day. And we *love* it. For a while we would have told you that they engaged in such antics because the team was terrible and they needed some other ways to occupy themselves on game day. But as of this writing, the Bills are actually good now, and their success hasn't dampened the maniacal resolve of their Mafia one iota. Hell, if anything, it has strengthened and emboldened it. May their burning passion for football-related insanity never smolder.

You may be wondering right now, *OK, that's all great, but where's the redneck part?* Well, the answer is the same as it is for pert near every state in the Union: the rural parts. You get ten minutes outside of any of Upstate New York's gen-u-ine city places, and you'll see a lot of trucks with a lot of flags on 'em. Yes, the Confederate variety, but also American and snake-and-skull varieties too! People get drunk in the woods there. Their uncles say *wild* shit on Thanksgiving, etc. However, we think it'd be more accurate to claim that—much like Southern states—they are blessed (or cursed, depending upon your perspective) with a surplus of gloriously unsophisticated white people, most of whom are in possession of a give-a-damn that is well and truly busted.

Oh, also they eat garbage. And they're proud of it. Which we can appreciate. OK, it's not literal garbage, but in terms of health impact, you might be better off dumpster diving. We're talking here about the tremendous affront to the concept of culinary decency that is Rochester's Garbage Plate. Y'all, they truly spit into the face of cardiologists everywhere (and also God) with this thing. In fact, we put it to you that this unholy trashterpiece may just be the single fattest damn thing we've yet concocted in this brilliant and gluttonous country. Which is truly saying something since America is the nation that looked at sandwiches and thought, *Yeah, that's cool, but what if the bread was like . . . doughnuts or fried chicken or somethin' instead?* We know you're probably screaming at the page right now for us to just tell you what the damn thing is, but it's honestly kind of hard to describe. Words fail it. Logic escapes it. It simply is. Perhaps the easiest way to define it would be to say it is . . . a greasy pile of trash food. On a plate. Hence the name. And it rules. But we know that definition will not suffice, so here we go. It starts with a base of two starches, something like fries, pasta salad, baked beans, or mac and cheese. Yes, we said it *starts* with those things. Then you pile on any assortment of hot dogs or sausages or entire cheeseburgers or eggs or just whatever you want to defile yourself with on this particular evening. Finally, you top it off with a chili-like meat sauce, onions, and mustard. Or, again, just whatever the hell you want to use to construct your own personal monument to excess and regret. Then you go in. And yes, you will likely want very much to die later. That's how you know it was a good fat. And the Garbage Plate is a fantastic fat.

Pages and pages more could be written about all the things Upstate New York has to offer, but hopefully we've established that it hits for us, and it would likely hit for you too. So in the future, when someone says they're from New York, ask them, "Oh yeah? The city? Or the good part?" Then watch their heads explode (into spaghetti and meatballs, probably).

BOSTON, MASSACHUSETTS

WHAT THEIR MOTTO SHOULD BE: It's Racist, but Not the Kind We Blame Everything On!

WHAT TO PACK: Lactaid for the chowder, Pedialyte for the lagers, and, oh yeah, a fucking quilt if it's fall or winter!

WHAT TO EAT AND DRINK AND WHERE: Boston is one of the few places in America that has truly historic stuff that still functions. We are a young country, but Boston can make you feel like you're in an old Harry Potter town from time to time. Head to the Green Dragon Tavern (established in 1654) and get you some chowdah and a beeya!

WHAT NOT TO MISS: All the gosh darn history! Take a tour . . . take a walk . . . take it all in! And if you see a Ben Franklin impersonator named Ricky, tell him he's full of shit and still owes us money. He'll know what you mean.

To the untraveled Southerner,[1] the North is the North is the North, and a Yankee is a goddamn Yankee. We ain't saying it's right to believe that way, but it is certainly . . . well, hilarious. Also, motherfucker, we hear what all y'all say about us, so you know what? How 'bout—OK, sorry. We'll calm

---

1. See: most everyone.

down now. Point is, only thing we ever really know about a place is what we see on TV, and since we grew up in a world before *The Departed*,[2] what we knew about Boston was as follows: They spilled a bunch of that gross-ass warm tea in their fancy lake; Ben Franklin got drunk there a lot; and Larry Bird is the best goddamn three-point shooter that ever lived! Need I say more? Yes, probably. Especially about the chowder.

As with anything, not only is there more to the story and a lot more nuance, but Bostonians also have a lot in common with Southerners.[3] For instance, they are *also* really big on war reenactments—and the one they reenact we can all sorta get behind.[4] First time we played Boston, we wound up at the Green Dragon Tavern gettin' shit-faced with a bunch of dudes dressed like John Quincy Adams's footmen and listening to them regale us with tales of America's revolution while in character. It was so awesome.

Another thing we were led to believe from what the moving picture shows and ladies with horn-rimmed glasses on NPR told us was that the American South had sort of a monopoly on racism. Well, turns out Boston would once again disprove some of our preconceived notions! Please don't think we are trying to disparage the boisterous blokes of Beantown. They are fine folks, and since there are assholes everywhere, we ourt notta let that define a place. It's just another one of them unfortunate similarities. That, and they are super argumentative and loud and have lots of Irish roots. Just like Pappaw! I mean, for God's sake, if you take the accent out of the equation, there are so, *so* many ol' boys down here in the South who go off exactly like Bill Burr after they've had a few whiskeys. And we mean that in the most loving way possible.

We were up touring in New England and stopped in Boston to do the historic Wilbur Theatre,[5] and because we are dipshit lushes, we went to one or two or twelve bars along the way. At almost every bar, some dude would hear our accents and say some version of "Oh, you guys will love this one!" and then proceed to tell us a racist joke.[6] Again, that does not represent all

---

2. What a bleak existence.
3. Well, the pasty-white ones, at least.
4. All us Americans, that is. 1776, eat a butt! SKEEEWW.
5. They spelled Corey's name wrong on the marquee. Please bring that up to him if you ever see him in person.
6. This became the basis of a sketch we did for Comedy Central called "Accent Problems."

of Boston, but it does need to be pointed out in order to maintain this whole "Ain't we all the same?" narrative that we are attempting to go for here.

Other similarities include having a white-trash culture! In Boston it's called "Southie,"[7] and in the South it's called "the South." We also think we are better than everyone. In the South it's because of Jesus or some such shit, and in Boston it's because of their proximity to Harvard—but the sentiment is still there.

Speaking of Harvard, one time we were on a press tour and were asked to speak and sign books at the Harvard Library. You have never met rednecks with more impostor syndrome than us in that moment, but we were certainly happy to do it and honored beyond words. When we got there, the library was full of hipster-looking folks standing in line to hear us, and some were already seated in front of the podium. *My God!* we thought. *We are drawing a crowd at the most prestigious university in the country. What a world!* As it turned out, however, they were all just the local homeless who had wandered in to escape the famous Boston winter. They were less attentive than the folks at the Wilbur, but we were happy to have them nonetheless.

---

7. Of fucking course it is.

NEW ENGLAND
Travel Ad Lib

Fill in the words below and tell your own clammy Beantown tale!

When we first got to Boston, we stopped off at the _____
(ADJECTIVE) + (FOUNDING FATHER'S SURNAME)

Inn for a _____ and some _____. Everything
(WHITE-TRASH BEVERAGE)   (DISH MADE FROM CRUSTACEANS)

was going great, until the jukebox played some _____
(PUNK BAND WITH AT LEAST ONE DEAD MEMBER)

and all the _____ started to get
(BLUE-COLLAR PROFESSION, PLURAL; E.G., "DOCKWORKERS")

a little _____. We thought it would be OK until a
(EMOTION TYPICAL OF ALCOHOLICS)

_____ walked in wearing a _____ jersey.
(MINORITY ETHNIC GROUP)   (FAMOUS BLACK ATHLETE NAME)

At that point, Corey said, "Let's get the _____ outta here before these
(CURSE WORD)

_____ lose it!" So we threw a
(ADJECTIVE) + (CURSE WORD) + (SLUR FOR WHITE PEOPLE)

_____ to distract them and left.
(ITEM OF CATHOLIC PARAPHERNALIA)

BURLINGTON, VERMONT

WHAT THEIR MOTTO SHOULD BE: If It Can't Be Solved with a New Pair of Corduroys, Then You Got You a Real Problem!

WHAT TO PACK: A jacket filled with bird feathers and a syringe of insulin to offset the ice cream and maple syrup.

WHAT TO EAT AND DRINK AND WHERE: Save room for a bunch of different kinds of pancakes at brunch (which was probably invented in Vermont).

WHAT NOT TO MISS: If you can pick your time to go to Vermont, obviously choose the fall. Vermont's foliage makes all other foliage look like a little bitch.

Burlington is one of those places that knows exactly what it is and does a damn good job of being that way. There's no way to measure this, but we'd bet Burlington holds the record for most times a person visiting there has said, "Well, isn't that neat!" Rumor has it that the Lands' End catalogue just goes to Burlington once a year, takes pictures of everyone walking around and existing, designs their clothes based on their research, and then marks the prices up so only people in Burlington can afford them. Burlington is also so white that Gwyneth Paltrow–types from all over point their yoga mats toward Burlington three times a day to say mantras and do them dog poses. It is certainly the mecca for syrup, and for that, we thank them. Here's looking at you, Bernie, you soup-eatin' son of a bitch! For real, though, if someone put a gun to your head and said, "Quick, tell me where the most poached eggs in America were sold last year!" I'm not sure if Burlington, Vermont, is the actual answer, but it's probably your best bet. Burlington also just *looks* like every pamphlet you have ever seen for a bed-and-breakfast. You almost expect to be greeted at the city limits sign by an old lady wearing a cat sweater, holding a basket of muffins, and apologizing to you because her husband ate the last of the orange marmalade.

The state of Vermont certainly has rednecks. We are told they are called "woodchucks," as a matter of fact,[1] and while that may be true, Burlington itself is not at all like what we were used to growing up. It's so neat and orderly. Everything has its place. The streets are made of brick, and it feels old-fashioned even though everything is very well taken care of and up-to-date. There are tons of "perfect" vacation destinations in the United States, but none of them feel as on-purpose as Burlington, if that makes sense. The whole place just feels like a group of Ivy Leaguers got together one day over brandies and set to creating a place that was the NPR listeners' equivalent of Disneyland. And I gotta tell ya . . . they nailed it!

All jokes aside,[2] Burlington is truly beautiful, and its scenery is inescapable. You may think you have seen the leaves change from vibrant green into the rustic cornucopia of fall colors, but once you see it happening in Vermont, all others will pale in comparison.

We perform in Burlington every year at the Vermont Comedy Club. That's right, baby; not the Burlington Comedy Club but the *Vermont* Comedy Club, by God. They have laid claim to comedy in the whole dad-gum state, and hell, I'll give it to 'em 'cause Nathan and Natalie (the cofounders) are the sweetest people on earth and do a hell of a job! They not only crush it as far as comedy goes, but also as great representatives of the good people of Burlington. Like almost everyone we have encountered there, they are kind, gracious with their time, super helpful, happy to see us, and unjudgmental of our redneck ways. Maybe it's just because we are

---

1. By "we are told," we mean that people said, "Hey, you guys are woodchucks!"
2. Well, maybe not *all* jokes. This is a comedy book.

there to entertain, but we've always been welcomed by the city with open arms—and that's hard to do considering how puffy all their jackets are!

Maybe it is because Vermontonians (Vermicians?) really do take kindly to rednecks because of all the "woodchucks" up there. I mean, they got plenty of farmers, they love beer, they put syrup on everything, they wear a shitload of plaid . . . Hell, actually, I totally get it now! They are just like us except, you know, we have Black people.

If you are looking for diversity, Burlington is not the place for you. If you are looking for different types of white people who have lots of beer, are super friendly, and know their way around a waffle maker and an eggs Benedict, then it certainly is! Do make friends with one of the woodchucks in case you need your tire changed or need help gettin' your beer bottle opened!

MOUNTAIN WEST

DENVER, COLORADO

WHAT THEIR MOTTO SHOULD BE: Every Kind of High You Can Be

WHAT TO PACK: Not a damn cowboy hat, apparently. (This will make sense in a minute.)

WHAT TO EAT AND DRINK AND WHERE: Well, last time we were there, we bought like two hundred dollars' worth of meat pies for some damn reason. Again, you really gotta watch how high you get in this town.

WHAT NOT TO MISS: The big-ass blue demon horse they got guarding the airport. (Before you ask, we have no idea.)

Denver: the land of crunchy white people with enhanced lung capacity. Both because they stay hiking and riding bikes and shit and also 'cause they *420 blaaaaze* it, are we right? They don't call it Mile High for nothin'. Weed jokes aside, Denver's awesome. One would do well to always consider the elevation though; it ain't no bullshit. Things affect you differently at that altitude. We once accidentally stayed high for sixteen hours in and around Denver. And when we say *high*, we're talking like "freak out and run away from an imaginary moose in the woods" high. You get drunker in Denver too. Which is all great, of course. We're just saying . . . be careful.

It seems like every few years in this country, young white people in search of novel climes in which to take their selfies gesture collectively toward a particular American city and say: *"There."* Then that city gets flooded with young professional DINKs (Dual Income, No Kids—i.e., people looking to trade some of their excess money and time for something to do with their life, basically) seeking exciting new opportunities for Living, Laughing, and Loving (white-people stuff). It happened to Austin, it happened to Nashville, and now it's happening to Denver. Not that there's anything wrong with that, but we'll put it this way: We talked to two friends of ours, one from Nashville and one from Denver (two people who have never met each other), and they both said about their respective cities, totally independently, these exact words: "Dude, the place is pretty much just brunch now." So it would *seem* to us that locals in these trendy cities are not altogether thrilled with the developments.

This might be unfair, but we think the general vibe of Denver is a combination of two things: (1) a weed-themed artisanal sandwich shop with menu items like "White Widow" and "Panama Red" that doesn't offer straws because straws kill turtles, and (2) John Elway hammered drunk on a Bird scooter. The place is crunchy and weedy and all that, but you can also get a kick-ass steak there. Like most American cities, Denver is a bit of an oasis—meaning that if you leave the city and drive into the surrounding areas of Colorado, things get *very* Alabama-y pretty quick. Personal liberty seems like a big deal to people there. Lot of snake flags flyin', if you catch our drift. And hell, that's fine too; the sight of 'em made us feel at home there. We also always considered Denver, Colorado, to have a Western-themed vibe to it, right? I mean, hell, they don't call it the Mountain *Left*, now, do they? But apparently this is a bit of a complex issue, which we'll let Trae expand upon with another personal story.

So I always thought Denver had a whole "Great American West" thing goin' on. I bought my favorite cowboy boots in Denver. Wasn't that whole deal a big part of Denver? And I'm not saying it *isn't*, but one time we were in a bar after a show with our buddy, the brilliant comedian, author, and Denver native Sam Tallent, and some dude came in there dressed like damn Wild Bill from head to toe. I'm talking jeans, boots, Garth Brooks shirt, ten-gallon hat. I think this sumbitch even had spurs on. I looked at him and thought, *Now, here's a guy who enjoys both rootin' and tootin'. Prolly eats beans beside a fire all the damn time.* All that shit. Or at least he wanted everyone to think that.

Buddy, we had to physically restrain Sam from challenging this guy to a duel for the Honor of All Colorado. Sam was *so upset* at this cowboy, I started wondering if my friend was more than the standard one-sixteenth part Cherokee or something.[1] But his fury was based on the same fury I had for all those TOBY KEITH 'MERICANS in Nashville that time: He could tell the guy was cosplaying as some version of a Denver avatar that existed in his head. It's not that cowboy culture doesn't exist out there, it's just that Sam knew this dude wasn't the real deal. He was a poser. His boots was too damn clean, and Sam wasn't havin' it. Gotta love a man who cares about where he's from.

One thing we should probably warn you about is that Denver isn't actually *in the mountains*. Lots of people show up there thinking they can grab a coffee before hitting the slopes and whatnot, but the mountains are like an hour away. And on that note, if you have this image of a snowy winter-wonderland mountain city in your head, that also isn't the case—which is a huge upside, in our opinion. Denver has an extremely mild climate, and for most of the year, the sun is shining, the humidity is low, and it just generally feels good as hell to be there. There's also tons of stuff to do, and most comedians would tell you that the comedy club there, Comedy Works, is one of, if not *the*, best clubs in America (and therefore the world).

So you absolutely should make it a point to visit Denver—just please remember to keep the elevation in mind and take it easy. Should you fail to do so, remember then that no, you are not having a heart attack, and no, your brain won't be stuck like that forever—but yes, that actually was John Elway you just saw, and yes, he was drunk. You'll be fine.

---

1. In case you're unaware, white people love to claim to be part Native American.

CHEYENNE, WYOMING

WHAT THEIR MOTTO SHOULD BE: Did Y'all See the Dick on That Bull?

WHAT TO PACK: Jeans stiffer than my thighs on leg day, a pair of muddy shitkickers, a belt buckle you could serve chicken on, and plenty of moisturizer.

WHAT TO EAT AND DRINK AND WHERE: Domestic beer, straight whiskey, steak, any goddamn where you please.

WHAT NOT TO MISS: A rodeo. You owe it to your life. They get made fun of, but them folks work real hard to put on a good family-friendly show, and you can get some pretty good fried eats to boot!

Cheyenne comes up in country songs almost as much as pickup trucks, shootin' guns, and women not remembering how to use a goddamn stove anymore. It's one of them places that sorta lets you know that redneck and "country" aren't necessarily divided by some imaginary line but rather are just ways of life. Do you like gettin' drunk at a bar with a rodeo clown and listening to him talk about how it all could have been different? Do you like dirt roads that turn into dirt parking lots that turn into miniature goat-roping competitions? Do you like feeling like you're on the set of a John

Wayne movie but within walking distance of a hotel and a great steak? Well then, go now, baby. If you hurry, you can still make Cheyenne!

Most cowboys are probably rednecks, but most rednecks are certainly not cowboys. In places like Cheyenne, "cowboyin'" ain't a term you just throw around loosely. These sumbitches are *legit*. Wyoming shocked us the first time we went there, but not necessarily because of their way of life (though we certainly weren't used to people practicing roping hubcaps on the side of the road). It was more that people behaved in a similar fashion to what we were used to growing up, but they sounded *soooo* much different. They all love shitty light beer, country music, spittin' tobacco, honky-tonkin', huntin' animals, eatin' animals, throwin' darts, bass fishin', and talkin' shit on the porch, but they don't put sugar in their tea and all sorta sound like they are from Canada when they are doing it.

We're not trying to make fun of or disparage the Wyoming accent (or the Canadian one, for that matter), but you gotta understand that we grew up thinking everyone who liked all that stuff sounded like us . . . a cartoon possum working as an auctioneer. And not only that, but we were led to believe that people who *didn't* sound like us were Yankees, and Yankees didn't like none of that shit because they were too busy eatin' couscous, avoiding manual labor, or reading a book for fun.

It's not just the stuff they do for fun or sport that makes a redneck feel at home in a place like Cheyenne, Wyoming, but also the general disposition of the people. Wyoming was the first place we realized rednecks weren't exclusive to the South, and it's also where we learned that hospitality wasn't either. Corey learned this firsthand.

There's a little town just outside of Cheyenne, Wyoming, called Kaycee. OK, sure, if you're looking it up right now, you will notice it is three and a half hours away from Cheyenne, but in the grand scheme of Wyoming, that may as well be right next door 'cause you gotta drive damn near forever to get just about anywhere. There are multiple signs in Wyoming that say something to the effect of: "If you didn't get gas at that gas station back there, you better turn your ass around and do so." I'm paraphrasing, of course, but they ain't kidding.

We were actually on our way to Cheyenne for some rodeo my buddy Jesse was gonna play music for. I can't remember where we were coming from, and trust me, Kaycee wasn't exactly on the way; but because Kaycee is the birthplace of Jesse's hero, country musician and rodeo legend Chris LeDoux, it was of paramount concern to my friend that we stop and pay our respects to the fallen idol.

As of this writing, the population of Kaycee, Wyoming, is 284, and I shit you not, I'm pretty sure that is double what it was when we passed through in 2009. I reckon everyone grew up and had a couple of kids. If there were 142 people in Kaycee back in 2009, then we damn sure met a lot of them at the Hole in the Wall Bar. Those are not my words; that was the literal name of this fine establishment. Everyone there had their own personal story of Chris LeDoux. A great handful of them carried pictures of them together in their wallets.

We had breezed into Kaycee having spent the very last of our money on a cooler full of beer, bologna, bread, and one squirt bottle of mustard. We parked at the first little dirt-parking-lot-gas-station we saw and decided to take our lunch on the back of Jesse's Ford F-250, the perfect vehicle for touring the country when you barely have enough money to eat. We pulled the tailgate down, made our sad little sandwiches with bread slightly damp from the cooler water, and began brainstorming our next move to scrape up a little gas money and get to the next town. We had been selling Jesse's country music CDs at various bars.[1] He'd sing, and I'd walk around telling jokes and closing the deals, CDs in hand. This town's bar didn't look as lively, though, so we thought we might be shit out of luck.

'Bout that time an old, dusty GMC Jimmy pulled into the parking lot. A man who I swear to God looked like Mater from *Cars* rolled his window down and said, "What you boys having for lunch?"

We described to him our pitiful feast, and he grinned and said, "I think I'll pass," then drove on. About ten minutes later, he circled back into the parking lot, rolled his window back down, and said, "What are you boys having for dessert?"

We informed him that our travel budget did not allow for dessert at present, and he let out a big belly laugh. "Well, how 'bout you all come on over to my house? My wife just made a lemon icebox pie, and we got plenty of iced tea. We can sit on the porch and get to know each other."

Jesse and I had both been raised by good parents who told us to never

---

1. Jesse is a singer-songwriter. We weren't just pawning his Willie Nelson albums.

take candy from strangers, but they had never said anything about a fresh piece of lemon icebox pie—so we accepted the offer and inquired with the stranger on the whereabouts of his house.

"Oh, it's just right there," he said, pointing at a tiny house beside the gas station. We looked and saw his wife on the porch, holding the pie and waving at us.

I'm choosing to leave their names out of the book, not because they shouldn't get credit for their hospitality, but because these are private countryfolk and I do not want to put their business out on Front Street without their permission. Further, I don't really have a way to get in contact with them as they are not, how do you say . . . internet-using people. They sure were hospitable though. We sat there and ate that entire pie, drank a couple pitchers of tea, and then they took us out to a nice dinner at a place that served biscuits and gravy all day long.

While we were at the restaurant, the momma noticed through the window that one of their bulls had gotten loose.

"Hey, honey." She turned to her son. "Looks like Rufus got loose!"

He turned and looked. "Ah shit, Momma. That *is* Rufus!" He went outside and, I shit you not, picked up a pebble, threw it at the bull, and said, "Goddamn it, Rufus. Get on back!" Rufus did exactly that.

After we finished dinner, the son took us to the pen where Rufus was standing, the obedient bull the family knew him to be.

They let us stay on their porch for three days so we didn't have to sleep in the truck for a while. They also fed us like kings, introduced us to everyone in town, invited pickers and singers to stop by on the porch to entertain us, and even hosted a poetry night where a ninety-some-odd-year-old woman recited "cowboy poetry" and 'bout made us cry ourselves to sleep. Every single one of them purchased a CD, and we made enough money to make it to Cheyenne and even enough to get a hotel.

I sure am glad we stopped to get gas before we got to Kaycee.

Everything said so far aside, Cheyenne is still the capital of Wyoming and therefore very much a city. Not a remarkably huge city, mind you, but I don't want to leave here implying that Cheyenne ain't nothing but tumbleweeds, dirt roads, and one copper spittoon after another. You can get Starbucks there, by God! However, you will likely be enjoying that Starbucks while a rodeo is going on not too far from you. If rodeoin' is a religion, then I believe Cheyenne would just 'bout have to be the heaven, the paradise, or the mecca depending on which one you wanna go with, at least if George Strait and all them fellers are to be believed. Unlike most "big cities," Cheyenne does still have a small-town feel, and that's no doubt due to the frontier sensibilities of its inhabitants.

SALT LAKE CITY, UTAH

WHAT THEIR MOTTO SHOULD BE: The Other Type of Christians

WHAT TO PACK: Running shoes so you can race the Mormons.

WHAT TO EAT AND DRINK AND WHERE: Salt Lake isn't necessarily a culinary bastion, *but* it's where fry sauce comes from, so go to a burger joint and enjoy the winning combination of mayo and ketchup, finally together in one convenient sauce.

WHAT NOT TO MISS: There's a big-ass Mormon church. Pretty sweet if you're into all that kinda stuff.

So we are probably about to unfairly shit on Salt Lake City a little. To begin, let us say that Salt Lake City is cool (and *definitely* the city we most think of when we hear the word *jazz*). We also very much love it there, always have great shows, and have met some supercool people—but some things stick out to us, especially because of where we grew up, that are too familiar and thus strike a nerve. We promise that by section's end we will circle back around to how pretty it is and how badass the goddamn salt flats are and whatnot, and as all of these travelogues should be taken, these are obviously just subjective opinions drawn from our personal experiences.

If you are visiting Salt Lake and are only interested in the scenery and the outdoor activities, then you are entering a virtual paradise. It is gorgeous as long as the smog ain't up, and there are so many great places to hike, ski, take Instagram pictures to make your girlfriend happy, blah-blah-blah . . . But if you are two fat drunks from the South looking to get sauced up and lose some money on a ball game or two, you'll have to do what no one in that situation wants to do and follow some pretty stupid rules. Here's Trae's brief account of experiencing this juxtaposition himself for the first time.

So, like every other worthless, entitled piece of lazy millennial trash,[1] I have a problem with the demon called *screen time*. I stare at my damn phone all day and oftentimes justify this by reminding myself that, as a traveling comedian with a social media following, my career *is on* my phone. If I've just gotten off a plane, I gotta check my emails! And don't forget the notifications! This is to say nothing of the views my last video got! Take my eyes but leave me my metrics!

Yeah, that's what I tell myself, but usually I'm just looking at cats. The point of this, and I swear I will soon be arriving at a point, is that I have on many occasions thought to myself, *Trae, you are traveling a beautiful country—get off your damn phone and* look at it. *You're in a fantastic city right now. The cats can wait. Right?* Well, I've never been more dumbstruck by the results of this particular internal monologue than when I went through it in Salt Lake City, Utah. There I was, visiting SLC for the first time, and *there I was*, in the back of a cab from the airport, watching a fat cat ride a Roomba around a Tokyo apartment. The non-sorry-as-hell part of my brain finally interceded, and I cursed myself as I reluctantly put my phone away, surveyed my surroundings . . . and literally stopped breathing for a moment.

I'm not just saying that; my breath caught in my throat, which I believe has happened to me only three other times: the births of my two sons and that time I saw Eddie George at LAX.[2] Maybe everyone else already knew, but I am, in the parlance of my people, purdy damn *ignernt*, so I had *no* idea how picturesque and striking the views are in Salt Lake City. Everywhere you look, there they are in all their snowcapped glory: the full-on Rocky

---

1. Just trying to butter up the boomers in advance of this section's playful blasphemy.
2. For a nineties Tennessee kid, this is like seeing Thor on a train.

Mountains. No matter which way you turn your head, you're looking at a beer commercial.[3]

Once I composed myself, I felt like I understood why the Mormons had chosen this place. Tailor-made for LDS, it feels isolated, special, spiritual, and *super* white all at once. If Brigham Young's charismatic, schizophrenic ass had told me that SLC was heaven on earth right after I first saw it, I probably would have believed him too. I dunno that I would have believed all that other truly *wild* shit that Brigham and company were about, but the "SLC is paradise" part I coulda got down with.

So now, fired up by this striking introduction to the city, I arrived at my downtown hotel, ready to join Corey and Drew for a podcast recording in Corey's room. Naturally this requires booze, so I went to the hotel bar and asked for a double vodka tonic (my go-to) to take up to my room. The bartender told me sure thing, but I needed to wait for one of the servers to become available to escort me. If I had been in Vegas, I would have defaulted to "Oh, no thank you, I don't need a hand job or anything," because that explanation would have made more sense to me than the actual one: that while you were allowed to have a drink in your room, it had to be hand-delivered there personally by an employee of the bar. You could walk *with* them, of course, but the bar staff had to physically carry the drink. I tried to explain that since the drink in question was not, in fact, the unmarried daughter of the bishop and I was not a sweaty-palmed teenage suitor seeking her hand in marriage, I felt a chaperone wasn't entirely called for. But they insisted, as people are wont to do where "laws" are concerned. I guess the worry was that I might take the booze out onto the street if they didn't escort it to my room? I have no idea, but either way, my first thirty minutes in Salt Lake had already demonstrated what I would come to view as the city's definitive dichotomy: so, so pretty, but *juuuust* a little bit weird.

In our experience, Salt Lake City is the only place outside the South that rivals our dipshit liquor laws, aka "blue laws," and you wanna know the common denominator? That's right. You guessed it: the Lord! Now, their Jesus is a little bit different from our Jesus in the sense that (if I remember correctly) they think he was actually from America or maybe rather came over here on a boat with some feller named John and tricked the natives

---

3. Because, as everyone in America knows, ever since the eighties, beer equals mountains.

into giving them their land. There was then an ancient and mystical scroll, perhaps made out of gold, that prophesied a mid-1990s championship run with another John, this one named Stockton, and his trusty sidekick Karl Malone, whom we will explore no further for various reasons. There was a feller named Brigham Young, which was Hebrew for "white quarterback," and he taught John Smith the secondary words of Christ that contradicted the "former" Bible. These were his "latter" teachings, and they would go on to institute what we know today as the Mormon Church or the Church of Jesus Christ of Latter-day Saints. Brigham Young and John Smith communicated with reptile aliens under a blanket of smog near the salt flats one night and went on to shape how the church operated.

Now I just made every bit of that up, but so did they at one point, which is now the reason why you can't get a beer over 3 percent in this goddamn town. You not only can't get beer over 3 percent or some such, but you are also required to order food every time you drink. You can't just belly up to a bar with a few of your buddies after a long day of riding bicycles, wearing pressed white short-sleeve button-down shirts, and spreading the Mormon gospel unless you get chicken tenders or some shit. And look, no one is saying chicken tenders don't go good with alcohol. It's just that if you are barhopping, you are either gonna get *very* full on chicken by bar number two, *or* a whole lot of chicken is going to waste just because you were trying to drink forty-six beers so you could feel six of them. It's just a silly law is all.

MIDWEST

INDIANAPOLIS, INDIANA

WHAT THEIR MOTTO SHOULD BE: We Promise There's Shit to Do Here

WHAT TO PACK: If you're white and wanna blend in, we recommend a bald head, a beard, and wraparound shades. Preferably adorned while behind the wheel of a truck for maximum efficacy.

WHAT TO EAT AND DRINK AND WHERE: A pork tenderloin sandwich, for damn sure.

WHAT NOT TO MISS: The comedy stylings of our good buddy and Indy's own Brent Terhune, but of course.

H ere's a thing you won't hear people say very often: The great thing about Indianapolis is that it's in Indiana. But that's exactly what we're saying right now. We love Indiana. Why? Well, because, as the saying goes, Indiana is the middle finger of the South. If you're from Alabama, you can drive around basically the whole of Indiana and feel right at home. (Maybe not Gary—as we understand it, Gary is infinitely more hard-core than its name would imply.) But we're not saying Indiana *is* the South, per se. It's more like a hybrid of the South and the Midwest. So you can count Confederate flags while also freezing your ass off! We kid, we kid. No, it means these people are sweeter than the sugar they are slowly killing themselves with. Sorry, we'll stop now. Seriously, though, the official state pie of Indiana is called the sugar cream pie, which is exactly as diabeetus-y (and delicious) as its name implies. Also we were about to make a joke about how Midwestern it is to even *have* an official state pie, but we looked it up (we do that from time to time, believe it or not), and apparently most every state has an official pie. The more you know, right? Lawd, this country fat. Anyway.

We have a theory that the South-like traits of Indiana are a result of the generations of Southerners who have moved there over the years. (Now *this* we did not look up, opting instead to pull it directly from the nether regions of our butts.) Trae is from Tennessee and has countless extended family members on both sides who long ago sought greener pastures in the Hoosier State. So when he was a kid, in his mind he thought, *Indiana . . . the Land of Opportunity. Indiana . . . Where Dreams Go to Bloom.* But in reality, it's more likely his trash cousins and their trash ilk simply went to Indiana and set about trashin' up the place. And therein is the basis for this theory of ours. Either way, Indiana definitely has a Dixie-esque feel to it despite being situated firmly in the Midwest. Before we get to Indianapolis the town, however, Trae wants to elaborate on his family's connection to Indiana.

All right, so I just said all my trash cousins moved to Indiana and trashed up the place. And . . . they totally did. But not across the board, which I was as stunned to learn as I presume you are right now. See, most of my wayward Indiana-bound family left Clay County and never looked back. I was going to make a joke about how that meant they were the smart ones, but it seemed like it might fall flat considering they picked Indiana, amirite? That's like some progressive twenty-year-old in the Middle East ditching Saudi Arabia for Qatar. Good for you, I guess, but how much better can it be?

Turns out the answer is: quite a bit, actually.[1] You see, because they never looked back, I spent most of my life not really knowing any of my Hoosier cousins. Then after my dad died in 2013, some of them came down for the funeral. One of whom—we'll call him Cousin DK—I stayed in touch with afterward. I had already started stand-up by this point, and he and his wife ran a theater and an art gallery, taught film classes at a local

---

1. Please note answer applies only to Clay County and Indiana. Your mileage in the Middle East may vary.

college, and did all this other creative and crunchy stuff that appealed to me as a burgeoning (and pretentious) artistic type. You have to understand: For me, finding out that one of *my* cousins was part of a progressive artists' community *in Indiana* was like a cast member of *Swamp People* finding out one of their cousins ran a vegan clean-living center in the Florida Panhandle, OK? This straight up did not compute for me. The whole time I was like, "Are you *sure* you're my cousin?! Are you *sure* you live in Indiana?!"

But years later, after I started touring professionally, Cousin DK took me to his Indiana town for a show, and it kinda blew my mind. It's a college town called Goshen in the northern reaches of the state, and my cousin and his crew are not particularly out of place there at all. It's got a welcoming downtown area featuring galleries and coffee shops, and it plays host to film festivals, which sort of puts one in mind of a smaller and less mountainous Asheville, North Carolina. It put *me* in mind of that, anyway. And listen, I know how stupid this is, but I genuinely did not realize that Indiana had towns like that. I know, I know. I just said it was stupid, OK? But it was a good reminder that pockets of awesome can be found all around this country, and everywhere has something to offer. Now back to Indy itself.

Indianapolis the city, like Goshen, is something of an oasis. Don't get us wrong, it's still Indiana, but you're allowed to like orchestras and shit there. In all seriousness, people who don't know anything about Indy just assume it's in Indiana and therefore is all crackerfied, but it really is a lovely town.[2] The people in Indy seem aware of their reputation elsewhere and just kind of roll with it. A good friend of ours who was born and raised there described the general sentiment thusly: "We may not be the best, but we're better than Kentucky." Which is neat because Tennessee has the same sentiment![3] Indy is a great time though. The downtown area has a lot to offer, including this big-ass statue that they project American flags onto at nighttime while blasting music, lest anyone forget how American America is. There's also the convention center, which hosts massive events every year, ranging from Gen Con, the world's largest tabletop gaming convention, to the National Future Farmers of America Convention and Expo. (Look, we said there was a lot of cracker stuff going on, didn't we?)

2. With a whole lotta crackers in it.
3. We're just joking. In Tennessee we say that about *Alabama*, not Kentucky.

137

One decidedly *not* white-bread thing about Indy is the city's affinity for the sport of basketball. Though, to be fair, that association derives at least in large part from *Hoosiers*—objectively the whitest piece of basketball-related material ever produced—but still, it's a whole thing. But that's unfair; Indiana isn't known for basketball simply because of *Hoosiers*. They also have . . . Larry Bird. Wow, Indiana really is super white, huh? Which is fine, of course. White people can love basketball too!

And you know what else white people love? Cars. And Indy has their own damn type of car, known as . . . well, IndyCar.[4] And IndyCar racing's premier event (really one of the premier events in all of motorsports), the Indianapolis 500, attracts hundreds of thousands of exhaust-and-fiery-crash enthusiasts to the city every May. For basically that entire month, the whole city becomes race themed. (Feels like this whole section has been kinda race themed, are we right?) People adorn their yards with banners that say, "Welcome, Race Fans!" as practice days and qualifying events occupy the weeks leading up to the Biggest Spectacle in Racing. Side note: We got a buddy whose uncle actually won the Indy 500 in the eighties, which we realize sounds like something a drunk redneck would say to impress his cousin in between cigarettes in a garage, but it's actually true. So that's neat.

When it comes to food, Indy, like the Midwest in general (and really most of America), is categorized by excess. We already mentioned the decadence of the sugar cream pie, but we can't omit the tenderloin sandwich, a comically oversized breaded pork cutlet served on a bun so woefully unequipped to the task it almost seems like the whole thing is a comedy bit they're doing. Seriously, the damn meat is the size of a plate, while the bun is the size of a . . . well, a bun. But when said bun is holding a fried heart-attack Frisbee, it looks pretty damn minuscule in comparison. And just so everyone is clear, we wholeheartedly support this sandwich in all its edacious lunacy.

Another thing served in excess in Indy is the official condiment/life-blood of the Midwest, ranch dressing. Now, first things first: Ain't a damn thing wrong with ranch. Indeed, most Southerners will gladly drink the shit *through a straw*. But if we're all keeping it real, the sauce belongs to our brothers and sisters in the heartland. In the Midwest, ranch is just a given. One needn't ask for it. Fret not, for one has to merely order from the

---

4. You ain't gotta be creative to go fast, dammit!

menu and verily ranch shall arrive. Really, you just about have to request that they *not* give you ranch in the Midwest. And you do so under threat of regional deportation. You ever seen a salad in the Midwest? Enough bacon and cheese and ranch to sate middle-aged Orson Welles. Legend has it that if one is of sound spirit and seasoned resolve, one can sometimes find traces of the vegetable known as lettuce deep in the bowels of a Midwestern salad. But no one knows for sure.

At the end of the day, while you may hear *Indianapolis* and think of "flyover country" or "hicks" or "corn" or "corn hicks," just spend a little time there to see for yourself why Trae's family members and countless others migrated there in droves. Now, you may hear that and think, *Sure, but if the place you're leaving is Clay County, Tennessee, then yeah, Indy would seem like Shangri-la*. And all we have to say to that is . . . we hear ya. But still, Indy is a cool place and absolutely worth your time. Holler at it.

DETROIT, MICHIGAN

WHAT THEIR MOTTO SHOULD BE: Eff What Ya Heard

WHAT TO PACK: We now recommend a Sunday-best suit-and-hat combo.

WHAT TO EAT AND DRINK AND WHERE: Two things people may not know about Detroit food: (1) the world-famous Coney dog is actually from Detroit, and (2) they have their own style of pizza (square and greasy and fantastic). Both are just gangbusters.

WHAT NOT TO MISS: Go down to the Riverwalk and talk shit to Canada!

We've always had a soft spot for any place that other people like to shit on, and Detroit is no exception. (Hopefully by this point you've realized that we are equal-opportunity shitter-onners.) A fantastic blue-collar city filled with people who have been subjected to years of misery by factors largely beyond their control (the changing economy, the whims of industry, and the goddamn Lions) and still stand tall, by God. They are also welcoming and hilarious. The last time we were in Detroit, we went to a casino downtown and were the only white people at the blackjack table. To boot, we were terribly underdressed. Everyone else was in Sunday-best suits and hats, just dressed to the nines. It was like losing your ass right next to the Original Kings of Comedy, which is generally the best way to go about losing your ass in a casino. An absolute blast.

Detroit is unfortunately one of those places that you rarely hear anything good about. Once again, in making a comparison to our upbringing, it really *really* sucks that because of a few loud, stupid, and violent assholes, the decent people who live there have to be lumped in with all that. It isn't fair. Can't we just focus on the great things about Detroit? Like how the people there have a self-deprecating humor about their city that rivals maybe only Cleveland? People in Detroit wear that shit on their sleeves, man! "Welcome to Detroit! Yeah, it's scary and dangerous here . . . Want some fucking square-shaped pizza?" And the answer to that is, 100 percent and all of the time, we want your pizza, Detroit![1]

The pizza doesn't get talked about enough, in our opinion. Their slice game is much like the rap game in the nineties when people thought only two options mattered: East Coast versus West Coast. Regarding pizza, it's always Chicago versus New York. Those rap-prejudiced sons of bitches always failed to acknowledge the shit that was going on down in Atlanta, and the pizza snobs far and wide always exclude Detroit-style pizza from any conversation. It's like the LeBron/Jordan debate going on while Detroit is over there like, "Can't we ever talk about Magic? Why does it only have to be about those two?"

According to some drunk guy at a casino who told us this, back in the old days there was a family who didn't have much of anything to eat. The wife had all the fixings to make a pizza but for one small problem: She didn't have a pot or pan to cook it in.[2] The husband, being both hungry and a tough, inventive Detroiter, had just the right idea. He'd get her a cooking pan from work the next day. You are probably wondering right now, *So did this feller work at a goddamn Williams Sonoma?* And the answer is no, he—like pretty much everyone who lived in Detroit back in "the old days"—worked at an automotive factory. Back then you either worked on cars or were a fat cat in a suit making money off the workers and then calling them lazy for wanting enough to afford, like, clothes and stuff for

---

1. Seriously, can we be sponsored by pizza? Detroit, let us know how many times we need to mention your pizza for free pizza.
2. This issue was compounded by one of the pots being designated for pissin', as was the poor-people custom at the time.

their kids. Anyways, got sidetracked there. Point is, he went to the factory the next day and procured some sort of metal pan that they used to store screws or nails or hubcap stuff in, or . . . Look, we don't know shit about cars except they get us to our shows and the beer store, OK? So he took this pan home and his wife used that to make the first-ever Detroit-style pizza, known for being square-shaped with a deep-dish feel.

I don't know if it's true, but if it is, they should name the damn Lions stadium after that family. Hell, just rename the whole damn team after them because they have certainly done more for the city than the Lions ever did.[3]

Don't wanna get too grim as—so far, at least—we've tried to make this a positive book. Sincerely, we love traveling this country and have had a blast everywhere we've gone. It don't matter where you are from or what the stereotype of that place is; wonderful, kind, and tremendous people live everywhere in this country, and we will go to our graves saying that.[4] Especially coming from a region that is so unfairly judged, we know a thing or two about how it feels to have people write you off because of preconceived notions. *However* . . . though we love the South and don't think it's as bad as people say, we have to admit there are systemic problems down here and some deep-rooted racism that may never go away. Likewise, Detroit has to admit it has a crime problem. And not only do they *have* to admit it, but they do! Whenever we play Detroit, we get messages from DETROIT NATIVES warning us about all the places we shouldn't go—which, when they draw it up on a map, usually only leaves us with the comedy club where we are playing and the damn hotel. When you are actually from Detroit and know it like the back of your hand, you have a good grasp on the spots to avoid without thinking about it—but for a couple of outsiders, it can be nerve-racking. We already don't really know where we are, but now we gotta listen out for gunshots too? That puts us in quite the pickle!

Again, please don't think we are unfairly piling on. Detroit is literally listed in the top fifty most dangerous cities in the world. Not in Michigan. Not in America. In the damn *world*! And unlike some other dangerous cities in America, reports show that it's actually gotten worse in the past

---

3. "Oh yeah? Well let's see those pizza people go winless and drive another future Hall of Famer's career into an early grave!"—the Lions, probably.

4. Yes, even Ohio.

couple of years. No doubt due to the pandemic. And look, if we could sit here and offer even decent half-baked ideas on what this country needs to do to stop crime and prevent its necessity, then we probably wouldn't be writing this book 'cause we'd be in a goddamn Mensa lab or something. But whatever it is, we know we need to do it, and fast. The good people of Detroit don't deserve to live in fear and constant judgment. Especially for all they have done for the world of pizza. We love ya, Detroit. Please don't stab us for saying all that.

CHICAGO, ILLINOIS

WHAT THEIR MOTTO SHOULD BE: Flyover Country Our Asses

WHAT TO PACK: Anything an off-duty cop would wear is gonna fly.

WHAT TO EAT AND DRINK AND WHERE: You pretty much cannot miss in this department in Chicago. With one very notable exception: the Satan's cocktail they call Malört. If a Chicagoan says, "You simply must try Malört; it's a Chicago tradition," you obviously do it since you ain't a coward, but be aware that it will curdle your innards and darken your soul.

WHAT NOT TO MISS: They got all these different kick-ass boat rides you can go on in the summertime, and we recommend them all.

Ah, Chicago: the capital of the Midwest. One of the few cities in that region that was largely spared from the Rust Belt economic desolation, Chicago has remained a thriving metropolis where go-getters from Omaha, Cleveland, and everywhere in between flock to lead a Big City Life, Midwest-style. What is Midwest style? Besides "with extra ranch, please"? People are polite yet tough. ("Ope! Just gonna scooch right past ya there" is a Midwestern phrase that loosely translates to "Get the fuck out of the way.")

They're hardworking, they know how to have a good time, and they're fat yet insistent on turning everything into a casserole (which is actually called a "hot dish," apparently? At least in Minnesota? We're unclear on the casserules [Sorry]).

In the Midwest, you graduate high school, go to a big state college, get a nice job with benefits, meet someone your mother approves of, get married, have some kids, give 'em names like Carter and Addison, and settle in for the long haul by thirty.[1] And if you wanna be all *metropolitan* about it, you do it in the fine city of Chicago.

When you picture a Chicagoan, you may picture someone's morbidly obese uncle wearing a satin Bears jacket and violently clutching his chest after the Bears' assuredly sorry-ass quarterback throws his fourth interception of the day. You can thank the "Superfans" series of *SNL* sketches for that. Or, depending on how much Fox News you've watched, you may hear "Chicago" and think, *Oh, you mean the Fallujah of gang violence, where rocket launchers are distributed to every South Side teen?* Both of these perceptions are overblown and unfair, though the former is the "just pokin' fun" variety and the latter is the "racist dog whistle" variety. As with any major city of its size, Chicago is massive and diverse and, like those little soldier figurines Mel Gibson turned into bullets in *The Patriot*, unable to be painted with a broad brush.[2] So rather than labor in futility by attempting to sum up Chicago in these pages, we're going to talk about a few of the things we love about it and call it a day.

There's an endearing amount of civic pride in Chicago. The average mom at the Chicago grocery store can tell you the names of both the city council members and the Bears' special teamers. Chicagoans love being from Chicago (as well they should). We feel like there are two types of places to be from: places you leave (unless you get stuck) and places you don't. And Chicago is the latter. In Chicago, massive Irish and Polish families spanning generations live within blocks of each other and still get together on Sundays to watch the game and play cards and get hammered. How wonderful. Especially the getting hammered part.

---

1. It's pretty much the same in the South, only with less emphasis on the college part, one of the kids is named Peyton, and twenty-five is the cutoff age. But still.
2. Remember? He had to use a tiny little brush to paint them? Listen, we thought we'd try out a twenty-five-year-old, ultra-specific pop culture reference, OK?

Getting drunk with your family is way more prevalent in the Midwest than in the South, which we assume is the Lord's fault. People get drunk in the South, but not generally with their mammaws. That wouldn't be fittin', see. But in the Midwest, Mammaw (or is it Grandma? Do they have mammaws up there?) will drink your sorry ass under the table and talk shit to you about running off another girlfriend while she does it. That shit is awesome. And when people build lives and families together in one place for generations, a deep connection with that place is formed. It's beautiful.

Speaking of beautiful, Chicago was also the site of one of our all-time favorite "what could have been" moments in American history. In the late 1960s, the Chicago Black Panthers, led by Fred Hampton, joined forces with a group called the Young Patriots, a collection of displaced hillbillies from Appalachia who had come to Chicago seeking a better life (instead they found the bootheel of the ruling class), as well as a Latino group called the Young Lords. They formed an organization called the Rainbow Coalition (the original one, pre–Jesse Jackson), whose goal was to fight back against systemic oppression of poor people of all stripes. And they made immediate headway, quickly growing in numbers and determination. If you need a stark visualization for how extraordinary this coalition was, consider the backdrop of the stage at their meetings: a Confederate flag set in between two Black Power banners. Wild, right?

But naturally, the powers that be determined very quickly that they absolutely *could not have* this shit. Poor people banding together? Why, that could bring the whole unjust charade to its knees! So they set about undermining the Rainbow Coalition at every turn, raiding their meetings, shutting down their food drives, harassing their members, and eventually murdering Fred Hampton in cold blood. His death scattered the remainder of the coalition's leadership and effectively ended the movement. Ain't that just the way. But Chicago was *that close*, y'all. Closer than we've ever come, before or since.

All right, let's lighten the mood a little bit. As comedians we would also be remiss not to point out Chicago's enduring legacy in the humor game. In the comedy world there are two headquarters: New York and Los Angeles. But beyond those touchstones, no one city has contributed more to the art of yuk-yuks and haw-haws than Chicago. As a matter of fact, Corey sojourned to Chicago at the tender age of nineteen, naught but a suckling babe, to take a summerlong intensive at Second City. He did this despite being an untraveled North Georgia hayseed because he wanted to be funny for a living—and if that's what you want, then Chicago is where you go. And so, he went and soaked up every bit of comedy secret sauce he could before returning home at the end of the session, riding high and ready to zing. (He could have stayed, but he's a Southerner. And as such, he lives in mortal fear of the mythic scourge known as "wind chill.")

If you have chuckled at an *SNL* sketch, a late-night bit, or, hell, most comedy movies ever made, then odds are you have Chicago to thank for it, at least in part. Between Second City and iO (formerly ImprovOlympic), Chicago has given us names like Belushi, Ramis, Radner, Fey, Carell, Farley, Murray, Colbert, Meadows, Mulaney, and so, so, *so* many more. We don't know if it's something in the water or if those frigid, windy-ass lake-effect winters just bring out the funny in people.[3] Either way, Chicago is to hilarity what Florida is to lunacy—i.e., an indisputable and widely recognized wellspring.

A brief note on an aspect of Chicago that, frankly, we are too dumb to discuss adequately[4] but deserves to be mentioned: The architecture there is straight-up incredible. If you are ever in the Windy City and have a chance to take any kind of architecture tour, you *must* do so. They have done some *wild* shit in that town. Back in the damn Civil War era, they raised the whole city up on jacks! For swamp reasons! Ain't that nuts?! During the age of skyscrapers, Chicago has been a hotbed of architectural innovation, and it shows. This fact is made evident before you even *reach* the city. And for our money, Chicago's skyline is perhaps the single most breathtaking urban vista in this entire country. They got good buildings, is what we're saying.

All right, we got one more aspect of Chicago to cover (even though we're leaving out so much), and you can probably guess what it is. So, recently we were discussing possible ideas for funny internet videos (like what a think tank does but with TikTok and farts), and one thing we bounced around was the notion of replicating a sumo wrestler's caloric intake—that is, twenty thousand calories in one day. Essentially, we would wake up, start eating and boozing, and see how many calories deep we could get before

---

3. You ever been stuck outside in the cold? You invent whole new cuss words.
4. "Oh, so you mean like the *entire rest of this book*?!" Yeah, yeah. You got us, smart-ass.

giving up, throwing up, or just fuckin' dying. (Our profession is absurd.) Due to a rare bout with sanity, we ultimately decided not to go through with it, but during the discussion, our biggest question was: What would be the optimal setting for such an escapade? Immediately, confidently, and enthusiastically we agreed the only city worthy of such an exercise in gluttonous depravity would be Chicago.

We've already said New Orleans is our favorite food city, and that's still true in terms of the fare NOLA is known for. However, when it comes to good, old-fashioned American *fattin'*, nowhere compares to Chicago. Which is to say nothing of the requisite boozing. Chicago is gloriously, unapologetically fat and drunk, and we love it. Sure, other people in other places might ridicule them for being fat and drunk, but then those people come to visit, step out the doors of O'Hare in the wintertime, and think to themselves, *Holy shit, I wish I was fat and drunk right now*. In Chicago, dammit, being fat and drunk just plain makes sense. And they make it so easy to do. You could spend every day of your life eating a different Polish sausage / Italian beef sandwich / pizza casserole[5] and never run out of new ones to try. Granted, you will absolutely die of a massive heart attack in under two years, but still, that's a hell of a run. We fuckin' love Chicago.

---

5. They call it deep-dish pizza, but it's a pizza casserole (y'all know how Midwesterners are with casseroles) and it is *awesome*.

SIDEBAR: CANADA AND MEXICO

When conceiving of a book called *Round Here and Over Yonder*, we had to determine how exactly to define both terms. Eventually we landed on "round here" being the South, the rest of the US being "over yonder," and "yonder yonder" being across the pond. But we realize there's, like, a *bunch* of places "yonder yonder." You got your Frances, your Japans, your Egypts—hell, you even got your Luxembourgs. However, we felt it wise to limit ourselves in these pages to "not the entire world," and ultimately Jolly Old Mother England (and Drunky Ol' Brother Scotland) felt like a good starting point. Yes, a starting point. If we had our druthers, we'd eventually travel to and write about pretty much every-damn-where. But that's another book for another day.

On that note, we thought of at least a couple more places one might consider to be "over yonder." Namely, our neighbors to the north and south—our hat and pants, if you will: Canada and Mexico. Now, we *have* spent time in each country, but more importantly, each place deserves more words and love than we have space for in these pages. So they will also be reserved for another book. However, we suppose we could share a couple of quick stories.

First up: Canada. We traveled through the western part of Canada in 2017 doing stand-up shows in Vancouver, Calgary, and Edmonton over the course of a few days. We probably don't need to tell you this, but yes, it was the summertime. As we understand it, they got temperatures in the winter up there that we ain't even heard of. No, thank you. But July was wonderful. We rented a Dodge Charger (we didn't ask for it—presumably they just met us and said, "Give 'em the most white-trash thing on the lot"), and let us tell ya, driving a rental car at speeds you literally can't comprehend (we don't know how "kilometers" work) across Alberta is a hell of a good time. We're lucky not to have been pulled over, but everybody knows Canadian cops wear red and ride horses, so it's doubtful they could have caught us anyway.

Being a hillbilly in Canada is fun. We were eating at one place in Vancouver, and from the moment we sat down 'til the time the check came, a different server came to the table for every single step of the meal. That is, one server greeted us, another brought us drinks, another took our orders, and on and on. Now we, being ignorant hicks, just assumed, "Huh . . . must be how they do it in Canada. The entire staff takes care of every table! We knew they were socialists, but damn!" But that, of course, is comically wrong. That would be a terribly inefficient way to run a service enterprise. But we are dumb.

When a completely brand-new server delivered the check, we asked, "So do you guys tag team all the tables? We've had like six different servers."

She goes, "What? Oh, no, Alexa just came back there and told us we had to come by this table to listen to you guys talk." Now we assume Alexa, sweetheart that she is, probably threw in a "dumbass" or two in reality, but either way, we found it amusing that our accents are apparently of note anywhere *actual* English is spoken. We walked outside and were smoking cigarettes (before you ask, we quit years ago) when a girl walked up and asked us for a light. We obliged, then heard her return to her friend group and say, "It's OK. Those cowboys gave me a lighter." Everywhere we went people asked us where the hell we were from. It was delightful.

One more quick Canada story, this one about stand-up. At one of our shows, our buddy Drew, who tours with us, was onstage, and he mentioned having been a quarterback in high school.

This prompted a heckler to yell out, "Yeah, right!" This set Drew off, and he went about "destroying" this heckler. You may know from YouTube that a big part of our job is destroying hecklers. (This is just a joke—please, for the love of God, don't heckle at comedy shows.)

"Wow, really?! What, just because I'm not that tall, or what? Ya know, I thought Americans were supposed to be the assholes! Everyone always talks about how polite Canadians are, but *apparently not*."

It got quiet, and an awkward silence filled the room. Then, from the back, the exact same unmistakable voice that had heckled Drew called out, in a comically on-the-nose Canadian accent, "SORRY." Not an ounce of sarcasm. It was completely sincere and absolutely hilarious.

Now for Mexico. We said we had spent some time there, but actually only Trae has done so. As the purest form of white trash, he has taken a variety of Carnival Cruises in his life, some of which stopped in Mexico. He and his wife also took a weeklong trip to Puerto Vallarta. So for this anecdote, we turn to him.

First of all, let me preface this by saying I love Mexico. It's a helluva good time, and the people are lovely. The trip my wife and I took to Puerto Vallarta was damn near magical. We ziplined over a mountainous jungle, drove ATVs down a tropical trail that ended in a breathtaking waterfall we then jumped off of, and enjoyed a multitude of brunches featuring beans. You know, gringo shit. Wonderful. So, having said that, this story is about a separate trip that was . . . decidedly less so.

When my now wife and I were dating, probably around 2009, we took a cruise with her sister and her sister's man to Cancún. Once off the boat, we took a cab downtown and wandered around from cantina to cantina, ending up in this little hole-in-the-wall that was advertising "Specialty Margaritas" for, like, two dollars. Now, my wife is a white woman who loves nothing more than a good deal, so that shit was like telling a barn owl, "We got buckets of crippled field mice half off on Tuesdays." Of course, I was more than down with it.

We ordered a round, and I swear to God, the bartender pulled out a plastic pitcher filled with neon-green liquid. You know that old, stained Kool-Aid pitcher your mammaw has had in her fridge since the Reagan administration? It looked like that but was filled with "Specialty Margaritas." Somehow, we were in no way deterred by this jug. (Being twenty-three is like that.) Her sister and her sister's fiancé, however, immediately bowed out and ordered bottled beers instead, as they have brains that work. There also was a group of three frat boys from Mississippi State who were on the same boat as us in this cantina, and they also ordered a round of Uncle Julio's Special Mystery Juice.

I sat there sipping the margarita (maybe "pounding" might be a more apt term) and talking SEC football with these fellers *annnnnnnnnnndddd* the next thing I knew, I was coming to in our cabin back on the boat *hours* later. Evidently, we blacked out right away and ceased to function. Well, *I* ceased to function. Reportedly I threw up multiple times and couldn't walk on my own. My wife, on the other hand, stole someone's sombrero and rode a mechanical bull. But neither of us remembers any of that. We lost pretty much the entire day, and I've literally never felt worse in my life than I did when I finally returned to myself later that evening.

Her sister kept talking about how drunk we had gotten, and I kept trying to tell her that I knew my way around some tequila. One margarita would never in a million years have had that effect on me. In retrospect, talk about a pretty hilarious argument to have with your future sister-in-law: "Nuh-uh, don't you tell me! I'm a *drunk*! I get hammered all the time! Ask your sister, she'll tell you!" But it's true though. I was fresh out of college, had come from a broken home . . . and knew how to fuckin' drink, god-damn it.

I also found out later that those Mississippi State frat boys who were drinking with us had to be carried back to the boat on stretchers. Something was off about this. I became convinced that it was some sort of predatory scam, where the restaurant drugged tourists and then waited for them to stumble out the door and collapse in the street. At which time they would . . . well, just let your imagination run wild. I know I sure did. I was convinced that I was lucky to have come away with both my kidneys *and* the sanctity of my back door intact.

I've told many people this story over the years, and I can always tell they're skeptical. They all think the same thing my sister-in-law thought, which is what she still probably believes to this day: that we just went too hard and couldn't handle our liquor. Then *finally*, in like 2018, almost ten years later, I saw an article in *USA TODAY* with the headline: "Tainted Liquor Seized in Cancún." Turns out, multiple different establishments had been serving unsafe alcohol, in what was apparently more of a cutting-corners type of situation than a stealing-kidneys one. Still, countless tourists over the years *had* been assaulted and robbed as a result, so I wasn't entirely wrong. It's nice to be vindicated, but it's also pretty messed up when you see an article about hundreds of people being victimized and your genuine first reaction is: "YES! I KNEW IT!" But I did though. I did know it.

Anyway, I still recommend Mexico to you if you've never been. Just maybe stay away from the Kool-Aid pitcher cocktails when you go. Since the majority of you reading this are presumably grown-ups who aren't stupid, that probably goes without saying, but . . . still. Mayhaps Corey and I will travel south of the border one of these days and live some more stories with which you may be regaled. North of the border too. And everywhere else while we're at it. If they'll have us.

PART 3

YONDER YONDER

ENGLAND AND SCOTLAND

As far back as we can remember, we have always wanted to be wankers. Well, not *wankers*, per se. We may be ignorant Americans, but even we understand that a *wanker* is not a designation to which one should aspire. But we wanted to be . . . somethin' Limey. We're both huge Anglophiles and always have been. Yet we'd never been across the pond in our lives, until now.[1]

At any rate, we're both big fans. Just for the record, however, neither of us chalks this up to our heritage. It's a big thing in parts of America to still identify strongly with the country from which your immigrant ancestors courageously absconded, but we don't really do that much in the South. Southern pride tends to override any form of ancestral affiliation in that way. If you meet a Southerner with a last name that sounds French and you

---

1. Who do you think came up with the phrase *across the pond*? Probably them, right? Isn't there a certain whimsical silliness to referring to the Atlantic Ocean as a pond that just screams Brit sensibility? Had to be them.

ask him about it, he will likely interpret that as you calling him gay and try to give you what-fer.[2] So taking this trip wasn't some kind of "the motherland calls" thing for us. We just really liked the way the Beatles talked when we were kids, OK?

Seriously, though, the accents are a big part of it for us. The two of us share an affinity for mimicry, and we each started cultivating that mostly-useless-but-nonetheless-amusing skill by trying to sound like eight-year-old knights of the round table. It's not just the way Brits talk but the words they choose—the way they combine verbosity with whimsy. Being insulted by a Brit is like being roasted by a thesaurus. And the effect is amplified tenfold by the accent. An American cannot simply crib from the catalogue of British epithets and achieve the same result. Calling someone a "numpty" or a "doughnut" in a hillbilly accent may have its own brand of confounding efficacy, but it's just not, and never will be, the same.

So here we find ourselves at the unenviable but also unlamentable ages of thirty-five and thirty-six (Corey and Trae, respectively), traveling for the first time to the object of our transatlantic affection, having been tasked with reporting back in the form of these here pages. We are writing these opening paragraphs in advance of our sallying forth (i.e., we haven't left America yet) with the intent of establishing what our preconceived notions and expectations are beforehand. So with all that said, let's discuss what we *think* this trip is going to be like for us.

First and foremost, we expect to feel like Big Dumb Americans for the entirety of the tour. Have you ever seen a foreign film that features a scene with an American tourist in it? Yeah, they're never erudite and worldly characters. They're obtuse, demanding, and oh-so very, very fat. Just standing around sweating and being pissed at a city for using kilograms and having stairs in it. We're both going to be self-conscious about asking anyone any question about anything, because in our minds, all Americans are stupid overseas. If that's not bad enough, we are very noticeably from the American *South*—that is, the place where America keeps all of its stupidest Americans. We'll be overly polite and excessively apologetic to everyone we meet in an attempt to offset our obvious ignorance. We doubt it will work. At best we'll be viewed similarly as one might look at two big, fat tongues-out bulldogs:

---

2. If you don't know what "what-fer" is, just know you should avoid being given it at all costs.

"Poor things. They're frightfully stupid and clearly shouldn't be here, but they seem harmless enough." We feel that's the most we can hope for.

We expect to be pleasantly surprised by the food. *Surely* it can't be as bad as all that, right? Besides, we are human garbage disposals who regularly eat things like canned chili and liquid cheese, so as long as they've got salt and an assortment of dipping sauces over there, we think we'll be fine.

We, for reasons we don't entirely understand, expect to connect more with the Scottish people overall. Maybe because many hillbillies are Scots-Irish in origin, or maybe because of their fondness for whisky[3] and speaking unintelligibly. Whatever the case, we think we'll hit it off with the denizens of the upper reaches of the island. We also expect them not to be particularly fond of the English. The English, on the other hand, we figure won't care too much either way. We don't know why we expect this, exactly. It just feels like after decades spent pursuing a bit of the ol' imperialism, England probably has collected a vast number of one-sided rivalries like that. Do you remember the scene from the *Street Fighter* movie wherein Raul Julia as M. Bison says, "For you, the day Bison graced your village was the most important day of your life. But for me, it was Tuesday"? Of course you do—who could possibly forget that cinematic touchstone? Anyway, that's England, we bet. We sincerely don't know how better to explain it.

We expect it to be gray and rainy. Like, every day. We're going there in May, but as far as we can tell, it's always gray and rainy there. You ever seen a tan Brit? You have not. No one has. You may, however, have seen a brutally *sunburned* Brit. This is because sun in Great Britain is like a snowstorm in the American South: They have no idea how to handle it, but it's not really their fault because it happens so rarely. We're obviously being a wee bit cheeky here, as they say, but either way, we're packing for gloom.

Lastly and above all, we expect to have an absolutely *lovely* time.

---

3. In Scotland, they spell it this way. We don't know why. This happens with a *bunch* of words over there.

JOLLY OL' LONDONTOWN

WHAT THEIR MOTTO SHOULD BE: A City So Awesome It Almost Makes Up for That Whole "Subjugating the World" Thing

WHAT TO PACK: Monocles and bowler hats and the like, of course. All the rage, innit? (Not really—just dress like a person.)

WHAT TO EAT AND DRINK AND WHERE: We know you're gonna want your fish and your chips and your bangers and your mash, but for our money, the best food was Indian. As far as drinking goes, leave your hotel and start walking; you'll be drunk afore long.

WHAT NOT TO MISS: Go down the Thames in Central London. You'll get the gist.

The first stop on our pondhoppery was, fittingly, London, where we were set to stay for five days. We didn't know exactly *what* to expect, but we expected a lot. London is in rarefied air as far as cities go. There are a number of organizations out there who maintain rankings of the world's "global cities," and on pretty much all of them, two cities rank a tier above the rest: New York and London. Name any industry—entertainment, finance, fashion, education, health care—and London excels in and influences them all.

Now, not much of that would be relevant to our little bromantic excursion, but suffice it to say, we expected to be impressed.

And we were. London is an incredible city, but our very first impression was more about its people. Like New York, it's a diverse metropolis filled with every type of person you can imagine, most of them operating with an air of "shit to do." But that's not what we mean. We're not talking about the way they *were* so much as the way they *looked*. And they looked, well . . . super British. You know: spectacles, top hats, big teeth . . . as if the phrase "Tallyho!" was a person. No, we're kidding. We did feel, though, like there was a particular expression many of them shared, one which seemed appropriate to us. Picture a perplexed individual at the tail end of saying, "Wot." That face. Lot of 'em were making that face.

We're takin' the piss a bit here, but it definitely wasn't like visiting Los Angeles for the first time. Corey has a comedic bit, the essence of which is "I'm a nine in Georgia, but I'm a six in Los Angeles"—and it really is like that. Any average-looking person—like us—will routinely see a heroin addict in LA who makes us look like a cabbage in comparison. We know this is true in other places as well. Like, we imagine you get off the plane in Stockholm thinking, *Jesus Christ, is this Asgard?* Well, in London, that's . . . not the case. We know this probably sounds mean, but all we're trying to say is that a regular person can walk around London and not feel like a bag of trash—and as two fellers who often feel trash-baggy, we appreciated that. So . . . thank you, people of London. Thank you for not being Swedes.

We landed at ten o'clock on a Thursday morning and intended to stay up all day to try to adjust to the time difference. So we had a bunch of London sightseeing lined up. And y'all know the sights we're talking about. The things everyone pictures when they think of London: the Eye, the Parliament building, a bridge that most people are wrong about, that building shaped like an egg, a pretty sweet clock, etc. Well, one thing we didn't realize until we got there is that many of those places are located basically right beside each other, along the Thames in Central London. You go down to the pier at the London Eye, get on a boat, and knock all that out in about an hour while a tour guide who talks like a sassy *Downton Abbey* cook makes PG jokes about princes. It's great fun.

We mentioned the bridge that most people are wrong about. We know that a goodly number of you will read this paragraph in annoyance at the notion that someone out there may not already be aware of this, but for the rest of you, those who *aren't* professors, here's a little fun fact: The London Bridge is not that big fancy-looking one with the towers on either end of it. That one, incredibly enough, is called Tower Bridge. London Bridge is kind of just a regular-ass bridge. Just all gray and flat and towerless. It ain't even falling down or nothin'. So one can understand why they never feature it in any establishing shots so the audience knows we're in London now. Tower Bridge is way better for that. If they used London Bridge, the audience would be going, "Why is this spy movie in Pittsburgh all of a sudden?"

We hopped around London quite a bit, and it was very easy to do since, unlike many major American cities, it doesn't seem designed to make you hate yourself if you don't have a car. Seriously, the public transportation system in London, and really in most of England, is incredible. It honestly kind of pisses you off as an American because it makes you realize how needlessly dumb and inadequate we are about the whole public transport thing. First of all, trains. Look into 'em, America. Most Americans think trains were just for cowboy bandits and hobo murderers, but they're actually pretty cool. Just imagine our surprise when we found out that *buses* are great over there too. Actually, we already knew their buses were better than ours. London's buses are famous for being red and double-decker and looking all storybook-y. Our buses are gray, have just one dumb level, and are famous for crackheads and/or being rigged to explode by Dennis Hopper in the nineties. So yeah, their public transit system is so far beyond our own it almost makes it seem like we don't even try. Oh wait.

In running around London as we did, we were pretty quickly enchanted by it. It's so many different things at once. Some parts of it feel like a pristine, ultramodern metropolis—some like Guy Ritchie, some like Harry Potter, some like *The Crown*. Some neighborhoods feel like hipster enclaves of Brooklyn, and others look like they could be straight out of a Dickens novel. There are buildings with windows that are still bricked up from the time when wealthy landlords essentially levied a tax on sunlight (classic wealthy landlords). Picturesque little alleyways and stone streets are lined with haberdasheries or stores selling assorted antique maps. Jason Statham characters hang out on the bridge running three-card monte and the shell game. Queen's Guard[1] chaps stand motionless in their elaborate uniforms and hats that look like microphones. It's all there.

One thing we did see less of than we expected (with some disappointment) were the classic English bobbies. You know: frumpy, red-faced gents with bushy mustaches and comically oversized caps, twirling their batons as they admonish ne'er-do-wells. Maybe we overlooked them, but we felt like we saw hardly any police around London, except for around Parliament, where the officers were heavily armed and not particularly whimsical-looking at all. It was striking to two Americans, accustomed as we are in this country to cops materializing out of the ether to start screaming and unclipping their sidearms as soon as someone crosses the street incorrectly. Maybe they just hide them better over there, but it's something we noticed.

Speaking of crossing the street incorrectly, Londoners seemed to be just about the jaywalkingest sumbitches you've ever seen in your life. Maybe it was just the confidence with which they navigated their native city, but it felt to us interlopers like crosswalks and signals were naught but suggestions to them, meant not so much to instruct as to be ignored. On a related note, we wondered if we were walking wrong the whole time we were there. We kept thinking, *Well, they drive on the left over here, so maybe they walk on the left too. We'll try that.* And maybe you *do* walk on the left over there, but it didn't seem to help us very much. No matter where we stood or which side of the walk we chose, we were constant obstacles to the good people of London. And for that we apologize.

Another thing that stood out to us about London, in comparison to major American cities, was the *volume level*. You may be aware that it's a stereotype that Americans are loud, but like . . . do y'all realize how damn LOUD we are, as a people? We didn't either until we spent some time in London. The city, much like NYC, is absolutely filled to bursting with people at all hours of the day, yet the sounds we have come to associate with a bustling city street were largely absent: no catcalling construction workers, no taxi drivers threatening sexual violence against mothers of pedestrians who also loudly proclaim where they are walking, no food vendors arguing loudly with Jewish mammaws over condiments, no gunshots, hardly any

---

1. Well, we suppose for you they're now the King's Guard, but when we were there, ol' Lizzy was still kickin'. Matter of fact, please keep that in mind for the rest of this book.

sirens, just . . . you know, city stuff. We didn't hear any of it. And it was lovely.

We know we've used the word *lovely* a lot when talking about England (and there are more instances to come), but dammit, it just feels so appropriate to us. It *was* lovely! London in particular was absolutely, perfectly, enchantingly lovely. Books and books could be written on what the city has to offer (and said books *have* been written), so we're not going to even attempt to be all-encompassing here. Suffice it to say that there is a reason London is considered to be one of only two cities on the planet that operates at such a level. It's modern and classic, inviting and overwhelming, impressive and accessible, more and more and all at the same time. It's just that kind of place, and it was a wonderful preamble to our UK adventure.

EATING YONDER YONDER

Perhaps the aspect of this trip we were most anticipating was sussing out the veracity of Great Britain's less-than-stellar culinary reputation. The stereotype goes that a Brit wouldn't know a good meal if it gave him a tut-tut on the sidewalk. For the record, a *tut-tut* is a mild clicking of the tongue, and in British culture it's considered an overt indication of extreme disapproval. So yeah, the stereotype suggests they don't know shit about food. It's probably one of the number one things the British are ribbed for by other peoples. They'll say, "Over there, they cook peas until they're paste and put fish in pie, for God's sake. You don't even *want* to know about spotted dick." And you think, *How could a country that conquered most of the world at one point* not *have good food?* Indian food's great, Caribbean food's great, African food's great . . . how could a people have empired their way through all of these rich culinary cultures and landed on *blood pudding*? Surely there's more to it than that. The UK is a modern, cosmopolitan country with a rich history and an increasingly diverse population; *surely* they've got some good food. Right? Well, after three weeks of fatting our way across their wondrous land, we can tell you the answer to that question is . . . *kind of.*

No, listen: Great food exists in Britain. We had plenty of it, and not just the dishes originating elsewhere, such as Indian, Thai, Mediterranean, etc. On that note, we feel it's only fair that the bulk of this section be spent on classically British cuisine. You can get some killer curry in Manchester, but should that count as British food or Indian food? Though we've never been to India, we know there are differences in the two places. As such, we feel strongly that when people say Brits have terrible food, they're not talking about the Indian fare—so we are limiting our commentary thusly. Having said that, we do want to emphasize that the offerings originating from other cultures are well represented across the pond. If you've been out at the pub for a few pints (which to Brits equals getting absolutely pissed—and to the Brits *absolutely pissed* means drunkern shit, but more on that later), and you pass by a kebab shop and think to yourself, *Now there's a good idea*, take it from us: It is. It is a good idea. You should do it. Possible gastric unrest be damned. But back to the Anglo-Saxons.

First, the good. The two of us have long lamented the fact that the States haven't properly adopted the meat pie. Isn't it insane when you really think about it? The fattest country on earth, a country known for such gluttonous obscenities as deep-fried Oreos and the KFC Double Down (both of which are *fire* as far as we're concerned), has somehow missed out on combining *meat* with *pie*?! Those are, like, *easily* two of our favorite things! Outside of chicken potpies, which are wonderful but yet have somehow not inspired other meat-pastry innovations in this country, the closest thing in mainstream American food culture has been the lowly Hot Pocket, a pale imitation of the real thing that was nonetheless a RUNAWAY SMASH HIT when it came out. So how are there not more meat pies around this place? Seriously, y'all. Explain it to us. Don't you feel like if you surveyed a hundred Americans and asked, "Hey, don't you think we should take a pot roast and put it inside a pie crust?" the over-whelming response would be, "[Brief moment of contemplation before the light bulb goes off] Hey! Hey, yeah! We *should* be doing that! Why aren't we doing that?! Who's keeping us from doing that? Is it Joe Biden? It's Joe Biden, isn't it? That son of a BITCH!"

At any rate, they do have meat pies in Britain. Everywhere. Just lousy with meat pies, that country is. And yes, some of 'em we ain't so sure about, like the ones packed with eels. Which, by the way, sounds like a cruel prank rich boarding school boys would play on the orphan down the street who's never had pie in his life. "Hey, Limpy! We 'eard it was your birfday so we 'ad the kitchen master bake you this 'omemade pie . . . Just kiddin'! It's got eels in it! HA-HA! You should see your face! Now get away from me 'orse!" Or whatever, you know what we mean.

But most of their meat pies are just filled with, ya know, meat. Regular meat, not snakefish meat. And gravy and vegetables and stuff. They are tremendous. Having said that, the meat pies are not all created equal.

Sometimes they're exquisite; other times they're absolute shite. The filling is lacking or the meat is tough or the gravy is brown water or the pastry is thick and dumb (we hate a dumbass pastry). This is obviously disappointing. But when a meat pie is done right? By Jove, is it lovely (please pronounce this "luhv-leh" in your head). It holds its shape, is jam-packed with gravy that neither spills onto the plate nor calls Jell-O to mind, and is flakier than a hippie babysitter. And when you get such a pie, well . . . proper scrummy that is, innit?

Continuing on, we will now make what will surely be a controversial decision: to separate fish from chips. We know, we know. In England that's like separating David Beckham from Victoria or the aristocracy's head from its arse. Still, we have to do just that. We simply cannot assess the dish of fish and chips as a whole because, in our experience, the consistency of the former far outweighs that of the latter. Fret not, we're not leaving out the chips.[1] Verily they will be covered in (likely far too much) detail here shortly. But for now, let's focus on the battered and fried golden slabs of delight one can find across the whole of England.

Generally speaking, and this will be discussed further as well, serving sizes in the UK are markedly different (smaller) than we're used to here in the States—but where the fried fish is concerned, this is not always the case. We received a number of haddock filets the size of which were, in a word, *alarming*. The fish comes wrapped in paper and reliably fried to perfection in exactly the type of beer batter one hopes fish to be subjected to. None of that baked pecan-and-breadcrumb bullshit you find in this country from time to time. No, sir. Greasy, golden, and gratifying, that's what. And in our experience, it's always cod or haddock, too, not some weird, probably-made-up new trendy deal like "barramundi."[2]

Now for the chips. All right. Here's the deal. Even the dumbest among us big dumb Americans know by now that the "chips" that come with fish and chips are really more what we would refer to as "fries," but it's a little more complicated than just that. The Brits also have what we call "chips," but they call those "crisps." *Furthermore*, they have "fries" as a menu item, and from what we saw, those items *also* are what we would refer to as "fries."

---

1. We. Would. *Never*.
2. All right, we have to be honest. Barramundi absolutely slaps for us, though we have always suspected it ain't a real fish.

So basically, their chips is fries and their crisps is chips but also their fries is fries. You with us? It's not quite as confusing as we just made it sound. What it comes down to is that their "chips" are more akin to what we would call "steak fries," whereas their "fries" are like . . . well, like the rest of our fries. Essentially, the thicker ones are chips and the thinner ones are fries. Savvy? Jesus, we hope so, because that took way more words than we thought it would.

We also feel the need to point out on a personal note that while neither of us has ever been a picky eater, we are in agreement when it comes to the inconsistent and hard-to-get-right nature of fried per-taters. French fries in particular really run the gamut from "Not only do I not need ketchup; I don't even need any other *food*, just shovel these right here into me until I give out" all the way to "If I wanted something moist, beige, and floppy in my mouth . . . I'd be eatin' *pasta*, not french fries! C'mon!"[3] So with that said, here's what, to us, constitutes a good french fry / chip: It's golden brown, piping hot, properly salted, and, most importantly, has the right CTTR, or "crunch-to-tater ratio." This number *must* be high—meaning the thing has got to be noticeably much crunchier than it is . . . potato-y. This is nonnegotiable. Far as we're concerned, if you ain't got crunch, you ain't got fries. Without the crunch all you have is a big mouthful of hot unseasoned potato, and at that point, why not just eat a cooked potato whole?[4]

As mentioned (have you ever in your LIFE had a person take this long to adequately express their opinion on french fries?), the chips that come with fish are more akin to steak fries, and as such, they are of a thicker nature. This is, in our opinion, to their extreme detriment. Never once did an order of chips automatically come with ketchup, which we know makes us sound American as hell. But since they don't customarily provide an alternative sauce, we can only assume the English are eating these big-ass chips just completely *un*sauced, and we simply cannot abide that. Further, and this is probably about to be a whole-ass thing, but the fries are pretty much never—and we do mean *never*—salted properly. In point of fact, we found salt to be an issue with a great many things on offer in England—a

---

3. You totally thought that beige-and-floppy thing was gonna be a wiener joke, didn't you? Naughty you.
4. Call that an Irish lollipop.

statement we are sure is likely to go over poorly. Still, though, it's the truth (as we saw it).

Which leads us to our primary takeaway[5] regarding English cuisine: When it was good, it was tremendous. But when it was bad, it was usually bad *not* because it was undercooked or way off base or insane or pungent or vile or off-putting or anything like that. Rather, it was just . . . bland. As hell. If you ask us, these people need Jesus and salt—hold the Jesus. And we already know what their retort would be: "Classic Americans and their excess. Should we fry it in butter and smother it with melted cheese before serving it too?" First of all, yeah, maybe you should. It'd probably hit harder than that bowl of Old Man Wheatbury's Classic Flavorless Breakfast Gruel you've poured yourself there. Secondly, we know we're fat and dumb, but when it comes to food, and in particular *fried* food, you really should think twice before questioning America. You think being this fat a country just *happens*? Hell no! This took *generations* of utterly shameless culinary self-flagellation to achieve, so show some respect. And believe us when we say: Y'all need more salt.

Now that we've said that, let's flip the script and baldly acknowledge one area where we as a country should 100 percent be taking a page out of the UK's book (which we assume is a big-ass, dusty old tome atop an ancient lectern in some candlelit antechamber somewhere), and that is on the subject of portion sizes. Now, listen. It wasn't news to us and won't be news to you that America goes just a *skosh* overboard when it comes to portion sizes. But now that we've been to a country that *doesn't* serve food in buckets as a general rule, we can confirm: American portion sizes should be illegal and/ or allocated to livestock. Hell, we don't even think a horse needs to be eating as much as your standard Olive Garden entree provides. Americans, you know how if you go out for a nice meal with your friends, afterward you're miserable and need to lie down for a while? And your wife's all like, "But it's two in the afternoon. That was brunch. Stop embarrassing me." And then you say, "Time is immaterial for I have defiled myself and must shun the light of day in favor of the darkness of my own private shame, *woman*! Now—*to my hovel*!" You know how we all do that? Every weekend, right? All of us? Right. Totally. Well, did you know that other people in other

---

5. No pun intended. (They call to-go food "takeaway," see.)

places *don't*? Yeah, we couldn't believe it either, but in the UK, receiving your meal in a restaurant is *not* akin to being downed with a tranquilizer dart made out of diabetes. Instead, you are served a regular meal for a regular human person. Isn't that just the damnedest thing you've ever heard? And probably because of that, they don't often have or take leftovers with them afterward. In fact, they presumably find it quite amusing that we not only take our leftovers home with us but also that we openly and willingly compare ourselves to stupid, fat little doggies (with bags) in the process. Christ, we are ridiculous. And the world knows it. Anyway, their portion sizes are what's up.

What is decidedly *not* up, however, is the standard for service in the UK. We know this is a real gray area of a topic here. To start, you don't tip much for service in the UK. Apparently the rules go like this: If you order at the bar, do not tip unless the bartender really crushes it, in which case you can say "and one for yourself" at the end of the night, telling the bartender to buy themselves a round on you (as you hand them this amount of money). As to whether anyone actually ever undergoes this whimsical and needlessly coded process, we couldn't say; but this is what we were told. We were further told that if you instead receive service from a waiter or waitress at your *table*, then yes, you can and *maybe* should tip 10 percent but not any more than that and also it's not required even then, oh, and *also* also you should make sure and review your check because a tip may already be included. If you can't tell for sure by looking at the bill, then simply consult with the spirits of your ancestors and let the wind determine whether, when, why, how much, and to whom you should tip in that damned country.

Before we move on, let's clarify some things about tipping. We *fully* acknowledge that it is unfortunate and also complete bullshit that tipping is a cultural thing in America at all. No doubt about it. The fact that companies can openly rely on the public to pay their own employees a living wage is, in a word, *fooked*. We'd even go so far as to say it's *proper fooked*, mate. That a widespread and profitable company with millions in annual revenue like O'Charley's (Trae worked there for years back in the day) can pay its servers $2.13 an hour and we're all just supposed to be completely fine with that is the height of America's capitalist bootlicking bullshittery. One hundred percent.

Having said that, though, we realized something about ourselves whilst across the pond: Not only do the two of us *like* to tip people well, but we also almost feel like we *need to*, especially when we're traveling far from home. And here's why, by way of a brief anecdote: In 2016, shortly after Trae had gone viral, he was invited to Boston to participate in the Forbes 30 Under 30 ceremony[6] and to be interviewed by Forbes as part of this process.[7] Separately, we had gone to a nice seafood place in West Palm Beach, Florida, just to eat lunch, and the Forbes interviewer chose the moment we were set to order our drinks to finally call Trae for his interview. So Trae spoke to this journalist from Forbes, trying to be respectful but still talking in his stupid hillbilly accent and all that, and our server, a Frenchman named Jacques (we shit you not), took his leave of the table. We never saw him again, for he had passed us off to a younger female server. We took this as confirmation that he had judged us to be unworthy filth who would not tip him well, and as such we looked at each other and wordlessly agreed: *OK, then. Guess we 'bout to put this girl through college, by God. Just to prove to Jacques he's wrong about us.* (By the way, Jacques almost certainly passed us off simply because we were men and she was a young, pretty girl, not because of what our paranoid inner voices were telling us. Hell, she probably traded him a table of South Florida mammaws for us and the move never had *anything* to do with us being white-trash rednecks, but good luck ever convincing us of that.)

So with that in mind, know that we have never in our lives felt more consistently and continuously like Big Stupid Dumb Americans than while we were in the UK. And in case you're wondering, yes: Even over there, they are aware that Southern accents "sound dumb." We were convinced that everyone around us was convinced that we were . . . Gump-y. By the way, we know how much more that says about *us* than the people of Britain, and further that we are insecure lunatics with chips on our shoulders, but hey. That's just what growing up smart in the South will do to a man. At any rate, we spent a lot of time lamenting the fact that we could not, in our words, "floss" on a particular server or bartender to make sure they did not think of us as Clampetts. This was the first time we ever realized how much

---

6. Ha, joke's on them. Trae's stupid trash.
7. Corey attended as well but spent his time bogging for cranberries in a virtual exhibit in front of an unimpressed Chrissy Teigen, who had the misfortune of having her book signing right beside our table.

the act of tipping meant to our own perceptions of our self-worth. We really need to stick with therapy.

Point is, they don't really tip over there, and we had a helluva time with it. And would you like to know what else they don't really do over there? Provide timely and efficient service in restaurants. Funny how that works. Nah, we're kidding. We don't wanna sound all Fox News by doubling down on "See, when they ain't got no incentive to work harder, they just get *lazy*, by God!" We don't wanna do that. We're not gonna do that. At all. But. But like. But like we kinda can't help but wonder if maybe the lack of additional incentive kinda makes 'em a little lazy. Just a tiny bit! Anyhoo, we should be paying servers a living wage in our country, dammit. It's just something we noticed.

In fairness, the lack of efficient service may not be related to tips at all. That is, they ain't in a hurry all the damn time like we Americans are, so the difference could just be cultural. You know how Americans be: so obsessed with working hard that they never stop to smell the roses . . . or properly assess the state of their mental health in time to avoid a complete nervous breakdown. Silly us! We never do those things! After all, as the old American saying goes, time is money and people are faceless cogs!

Maybe they're just not like that in the UK—all rush rush and hustle bustle and rise and grind and all that other "I'll be dead by forty" horseshit we're so obsessed with. For example, we went for afternoon tea at the very posh Fortnum & Mason in London and stayed for an hour and a half. When we said (very politely) that we were ready to go, we were met with very surprised reactions. "Truly? But you've only been with us for such a short time!" And in our heads we're like, *Motherfucker, in America we never spend more than an hour on just one fat. Not with all the other fats we gotta get to in a day.* We were so confused. But ya know, c'est la vie and all that. At any rate, we kept expecting to adjust to the slower rate of service over there, but to be completely honest, we never really did. We had a tremendous time (and some outrageous meals) anyway.

JUST WHAT EXACTLY IN THE HELL IS "PUDDING"?

After our travels, we have one major question for our British cousins in terms of food: Do y'all know what pudding is? Do we? Does anybody? Is your usage of the term *pudding* an elaborate joke you're playing upon the rest of the Western world? Do you understand how confounding and non-sensical it is? Why can't you just call one thing *pudding*? Why? For God's sake, *why*?

All right, so that was a bunch of questions, but just go with the first one: *Do y'all know what pudding is?* If you're an American, you probably think you know what pudding is. And as a fellow Yank I would wager that you do. You *do* know what pudding is. You know what pudding is because (a) it's a simple word for (b) a simple dish with (c) only one definition and because (d) you are neither a child nor a madman. Pudding is a custard-like confection with a thick creamy consistency, often flavored with chocolate or vanilla (though not always) and eaten with a spoon by necessity. That's pudding—or *puddin'* if you're using it as a term of endearment or tend to sound dumb when you talk, like us. Right? We're all in agreement on that?

Yeah, not the British. They evidently don't have a clue what pudding is. That, or they decided that *pudding* is such a lovely word that by all rights it should mean like fifteen different goddamn things. When first encountering this phenomenon, you may think you've parsed it relatively quickly. *Oh, oh I see*, you'll think to yourself. *Based on this section of the menu, I now understand that* pudding *is their word for* dessert. *Different, but fair enough.* Yeah, well, joke's on you, idiot, because that would make far too much sense to actually be the case.

Pudding is their word for dessert. Except they still also use the term *dessert* for dessert. (Apparently it's more posh to say *dessert*? Whatever you say, Viscountess!) To make matters worse, they use the term *pudding* for just *sooooo* much other shit as well. For example, a pudding apparently also is a . . . well, a pudding, we guess? That is to say, the stuff we call pudding, they might also, sometimes, on occasion, maybe, if they feel like it, perhaps, but not necessarily, call pudding. Further, if someone tries to bake a cake but undercooks it, that would-be cake is now "more akin to a pudding." Why, you ask? We'd sooner lasso the moon than answer that question.

It doesn't stop there. Oh, no no no. The madness has only just begun. Have you ever heard of Yorkshire pudding? Take a guess at what that is. "A dessert popular primarily in Yorkshire?" Good guess, but *heavens no*, dear sir or madam. "OK, so maybe it's a really gooey cake or something resembling what we call pudding in the States then?" *Poppycock!* No, Yorkshire pudding is not sweet at all—because of course it isn't. Why would a pudding be sweet? Except for literally everything else about it, anyway. At any rate, Yorkshire pudding is a pseudo-bowl-shaped type of bread, which they often fill with meat and gravy and the like for use with their Sunday roasts. It's wonderful, but we just think calling that *pudding* would be like us calling corn bread, well, *pudding*. Maybe Alabama pudding. Either way it would be dumb.

Right now you're likely thinking, *This is a much more pronounced level of vitriol than I was expecting in a section on pudding.* And you are correct. We're almost done. But this last part is the most flabbergasting part yet. Y'all ain't gonna believe this shit they call *black pudding*. Now, first of all, it ain't half bad in terms of taste, but the name combined with the thing itself is one of the damndest things in all the British Isles, based on our opinions and given all the context to this point. So what do you think black pudding is?

The most creative and long-winded among you might think, *I remember reading somewhere that they call molasses* black treacle *over there. So maybe this is a molasses-based confection. Or just a really dark chocolate. Something like that.* First of all, why are you still guessing sweets? Did you really think that after the whole Yorkshire pudding thing that guessing something sweet was going to be a winning strategy? Seems silly to us, but whatever melts your butter. And *now* you're thinking, *Is this book really insulting me for a thing it made me do? I'd have called my mother if I wanted that kind of treatment.*

Sorry. Anyway, black pudding is sausage made from blood. Yeah, we don't know what kind of stygian eldritch madness led to giving the most metal-as-fuck of all the sausages a dessert's name. Did a medieval witch make it and give it that name in an attempt to lure illiterate peasant children into her magic murder forest?

Probably. Yep.

After all, that would make just as much sense as anything else surrounding the Brits and their relationship with "pudding."

CANDY

There are a few things that, regardless of whether you are proud of them or not, America kicks ass at. Barbecuin'? Check. Having a diverse and breathtaking array of landscapes? Check. Turning our flag into swim trunks and overalls? Check, and hell yeah, buddy! One thing we were absolutely certain of before we embarked on our trip across the pond is that America is also number one at anything that will make you spill out of your blue jeans—especially when it comes to fatty or sugary treats that are nothing but empty calories that make your teeth fall out. Candy, that is.

No way could any country touch us when it comes to nonnutritious items. America don't give a fiddler's fuck about nutrition, y'all! Remember when Michelle Obama dared to suggest that our kids could eat more broccoli? Why, we treated her as if she just squatted over the Constitution and took a big ol' country shit on it! "Take that communist vegetable talk somewhere else, lady!" we said. "I ate doughnuts dipped in butter for breakfast, my daddy ate doughnuts dipped in butter for breakfast, and by God, my son is gonna eat doughnuts dipped in butter for breakfast!" We're . . . *sigh* . . . number one.

The two of us consider ourselves candy and junk food connoisseurs. Thanks to our jobs, we basically live in hotels and often survive purely on sustenance that can be found in the hotel sundry. Which reminds me: If you're from the UK and reading this, you don't know what a hotel sundry is, do ya? That's right, y'all. *They ain't got hotel sundries!* So let me explain hotel sundries to those of you who are either from the UK or from America but have dignity. The hotel sundry is the little shame-pantry right beside the check-in desk where one goes at three o'clock in the morning to fill in the Cheetos-and-Butterfinger quadrant of the food pyramid. You will rarely find any actual meals there, but if you do, they are of the Hot Pocket and Cup O' Noodles variety, which is good because we all know you sleep better if you go ahead and get your year's worth of sodium right before going to bed. Hotel sundries are for the weak, the shameful, the desperate, and the forlorn. We love them.

Even though we are talking a pretty big game about being bags of shit, the two of us had actually been adhering to a pretty decent diet before this trip. Trae had gotten in better shape recently, and Corey was actually down a whopping sixty pounds. The portion sizes being what they are in the Queen's country was actually helping us maintain our svelte figures.[8] It was only when waiting to board a train at London Paddington Station that Corey stumbled upon the candy aisle of Boots (like a British Walgreens or CVS drugstore).

He was taken aback by the array of sweets. The beautiful wrappers, the variety of flavors, the whimsical names. The Flake Bar, the Twirl, the Yorkie, a Dairy Milk, my God, a *Curly Wurly*? Surely someone was playing a joke on us! We thought this was a drugstore, not a Harry Potter–themed chocolatier! The first thing he noticed was that Cadbury had significant representation among the candy bars. We are, of course, familiar with Cadbury, but only because of their once-a-year treat that passes as quickly as it arrives: the Cadbury Creme Egg. The Cadbury Creme Egg is a fleeting treasure! As soon as we see the thirty-some-odd-year-old commercial with the lion wearing bunny ears every spring, we know it is time to hit the stores to stock up on that ultrarich delicacy before it's whisked away for reasons we'll never know. Why do we treat something as good as the Cadbury Creme Egg the way we treat something as bad as the McRib? It should be available 365 days a year as far as we are concerned, and if one of us ever runs for office, you can bet your sweet ass it will!

Apparently, though, yonder yonder, Cadbury is like the Don Dada of the chocolate game. Please understand that what we are about to say is not the result of any actual research or even peeking at Google for five seconds, but to us it seems that, over there, Cadbury is to them what Hershey's is to us. And by that we mean the primary source of chocolate candies, at least from a mass-produced commercial aspect. For pretty much every candy bar or candy nugget or candy stick we have over here, they have the equivalent in British form. Candy bars are, of course, a little like food at an Americanized Mexican restaurant[9] in that every item is basically a mixture of the same ingredients, but those ingredients vary as it pertains to their distribution throughout said item. You got your peanuts, your chocolate, your crispy crunchies, your caramel, and then your nougat. Oh dear God,

---

8. OK, we are only considered svelte back in our hometowns, and mainly just according to our grandmothers.
9. See: Our Almighty Taco Bell, praise be its holy name.

the nougat. To this day we have no idea what in the hell "nougat" is, but much as we can't identify the "beef" at Taco Bell, we don't really give a shit but we'll take some more, please and thank you. Quit judging us, and don't look us in the eyes!

We wish we could remember what the first British candy bar we ate was, but it was all a blur. Once we took the first bite, we moved into a near transient state. We scarfed them down like we hadn't eaten in days, when in reality we hadn't *not* eaten in days. *Dear God, could it be?* we thought. *Could it be that the snooty Brits have bested us in the candy game? Perhaps this is why they have such bad teeth!* [10]

The candy bars burst in flavor but also literally burst with gooey caramel and nougat. They seemed so fresh. So magical. So much better than our candy. We sat in dismay for what felt like hours. Our whole lives had been a lie. We started looking into it, and apparently chocolate used to cost, like, a shit ton of money until some feller named Hershey figured out a way to make it cheaper and more available to the masses. That became the standard in America, and no one ever felt the need to raise the bar. For shame. *For. Shame.* If you are reading this in America, you should know that whatever your favorite chocolate candy bar is, it is pure dog shit. Our eyes have been opened to the truth, and now, unfortunately, there is no going back. We haven't been able to eat an American candy bar since this trip. It is simply not worth the calories.

Want even more proof? Trae's favorite British candy bar was the Starbar, and Corey's was the Picnic. We did a little internet searching to see how the people of the UK rank their candy bars. According to multiple listicles and Reddit threads, the Starbar and Picnic consistently rank among the least favorite of the lot to the Limey bastards—meaning that their *worst* candy may be better than our *best* candy. We're number one? We don't think so. Get your shit together, America!

---

10. We are kidding, but considering Southern people share the stereotype, we feel we can make the joke.

INTERNATIONAL CHAMPIONSHIP

★

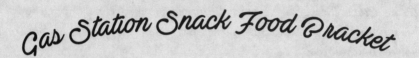

THE CONTENDERS

FROM THE SOUTH

Boiled Peanuts: Arguably the steak tartare of the South. They're mushy, they're wet, they're salty, they're an abomination to God soaking in a germ-riddled Crock-Pot. They're delicious.

Pickled Eggs: You ever see them jars with little floating pink orbs that look like the workings of a witch doctor? Them's pickled eggs, and every woman named Betty Lou loves 'em.

FROM THE WEST COAST

Avocado Soda: The standard beverage order for the trust-fund baby on the go!

Wheat Grass Jerky: Who doesn't like it when you take something good and make it bad? It's all the rage in LA!

FROM THE UNITED KINGDOM

Salt and Vinegar Crisps: UK crisps = American potato chips except surprisingly better! These sumbitches are so tart they'll make your jaw hurt in a good way.

Wine Gums: Sort of like gummy bears except wine-flavored. No, they are not like weed gummies. If you eat a bag, your belly might hurt but you're good to drive.

FROM THE MIDWEST

Cheese Curds: Bite-sized cheese that, if they are fresh, make a squeaking sound when you eat them! They not only taste delicious, but they *sound* delicious.

Premade Tenderloin Sandwich: Far as we can tell, this is sort of the Midwest's version of a gas station burrito. Super tasty but you'll likely explode the next rest area toilet.

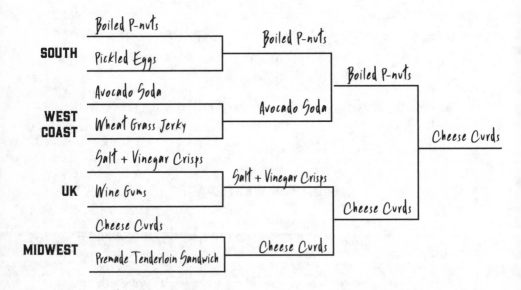

And the Winner Is . . .

This was a difficult decision that could have gone many different ways. At the end of the day, a perfect road snack needs to be enjoyed while driving, and this takes boiled peanuts and pickled eggs out of the equation. Can't give it to wine gums because (unless we missed something) they are bereft of the heavenly "sour dust" that takes gummies to the next level. Avocado soda and wheat grass jerky can't win because we made them up. So after much deliberation and soul-searching, we claim that the winner is . . . cheese curds! I mean, come on, y'all! Did you really think cheese was gonna get knocked out? It's the strong number one seed and a first-ballot Hall of Famer in basically every iteration!

THE COTSWOLDS

WHAT THEIR MOTTO SHOULD BE: Not Your Pappaw's Countryside

WHAT TO PACK: The opposite of what you would pack if you were going to "the country" in America.

WHAT TO EAT AND DRINK AND WHERE: Find ya a cozy pub in a quaint village for a scrummy meat pie and a pint of [insert other stereotypically English fare here].

WHAT NOT TO MISS: Do you like pretty green stuff? They got plenty of it!

Being rural Americans ourselves (or "hicks" if you're of the high-horse persuasion), we wanted to make a point to travel at least briefly to some rural parts of England. Our travel agent heard this and, very reasonably, thought, *Oh, I know just the place: the Cotswolds!* Hence, we went. We couldn't wait to take in the English countryside and some proper English countryfolk. Well, we've since done so, and the number one takeaway we had from the experience is this: The word *country* means a *rather different* thing over there.

We're country fellers. Grew up in the country, love country music, have been privy to a big ol' country ass-whoopin' or two. So we thought we had a fair idea of what "country life" was like. And we do. In America. In England, it's a whole other kettle of fish.[1] In America, a country boy is a big burly book-hatin' barefoot sumbitch in overalls, cussin' at something for being different from the sky-high window of his coal-rollin' truck, the transportation utility of which is secondary to its effectiveness as a canvas for any number of offensive bumper stickers. He dips snuff, talks tough, and takes no guff, by God. To hear him tell it, anyway. He works where his daddy works, married at nineteen, had three kids by twenty-four, and believes the game of football has long since been "pussified." He ain't got much besides a kick-ass stereo, but he works hard, pays his taxes, and looks out for him and his. Also guns. Just everywhere.

Now we're not saying that's an *accurate* representation. Hell, only 'bout 25 to 30 percent of that applies to us, for starters. But it is absolutely the image that most Americans call to mind when they hear the term *country boy*. On this side of the Atlantic, countryfolks are simple, unsophisticated rubes. Hayseeds. Yokels. Bumpkins. And any other number of ways to say "big dumb barn person." And some of that may also ring true in England. For one thing, England absolutely has a "town and country divide." Like in America, the rural parts of the country tend to be more conservative than the cities. In light of that, we have to imagine that many English city dwellers have a less-than-favorable perception of those out in the boonies. Still, though, having now spent some time over there, we decided *the countryside* and *country living* as concepts have a very different color to them than in America. And that color is green. And not like the rolling-hill-vistas type of green either. In the US, the rural parts of the country are the most impoverished and economically destitute regions of all. People struggle, and they're not happy about it (nor should they be, even if some of that anger is misplaced, in your authors' humble opinions). Things here are rusting, in a constant state of disrepair. In England, the countryside is lush and affluent—idyllic, even. Things there are rust*ic*, in a constant state of "Instagrammable." It's a whole different vibe.

Before going further, we should probably offer a massive disclaimer. The Cotswolds in particular, where we spent our time, is likely not representative of country living in the rest of England. Our experience may have been

---

1. That phrase has *got* to be English in origin, right?

like that of an English travel writer who visits wine country in Northern California and then comes back saying, "I dunno wot all this trailer talk is about. It was luhv-leh! I smashed grapes with a billionaire!" Regions of rural England may be positively filled with their own versions of the hypothetical Bubba outlined previously, with their own rendition of "Dueling Banjos" playing in the background. Just gargantuan, ill-toothed peasants, holding a torch in one hand and a dead goose in the other, forming an angry mob to harass the local school board for teaching a course on the Quran. That may exist. We acknowledge that. But we did not experience it.

Even outside the Cotswolds, country life seemed even more idealized over there than it is at home. Just look at the names. Rural towns in America have names like Bucksnort and Lick Skillet. Rural towns in England have names like Buxton-upon-Thames and Somethin'shire. And they're *like* the Shire too. Green rolling hills surround cozy hamlets where everything is made out of stone, and each village has a welcoming pub with a lazy plume of smoke billowing from its precious little chimney. It really be like that, y'all.

This seems to be because, as we alluded to previously, the English countryside is *wealthy*. We're not saying that everyone who lives there is loaded, but the regions have a pronounced "landed gentry" feel. Take the Cotswolds, for example. The Cotswolds region comes from old money. Old sheep money, to be specific. In fact, the name "Cotswold" comes from Old English words meaning "sheep enclosure in the rolling hills."[2]

Money has a way of keeping things up. Everything in the Cotswolds feels old, but old in a pleasing, romantic way. You pass through these little villages in the Cotswolds, the very definition of "quaint," and you feel transported back in time. The golden-stoned cottages have thatched roofs, the streets are narrow, and the (few) shops are picturesque. Exactly one church and one pub grace the town. Then you see a minute, cylindrical stone structure in the middle of the village no bigger than a mall kiosk and find out that it used to be the jail they'd throw a pheasant thief into after stripping his clothes off but before tarring and feathering him (or something along those lines). Then you remember, *Oh right, the past was an abject nightmare.* Even so, the villages are very cute.

---

2. Isn't it funny how the names we have for things now used to just be words for whatever that thing was? Y'all ever thought about that? Maybe while high? Bet you will now.

Whilst in the Cotswolds, we stayed at a country inn called the Hare & Hounds (because of course it was called that). The front-desk clerk was a Great Dane wearing a Sherlock Holmes hat and smoking a pipe. That isn't true, but it should be. It was that type of place. We felt like we should've been hunting foxes and shushing chambermaids the whole time we were there. And we loved it. We drank many a pint and had some of the better meals of our entire trip at this establishment (including oxcheek croquettes, and *hoo-wee* were they somethin'). Truth be told, there's not much else to do at a place like Hare & Hounds. Just eat, drink, and look at pretty stuff. Maybe *talk* about how pretty the stuff is. We did a lot of that. It also seemed a lovely place to pen a murder mystery, if you're looking to do that. But that's about it.

For us, it served as a base of operations. We stayed there at night while we explored the countryside, including sojourns to Stonehenge and the breathtaking city of Bath. So let's cover each of these in detail. First, though, a note on the method by which the exploring took place—i.e., a positively harrowing experience known as "driving in England."

DRIVING YONDER YONDER

Neither of us is overly fond of driving. Our fathers-in-law would probably tell you that's because we're not overly fond of *bein' real men* either, but oh well. As traveling comics we have to do an awful lot of driving, regardless of our feelings on the matter. But we'd really rather not, as a general rule. And that rule is compounded exponentially by the prospect of driving in a place where everything is totally bass-ackwards, such as England. You probably already know that they drive on the wrong side of the road over there. (You heard us: the *wrong* side.) But they also got totally different signs and lines on the road and intersections and just ever' damn thing. Did the rest of the world not get the memo that they were supposed to be changing their stuff to match America's stuff? We're pretty sure that was in the Geneva Conventions.

We also were surprised to learn we would even be *allowed* to drive over there. Isn't it sort of weird that they'll just let you do that? Sure, we've got licenses to drive in our home country, but it seems a bit cavalier to assume that means we'll be good to do so over there. The attitude seems to be: "So you know how you drive in America? Right, well . . . just flip that. Now here's a Mercedes. Steering wheel's over there. Ya know, where it shouldn't be. Have fun!"

We're kidding about the American way being the correct way, but that doesn't change the fact that it's the only way we've ever known. And you probably think we're exaggerating the effect that had on us, but we were nerve-racked for every second we spent on English roads.[1] We don't know what it is, but it happened to both of us. There's just something about

---

1. Maybe our FILs are right.

driving on the other side of the road that makes you completely incapable of properly judging how close you are to the shoulder. We musta hit about fifty-'leven curbs on this trip. And one side mirror. Sorry about that, DHL man. No pedestrians, though, so perhaps we should count ourselves lucky. Especially considering the English propensity for jaywalking.

Add to this that their roads are so damn *narrow*. We understand that everything is bigger in America and that Great Britain's roads date back to a time when the most common form of transportation was damn Roman sandals, but still. The roads in a lot of these villages are literally not big enough for two cars at once, and you're expected to just sort of roll with that. Which the English do constantly and with little issue, but we were in constant terror over it.

The other thorn in our sides while driving over there was a feature of their infrastructure that logically and intellectually we understand to be superior but that we found confounding and frustrating all the same: the roundabout. Most Europeans are aware that Americans, us included, are roundabout-dumb. The first time Corey ever encountered a roundabout in Minnesota, he got stuck in it and eventually just gave up, resigning himself to a lifetime of slowly circumnavigating that particular intersection. He finally escaped, but he's had a phobia of roundabouts ever since. And for a person with such a phobia, driving in England is like taking your fear of clowns to the big top. Every new encounter with these circular convergences brought with it a fresh bout of anxiety. Sure, we had successfully negotiated all those preceding, but that was no guarantee! Also, *successfully* is a strong word. We couldn't tell you how many times we panicked and took the wrong exit from a roundabout, all the while screaming, "This one is it this one I DON'T KNOW, I DON'T, FUCK, it was that one, wasn't it?!"

Again, we understand that roundabouts are the superior intersection mechanism. We know. But we still feel England gets a little too cheeky with 'em. At least some of the ones we encountered must have been the products of some transportation engineer outsmarting himself. If you don't believe us, do us a favor and google "Swindon roundabout." Do so, and behold the arrogance of man. It's made up of five mini-roundabouts arranged into one gigantic, labyrinthine monument to the merciless god of traffic. That's the most egregious example, but there were plenty of times we left one of these devil disks thinking, *Why do these people hate us so?*

We are making Americans look bad here, but that's sort of Americans' thing abroad, innit? We should also state for the record that on the rare occasions we were able to overcome our existential dread, we found that if nothing else, the experience of driving through the English countryside sure was pretty. We've mentioned it already, but it cannot be stated enough just how damn *green* that country is, y'all. Lush and vibrant and inviting, the land begs to be driven through, top down and music blaring. But then you remember that at any given point in England, there is at least a 67 percent chance that the sky will start to piss on you, and you think better of it. Still, it's an aesthetically pleasing, if frightening, experience.

STONEHENGE

WHAT THEIR MOTTO SHOULD BE: Listen, We Honestly Still Have No Idea What They're For, Really

WHAT TO PACK: A windbreaker. Maybe a wizard staff if you're cool.

WHAT TO EAT AND DRINK AND WHERE: You will eat and drink at the official Stonehenge café and you will like it. (Seriously, it's your only option; although, we guess . . . we guess you may not like it. But still.)

WHAT NOT TO MISS: Them big rocks. Kinda hard to miss, but yeah, don't.

Stonehenge is more than a bit of a cliché at this point, the furthest thing from a "hidden gem" one could imagine. By now we've probably all heard from at least one source that Stonehenge isn't all it's cracked up to be. "It's smaller than you'd think." "It's in the middle of nowhere." "It's just a bunch of rocks." And on and on.

We'd heard all those things, too, but we were frankly never *not* going to go to Stonehenge. The two of us share a number of nerdy interests: heavy metal, high fantasy, aliens, Satan, etc. And we believe we have covered our fondness for Really Old Shit by now. Well, Stonehenge ticks a lot of those boxes. When you think of Stonehenge, it's easy to conjure up images of ancient white-bearded Druids drawing runes in goat's blood while chanting in unison amid a thunderstorm featuring purple lightning. That sort of thing. And we like that sort of thing. So off we went.

First, the location. We were never deterred by those who lamented Stonehenge's "middle of nowhere" status because, as Americans, we figured that in England "middle of nowhere" probably meant something along the lines of "Why, it's almost *for'ee moiles* uh-way frum any-fin!" And we were right not to worry about it. We met our tour group outside a hotel in Bath, and it took less than an hour to get to Stonehenge from there. An hour's ride may be the height of inconvenience in England, but to us (especially to the LA-based Trae), that's naught but a hop and a skip. Also, it's an hour spent traversing the English countryside, which is, once again, super purdy. What's to complain about?

And frankly, "Stonehenge is in the middle of nowhere" is a weird complaint to have in the first place. Where do these people *want* Stonehenge to be? Beside a damn shopping mall or something? "Stonehenge was garbage; there wasn't even a Sbarro!" It's a prehistoric stone monument, not a parking garage! In our opinion, you absolutely *want* something like Stonehenge to be out in the middle of nowhere/nature. That way you can look around and imagine the dragons and stuff. Hard to do that in a town center. So yeah, they can miss us with all that talk. The location is fine.

Second, people have said that Stonehenge is "underwhelming," "smaller than expected," or "less impressive than you'd think." To those people, we would simply say, "You have weird and dumb expectations regarding the bigness of things. Are you from Texas, perchance?" Because them rocks are plenty big, y'all. We feel confident in saying that most people would not be underwhelmed by the stones. You will more likely gaze upon them and have a version of the thought, *Damn . . . How them Druids did that shit?* You will have these thoughts because (a) it's super wild that them Druids did that shit, and (b) we still don't know exactly how (or why) them Druids did that shit.[1]

And finally, to the "it's just a bunch of rocks" people: Yeah, no, we were aware of that. We did not expect a roller coaster or anything. We expected

---

1. Our guess is slaves. It's usually slaves.

the rocks. But thank you for the insight. Also, it's not *just* a bunch of rocks. It's a bunch of *rad, huge, super-old rocks*, thank you very much. And it's not just the rocks themselves either. It's the *aura, maaaaan*. It's the fact that they're shrouded in eldritch mystery, ancient almost beyond comprehension. Stonehenge was built by peoples so distantly removed from us they might as well have been aliens (who nonetheless were human) lost forever to the cryptic sands of time (and yet perhaps known somewhere across the vastness of space). And that shit is *sweet, OK*?[2]

Long story short, we do recommend Stonehenge. We were there on a beautifully sunny and pleasant day, and it was simply lovely. Also there were a lot of blackbirds around, and we thought they were gonna give us a side quest. Alas, they didn't. Still, you should go.

---

2. Yes, we do sometimes smoke weed.

DRINKING YONDER YONDER

C an we all agree that one of the best parts of traveling is getting drunk, but in a whole different place? Outside of the first-names-and-folding-chairs crowd anyway. Getting drunk at home is great (again, as long as you don't get all shouty about it), but getting drunk *elsewhere*? The best. And as far as elsewheres go, there are few better drunk-getting destinations on earth than across the pond. It's one of the primary things everyone knows about them: They talk funny and they drink. That's what they do. And their version of drinking always felt like it had a different vibe to ours. A more . . . acceptable vibe. Hell, kids do it over there, right? Don't they? Either way, it's definitely different.

Over here, we have bars. Over there, they have pubs. Bars are seedy. Pubs are quaint. Bars are filled with sad people and horny people. Pubs are filled with jovial people and probably also horny people. Horny people are legion. Bars have fights. Pubs have disagreements. Bars have names like Bubba's Bad News Bar and Grille. Pubs have names like the Goose and Whistle. Bars are where you go after a divorce. Pubs are where you go after noon. Bars are a staple of the police report. Pubs are a staple of the community. You get it.

It probably goes without saying we were very much looking forward to the pub experience. However, we also wondered just how different the entire pub experience would be, and we felt very dumb and American about the whole thing. Having now gone and done the thing (at a great many pubs all across England and Scotland), we are happy to report that pubs do, in fact, live up to their delightful reputation. Here are some more takeaways we found noteworthy.

One of the foremost questions we had, as is probably the case with most Americans sojourning thataway, was: *Is it true the beer is warm? Surely not, right?* Every red-blooded American knows that beer is supposed to be colder than your ex's blackened heart or it ain't worth drinkin'. Hell, entire American beer companies focus their branding exclusively around how cold their beer is (which we always found funny, by the way). Isn't the coldness of any given beer entirely up to the consumer? "Drink our beer; it's as cold as the Rockies!" Yeah, well, not if our fridge sucks, buddy. As a company, aren't you setting yourself up for the moments when someone tries one of your beers in a less-than-ideal cooling scenario and thus thinks to themselves, *I* knew *them commercials was full of shit!* Seems risky. But we digress. The point is, Americans like a good beer, but Americans *love* a good *cold* beer. As such, we were a little apprehensive about the temperature situation in these lauded English pubs.

So, *is* the beer warm? Well, based on our extensive and studious research on the subject,[1] the answer is, sometimes (oftentimes, really), yes. The very first beer we got from the very first pub we went to in Central London was tepid at best. It also seemed damn near flat. *They like it like this?* we thought. *Surely they've heard of the American—and thus correct—way to serve this beverage, yes? Are they doing a bit?* No, they are not doing a bit. In fact, they are deadly serious about beer and beer-drinkin'. In the estimation of many Brits (and other Europeans), beer cannot be properly appreciated when served ice-cold. This estimation would, of course, differ wildly from that of most Americans: "How the hell is a man s'posed to yell at a softball ump or shank a tee shot while drinking a *warm* beer?"

Brits likely think we are philistines in this regard—and, dear audience, your humble authors reckon that, even though our 23andMe results never indicated it, we must have roots in ancient Palestine, because on this subject, philistines are we. Give us cold beer or give us . . . well, give us a warm beer, we guess, because warm beer is still better than no beer, but y'all know what we're saying.

Having said that, it's not impossible to find a frosty brew over there. In fact many pubs have a dedicated "cold tap," typically of Guinness, which we presume was installed for the express purpose of catering to any knuckle-dragging Yanks that happen upon the place. Fine by us. Also,

---

1. We were very dedicated to the cause.

we found—as with anything in life—that eventually you get used to it. We got plenty drunk on plenty of not-cold beer in our travels and didn't regret it nary a bit.

We also wondered what the process itself would be like. Do you order at the bar? (Yes.) Do you tip? (No.) Are there servers? (Sometimes, but not typically.) Are said servers orphans with soot on their face? (Not anymore.) Is there a special lingo, something like, "Proffer a pint of the ol' scrummy wallop, would ya?" We had lots of questions. And we found that there were some intricacies, but nothing outrageous. Basically, you ask for the beer you want by name, and unless otherwise requested, it will be served as a pint (you can ask for a half-pint). You order at the bar, which is usually much easier than in America, because a majority of the pubs we patronized did not have barstools in the way. We found this odd at first but quickly grew to appreciate it. Much easier to hail the barman when you don't have to squeeze between two bricklayers arguing about rifles to do so. You generally pay as you order, and as mentioned earlier, tips are not expected. The few times we used the "And one more for yourself" line, the bartender acted either confused or amused by it. "*Someone's* been googling pub tips," their eyes seemed to say to us. Many pubs do offer meals. One more note on food: Pretty much every pub we went to had chips (excuse us, *crisps*) for sale, which we thoroughly enjoyed. Also, if you're going to a pub in a group or happen to find yourself part of a group at said pub (you charmer, you), then you need to know about *rounds*.

If you're any sort of public drinker, you presumably already know what a round is. You buy a round of drinks for your companions or for the entire bar if the home team just won a big game or if you're a mobster whose muscle just smashed a guy's face for cracking wise or something like that. Generally, in America, we order rounds on occasion, but it's more typically every drunk for himself. Well, over there, rounds are everything. The only thing. One does not simply order oneself a drink when one is accompanied by others. The standard is that each person in your group will buy a round for everyone, in whatever order you determine, and this process will repeat itself in an orderly fashion until everyone has reached a mutually recognized appropriate level of pissed-ness. Or the pub closes. Probably the latter.

The etiquette surrounding rounds may sound simple, and it is, but it is also deadly serious. Let's say you're in a group of four, and you're not much of a drinker. Three rounds have been bought and it's your turn to pay, but you feel as though you've had enough and would rather pack it in. No. No, you will not pack it in. You will buy your round. You will and you *must*, whether you get one for yourself or not. Rounds are sacrosanct. Let's say you're in an American bar and you either hit it off with someone at the bar or you accidentally step on their shoe or you want to initiate a conversation with / hopefully pork a stranger or the like. You might offer to buy them a drink, yes? Yeah, well, none of that horseshit in a pub, thank you very much. You *can* offer to buy someone a drink, but that person will then owe you a nonnegotiable blood debt. And if they're already part of a round-buying group, well congratulations, now you've gone and monkeyed up the whole thing. Hope you're proud of yourself. Lastly, you should work on your server skills because when it's your round, you are expected to obtain and deliver those drinks to the table yourself.

Part of the reason rounds are so important in the pubs is because Brits are big "session" drinkers. They like a nice session beer. If you're wondering what a session beer is, it's any beer you can drink a metric shit ton of. Anything lighter or with a lower ABV (generally 4 to 5 percent). And the Brits love them, which honestly is responsible of them. Because if you're gonna drink an alarming number of beers, then it really should be something light. And they are absolutely going to drink an alarming number of beers. Whereas a German might savor a nice Doppelbock sip by sip, a Brit generally prefers to house a barrel of lager by eight o'clock. It's all great fun, really.

Pubs are such fun, in fact, that they tend to be packed to the gills. We don't know if you remember or not, but they like to drink over there, and the pub is the place to do it. So every day after quittin' time, in any kind of business district (or even just a crosswalk in a village), the pubs will quickly fill up with Limey imbibers. So our recommendation would be that if you are there on vacation, and if you do not have to work or be generally worth a damn for anything, then you should go to the pub either a little earlier in the day or a little later in the evening unless you're the crowd-lovin' type. Be careful, though, because they tend to close much earlier than any American would expect. In America, the lights come on sometime between 2:00 and 4:00 a.m. in most places, and the few desperate stragglers are faced with the well-lit truth of their intentions and then generally say "to hell with it" before making those bad decisions anyway. It's all part of the experience. But in England, particularly London, the pubs close (for the most part) at 11:00 p.m., which is wild to us Yanks. "What the hell! The damn ball game ain't even off yet!" Apparently it's a tradition that goes back a long ways and, as many traditions are (especially the older ones), it is steeped in war and sadness.

The story goes that the pubs used to be open for longer, but during World War I, people were spending more and more time getting plastered, probably on account of the whole world being at war. It got so bad that at one point, the soon-to-be prime minister, David Lloyd George, famously said, "Drink is doing us more damage in the war than all the German submarines put together." So in light of that, he and the country's leadership enacted various temperance rules, one of which closed the pubs at an earlier hour. That particular law has been lifted for years now, but it's sort of become a tradition all its own.[2] Anyway, yeah, be wary of the clock when you're pubbin' it up.

One of the best parts of the pub experience was the lively, communal atmosphere. The pubs we visited were buzzing with conversation, or as the British would probably say, people are always "chattin' each other up." Or maybe they'd say, "Everybody's 'avin' a talkity-doo, innit?" Either way, you know what we mean. The pub is a great place to shoot the shit with people, and on our trip we were shootin' more shit than a drunk pappaw in a junkyard. We had an almost entirely incomprehensible but nonetheless enjoyable conversation with a London pensioner that we *think* centered around the inadequacies of the Scotland rail system as compared to England's, at least as he saw it. In the bar of the Bill Murray, an incredible London comedy club, an Irishman quizzed Trae on how he managed to perform comedy considering he was "obviously a rather serious and nervous person." Which was nice of him to point out. A mid-forties Scottish mom gave us a crash course in proper queueing technique. In Inverness, we got into a joke-telling session with some Scottish workmen, and our dinner reservation came just in time, as it was clear that they were *just* about to bust out all their best racist material. As an aside,

---

2. Ain't it wild that Germany tried to whoop the whole world's ass twice in like twenty years? They was on one.

though we're obviously biased, we truly believe the two greatest accents in the English language for jokes are Scottish and Southern. You don't have to agree with it; hell, people disagree with true things all the time. We also had many, *many* conversations on the subject of American Insanity, as one might expect given how insane we are. For more on that, see the "What They Think of Us" section of this here book. All of this is to say: If you visit the UK and frequent the pubs, please make it a point to talk to people. You will not regret it.

We must report on one negative aspect of the pub experience, however. You may have noticed that so far every note on alcohol in this section has been about beer. So what of cocktails? They love a good G&T, right? You'd think they have all kinds of nigh-ludicrous-sounding mixed drinks over there. Such as: "Lemme get a Witch's Kiss and two Buttery Bum Bums, please." Alas, and we are sorry to any Brits reading this, we found that compared to American bars, they don't make cocktails worth a damn. Every American lush knows to find the right bartender—the one that will, as the kids say, "hook it up."[3] Anyway, a good American bartender understands that the mixer in a cocktail is basically there for color. A liquid garnish, if you will. The best martinis are made by shaking the vodka in the general direction of some vermouth and then pouring it up. Good cocktails hurt a little bit. They incite a quick intake of breath followed by a reserved, "*Goddamn.*" We all know that. *In America*, anyway.

Over there, cocktails are a whole different and very sad affair. Apparently there's a law called the Weights and Measures Act, and it dictates the specific amount of liquor to be used in a mixed drink. Well, we have weighed and measured the Weights and Measures Act and found it wanting. Most every bottle of spirits we saw behind a bar in the UK had a governor on the spout that took any guesswork (or fun) out of the equation. It's the same amount always, and the amount is: "This ain't it." Add to this the fact that they seem not to be overly fond of ice in the Land of the Queen, and that they for some reason will typically give you the mixer in its own separate bottle for you to pour yourself. The end result is an inadequate, depressing beverage. No stiff pours, no hookups, just the same impotent puddle of liquor where you had hoped a cocktail would be. Every time.

---

3. Actually, the kids don't say that. We say that, and we're old now. God knows what the kids say.

We couldn't *not* say all that because we as authors are as committed to the truth as we are to wiener jokes. Still, cocktails aside, we were immensely pleased with our time in the pubs and would rank them an absolute can't-miss for any UK trip. Cheers.

YONDER YONDER
Travel Ad Lib

Fill in the words below and spin a proper British yarn!

Once whilst having a pint of _____ lager at the
$\quad\quad\quad\quad\quad\quad\quad\quad\quad$ (WHIMSICAL ADJECTIVE) + (FANCY BREED OF DOG)

_____ Inn, we met a man by the name of
(COLOR) + (ANIMAL)

_____
(NORMAL ONE-SYLLABLE MAN'S NAME + "BERT") + (ADJECTIVE ENDING IN ~Y + "BOTTOM"; E.G., "TOMBERT WISPYBOTTOM")

who informed us that his family had been in the village of _____
$\quad\quad\quad\quad\quad\quad\quad\quad\quad\quad\quad\quad\quad\quad\quad\quad\quad\quad\quad\quad$ (CARDINAL DIRECTION)

_____ for so long that his
+ (MADE-UP WORD THAT RHYMES WITH "ODDS" + EITHER "BURY" OR "SHIRE" AS A SUFFIX)

great-great-great-great _____ had been _____ in the
$\quad\quad\quad\quad\quad\quad\quad\quad$ (FEMALE RELATIVE) $\quad\quad\quad\quad\quad$ (MEDIEVAL TORTURE METHOD, PAST TENSE)

town square for knowing _____. We were unsure how to respond
$\quad\quad\quad\quad\quad\quad\quad\quad$ (ELEMENTARY SCHOOL SUBJECT)

to this, but luckily for us a Scottish man named _____
$\quad\quad\quad\quad\quad\quad\quad\quad\quad\quad\quad\quad\quad\quad$ (VARIOUS THROAT-CLEARING NOISES)

entered the room and immediately started a _____ over
$\quad\quad\quad\quad\quad\quad\quad\quad\quad\quad$ (OLD-TIMEY SLANG FOR FIGHT)

something that happened _____ years ago, and we took our leave.
$\quad\quad\quad\quad\quad\quad$ (NUMBER > 500)

BATH

WHAT THEIR MOTTO SHOULD BE: When in Rome . . . It'll Kind of Look Like You're in Bath!

WHAT TO PACK: A selfie stick for all the Instagram pics you'll take trying to look cool.

WHAT TO EAT AND DRINK AND WHERE: OK, please know this is coming from two trash bags, but they had a stand in the middle of town selling sausages and it was *fire*!

WHAT NOT TO MISS: The Circus! No . . . not that kind of Cir—look, we'll tell you all about it!

After our lovely visit to Stonehenge,[1] our redneck asses spent some time exploring the historic city of Bath. Yes, go ahead and make your jokes: "I never thought I'd hear the words *redneck* and *bath* in the same sentence!" Hardy har har. You are so clever and hilarious.[2]

This is yet another example of just how small this part of the world is compared to where we are from. It seemed like every time we saw some insanely famous landmark, another one was but a stone's throw away.[3] We were on one of them big chartered bus gimmicks. Please understand, the

---

1. Where we definitely didn't re-create the iconic scene from *Spinal Tap*.
2. No, seriously, you are. We were hoping you'd get there before we did.
3. BTW they will kick you out of Westminster Abbey if you throw stones.

roads in the UK are barely big enough to fit them itty-bitty Austin Powers cars they drive, so to say this bus ride was a harrowing experience is to put it lightly. Well, maybe not for Trae, but Corey was losing his mind. Granted, Corey gets anxious going to get the mail. Along this bus trip the driver educated us on a little history of Bath.

> **BUS DRIVER:** The city of Bath is the largest in the county of Somerset.
>
> **COREY:** Somerset? I used to do them back in gym class to impress the girls!
>
> **TRAE:** That's somersaults, and no, you most certainly didn't.
>
> **BUS DRIVER:** Though the hot springs predated them, the city was turned into a spa after a temple and baths on the River Avon were built by the Romans.
>
> **COREY:** I know they didn't build it in a day!
>
> **TRAE:** I regret being your friend.

The bus parked atop a hill overlooking the city, and when we first gazed upon it, echoes of our meemaws ran through our heads: *If this don't beat all I ever seen!* We know we've worn out the phrase "It was like a whole different country!" but, y'all, even while *in* a whole different country, this seemed like another country. Which means they pulled off what they were going for, and we were now entering a "Little Rome" smack-dab in jolly old England.

The movie *Gladiator* came to mind because, as proud Southern dum-dums, that was our introduction to the Roman way of life—but believe us, we *were* entertained![4] This damn place had more ivory towers than a Garth Brooks song on repeat. It looked like how your meemaw *wanted* her bathroom to look back in the eighties but couldn't quite pull it off.

If you will allow us to do our best impression of someone who knows what they are talking about: [clears throat] The Georgian architecture of Bath makes the city feel ancient and timeless simultaneously. The cream-colored homes peering over the River Avon seem both inviting *and* intimidating. This same dichotomy is also present in the hot springs found in Bath. You feel as though you could go for a nice swim or perchance be portaled into

---

4. You . . . you get it? Like in the movie . . . *Gladiator*?

another realm where the ancient gods await you for your judgment. The city is diverse in its altitude, with rolling hills of cobblestone streets just begging you to stroll into the past and make better your present. All roads lead to the city's epicenter, an engineering and architectural marvel called, quite aptly, *the Circus*.

In other words, it's fancy and pretty as shit, y'all. [Spits dip.]

That Circus really is something else. It's a big ol' circle of houses segmented equally into three parts with this big ol' yard in the middle where you can play a hell of a volleyball game. I mean, you *could*, but we doubt they'd let you. Hell, they won't even let you swim in the damn hot springs and it's like, well, hell, who gets a pool just to show it off? Must be nice!

But back to the Circus. Y'all know by now that this ain't no damn history book but rather our silly little perspectives on immaculate wonders, so we ain't gotta get into all the specifics. But what blew our minds about this particular landmark is that it was built from 1754 to 1769. And we don't mean it blew our minds that it took fifteen years—hell, they've been workin' on the road between Corey's house and the Mexican restaurant since he was in middle school. We mean the fact that *over there* 1754 may as well have been damn yesterday. That building is *young*. No more than a suckling babe compared to the shit around it, which was there when Joaquin Phoenix stabbed Russell Crowe in the gut (the bastard). We don't know if there is such a thing as a *perfect* building, but if there is, the Circus is that. It almost seems like something from a damn Jane Austen novel and—oh, wait—*she lived there.* DUH!

It was also interesting to see that no matter how fancy a city is, there will always be someone on the sidewalk with a portable speaker and microphone doing the absolute worst Bruno Mars impression you've ever heard. And that's not a knock. We love that type of shit. As fancy as Bath is, because of the tourists waddling around and the street vendors and karaoke singers, it manages a Gatlinburg vibe. That is, of course, if Gatlinburg had been built by a bunch of sweaty Italians who liked to have orgies and sculpt naked babies.

Bath is an adorable little market town, and by *little* we mean there are eighty-five thousand people there. But I assure you, they are all (as our pap-paws used to say) *wedge-ass* in there.

If you want a Gucci bag, Bath has got you, boo-boo. If you want to whittle a stick while sittin' atop the Pulteney Bridge and overlooking the River Avon while your wife goes and gets said Gucci bag, bring it on, hoss! Something for everyone, this visual masterpiece has. So while on your trip across the pond, we highly suggest that you (dad joke coming in three, two . . .) take a bath![5]

---

5. You've already bought the book. You can't get your money back now.

WHAT THEY THOUGHT OF
US YONDER YONDER

We have mentioned countless times how much and how often we felt like big, dumb Americans while on this trip. This sense was rooted in our understanding that, to 90 percent of the world, Americans are basically patriotic gorillas. But even that analogy doesn't work because people actually *like* gorillas. Hell, gorillas have a *much* better reputation than Americans do. So we would like to formally apologize to gorillas for insulting them so. Moving on.

Point is, we do not have the most sterling of reps abroad. To such an extent that our travel agent offered us this helpful travel tip: "Pretend to be Canadian." Apparently this practice is all the rage among Americans traveling abroad. Evidently, if Europeans think you're American, they'll assume you're a wound-up racist who's sexually attracted to high-powered assault rifles, but if they think you're a Canadian, they'll assume you're a laid-back lumberjack who chugs maple syrup and knows how moose work. And we would find that to be unfair if we didn't totally get it.

Obviously we shot down the Canadian Pretense Approach, on account of our thick Southern accents. Canada has its fair share of redneck equivalents, but none of 'em sound like we do. It woulda been kind of funny if we had attempted this approach anyway though. We'd get to London just like, "Ay, y'all. We're from Canada. Hockey hits. So . . . yuns got any biscuits what ain't cookies round here? We ain't had no sausage gravy since we got here and we're plumb fit to be tied . . . uhh . . . hoser." Yeah, don't think we'd've made it too awful far going that route.

So, as we've mentioned, we took the slightly different tack of just apologizing profusely for our own existence to everyone we met. "Hi. We're Americans, and we're sorry. Do you know where Pinkelnickems is?" Or "Hi. As you can already tell by my accent, I am dumb. What's a *rasher*?" That sort of thing. So having spent a fair amount of time there employing this strategy, we can share the impressions we got from most people regarding their opinions of and expectations for Americans.

The first thing we would say is this: Whatever silly, unfortunate, or horrific bullshit the Land of the Free is up to while you are traveling abroad, you can absolutely expect to hear about it from people. They keep up with our shit, for reasons we will never understand. Do they not realize that most of us only keep up with this country's lunacies because we feel we have to? Well, it seems that many of them feel the same way. To them, America is sorta like the crazy drunken uncle at the family holiday. You can scarce believe the shit he says and believes, but still . . . you're *gonna* keep an eye on him. Especially since he just pulled out a gun.

At any rate, they have something of a fascination with American politics and will probably want to talk to you about it. Generally this is how that will go: They will start by being diplomatic because at this point they still think you might be One of the Insane Ones our country is so known for. If at any point you give them reason to suspect that you are *not*, in fact, a maniac, they will visibly relax and say something to the effect of "So, mate . . . what are you lot *on about*?" Now you're fully in it. To illustrate, here is a personal anecdote from Corey about a conversation he had with some lads in Stratford-upon-Avon while Trae was in the room FaceTiming with his family.

We had spent much of our first day in Stratford-upon-Avon stumbling around full of pints and meat pies, soaking up the aura of the Bard's home-town, even doing our touristy duties and taking in multiple tours, including one of Shakespeare's house. On our way back to our hotel to take much-needed showers and, well, to relieve ourselves of the meat pies and pints, we strolled past a pub that was perhaps the pubbiest of pubs we had ever seen. The Garrick Inn was old. It was made of stone and wood. It was tiny. Like, *very* tiny. It looked like somewhere Bilbo Baggins would work to pay his way through hobbit school and be able to afford all the elevenses he wanted.[1]

---

1. If you're not a nerd, elevenses is a meal the hobbits in *The Lord of the Rings* would eat at—you guessed it—eleven o'clock.

Because Trae decided to be boring, aka a "good dad," I decided to get gussied up and head to the Garrick Inn. It should be noted that I don't often gussy up. I am, in fact, rather un-gussied and am not prone to gussiness in any shape, form, or fashion. But for some reason, when we were across the pond, it just felt . . . proper, as they would say.

I strolled down the street in my new tweed jacket, form-fitting jeans, and *Peaky Blinders* hat, feeling as dapper as dapper could be while also sweating my entire ass off because England decided to have good weather for a change. But I sweated with glee, for tonight, my dear . . . tonight, I would drink and dine with the noblemen in the hometown of the Bard. Huzzah! Upon entering the Garrick Inn, I was surprised to find that it was somehow smaller on the inside than it looked on the outside. A sort of reverse-TARDIS situation.[2]

The second thing I noticed, much to my—Er . . . what's the opposite of "my chagrin"? It hit for me! *That's it!* The first thing I noticed that really hit for me was that unlike the multitude of pubs we had been to by this point on our journey, the Garrick Inn had seating at the bar!

I sat at the corner seat next to the wall so I could lean back and observe all twelve square feet the joint had to offer. I pulled my phone out to take notes but then quickly put it away, as I didn't want to be labeled a millennial-constantly-on-his-phone-not-experiencing-life type, even though that is 100 percent who and what I am. I ordered a pint from the feller behind the bar, who sort of looked like he would either be into magic or play bass for the Smiths. There's probably some overlap there. I didn't recognize any of the beers on tap, so I just asked him to surprise me. I didn't care for his choice, but I ordered another one and choked it down because I didn't want him to think I didn't like it, a tendency of mine that gets me into more bad than good.

About that time, a pair of jovial young Englishmen walked in and bellied up to the bar next to two older men who had been drinking in silence. The older men now perked up as if the party had just arrived. By body language alone, I could tell these blokes were regulars, and I began to get excited about the authentic UK jibber-jabber I was about to overhear.[3]

---

2. The TARDIS is Doctor Who's spaceship / time-travel thingy. I promise I know adult stuff.

3. *Jibber-jabber* sounds like a whimsical British saying or, with the wrong accent, an ethnic slur.

I do not remember any of these fellers' names, and even if I did, I wouldn't use them in print so as not to rat them out in case they had told their wives they wouldn't spend so much time at the pub. For the sake of this story, though, I am just going to assign them the most British names I can think of. The first guy that walked in—let's call him Nigel—was around thirty-three years old and was dressed in tech-bro chic: a nice pair of dark-washed jeans and a form-fitting salmon-color button-down shirt, which was, of course, tucked in, all held up by a classic braided belt. I was very much prepared to hear all about the UK's crypto market and was anticipating learning about its English equivalent, likely called Bittlesby Coin or Digitee-Doos.

His buddy beside him, Ian, also thirty-three, was in a more casual getup—T-shirt and jeans—and had sort of a Pete Davidson thing going on. By that, I mean I couldn't tell if he was white or if he was good-looking, but my wife would probably bang him if she weren't with me. You know the type. The two old men they were meeting, Farnsworth and Lowell, were a slightly younger version of Statler and Waldorf from *The Muppet Show*, and each had nose hairs longer than the line to a Billie Eilish concert in New York City.

The group sparred with English insults that I wish I could have understood enough to remember and write down.[4] I was apprehensive about engaging in conversation with a group as established as they were. Besides, I know that when I'm out drinking with a few of my buddies, we don't always care for some outsider butting in and ruining the flow of the night. I assume this goes double for people across the pond when some slack-jawed yokel cosplaying as a Dickens character chimes in with some "Yankee Doodle" nonsense.

Then one of them brought up the Queen's Platinum Jubilee. This was my chance. They weren't talking about their relationships or something I had no business intruding on; they were talking about *the* cultural happening of the moment, and I could finally organically work my way in. I hit them with the "Excuse me, fellers, but I couldn't help but overhear," then gave the obligatory prefacing apology for being American, Southern, and stupid. "So being from America and not having a clue, I've been curious as to how regular folks over here feel about the Queen's Jubilee?"

---

4. Imagine Buddy the Elf calling someone a cotton-headed ninnymuggins but with a thick English accent and curse words peppered throughout.

I would like to point out that these gentlemen could not have been more welcoming to my conversation. They jumped at my greeting as if I was an old friend they had been waiting to see. As is custom virtually everywhere I and my accent go, the chip on my shoulder was not warranted, as they assured me that they loved Americans and especially loved that I talked "like a cowboy." The conversation went a little something like this:

NIGEL: Well, mate, the Jubilee, I mean, come on . . . it might seem a touch of a kerfuffle, and sure, it's annoying, but seventy years!

ME: Yeah, seventy years. That is something.

IAN: You're fookin' right, it is.

NIGEL: I mean, even if I worked in a shithouse fer seventy years, you bet your arse we are throwin' a party!

FARNSWORTH: Yeah, plus the Queen deserves it. It'll probably be her last romp.

ME: Yeah, in America we just can't fathom anything of this magnitude because—

NIGEL: Because your fucker only gets to be up there for four to eight years!

ME: Yes, exactly!

I then explained to them that the closest thing we have to anything like this is maybe when the president comes to your hometown or the big city closest to your hometown. I mentioned that even though I liked Barack Obama, when he visited Chattanooga several years ago, it was a *huge* pain in the ass because of the traffic, the chaos, and the overbearing smell of Sharpies from the not-at-all-clever protest signs made by people who, for some reason, decided to pick 2008 as the year they started caring about politics. When I said that, Ian sparked up.

IAN: Oh, I mean everything *they do* is a pain in the ass, mate, but you know, it's good for the economy and all, innit?

NIGEL: Oh yeah. It's a pisser for all that, no doubt, but you know, we probably like our queen more than you like your presidents. Especially this one.

I mentioned Ian's point about the economy to Trae when I got back to the hotel room, and we felt so stupid that we had never considered it from that position. To us, the royal family had always just been a brazen display of opulence with no benefit to society, but when Ian said that, I was blindsided by how dumb a thought that was for me to have. *Of course* the royal family brings money into the economy because of tourism. Hell, considering how riled up people were for the Jubilee and how many of them came from all over the world to see it, the entire UK was going to see an economic surge from that. And how about the other three-hundred-plus days of the year? Do you think there is ever a moment when Buckingham Palace isn't the backdrop for some dumb duck-lipped teenager's Instagram post?

I would like to point out on behalf of both of us that we are *in no way* meaning to imply that we support the monarchy. Hell no. Kings and queens and shit ain't it, far as we're concerned, but I do now feel a *little* less "let's put their heads on sticks" about the whole thing. Especially when the guys started lamenting the loss of Princess Diana and praising what she meant for the underprivileged, downtrodden, and voiceless among us: "Aye, what she did with just a wee handshake meant more to the cause for AIDS than anything that had been done for it previously. Pretty incredible, innit?"

OK, so I gotta come clean. Because of how Nigel and Ian seemed all tech-bro and because Farnsworth and Lowell were older men, I went into all of this with the assumption that they were super conservative. Tories, I believe they are called over there. Now to each their own, and trust me, growing up where I grew up, I can get along with anyone—but let's just say I have an easier time getting along with a certain type of people, and depending on how someone leans, I may choose to keep my guard up. To me this was all but confirmed when they mentioned how much they loved the Queen. Because in my dumb American brain, that meant they were monarchists, and monarchists *have* to be the British equivalent of a corporate bootlicker. But they also appreciated charity and had empathy for AIDS patients? I almost didn't know what to think! Was this . . . was this nuance? WE DON'T HAVE NUANCE WHERE I COME FROM, CHAPS. *Which side of the aisle are you on?*

We laughed a bit more, downed some more pints, and then there was a rare silence that was broken by one of the scariest questions I had ever been asked. "So, mate," Ian said. "Since you're an American . . . elephant in the room . . . how do you feel about guns?"

Oh. Fuck.

Well, so much for our pleasant evening. I had really assumed that since they didn't have them over there, a conversation like this didn't stand a real chance of happening. That was stupid of me to think, though, because earlier that day the shooting in Uvalde, Texas, had occurred. It was world news that made Trae and me slink around in shame, as we knew everyone on earth was once again looking at the United States and going, "What the fuck is wrong with you?"

I grew up in the South, and oftentimes my ideas don't align with those of a stereotypical Southerner.[5] But I learned early on how to behave if I don't wanna get punched, be screamed at, or, at the very least, ruin a party. I'm not proud of all the times I stood idly by when people said some horrific things I disagreed with, but I *am* saying I like to party.

I'd like to think I've grown, so regardless of what was going to happen when Ian and the fellers heard my honest answer, I decided to give it anyways. "Well, I don't think anyone should have access to something that can mow down an entire classroom in seconds. We have a very sick relationship with firearms in my country, and we put some feigned sense of freedom above a child's right to breathe another breath. And while shotguns and hunting rifles are perfectly fine in the hands of a hunter, even then I think there should be stricter background checks and more safety-class requirements."

I took a deep breath, a swig of my beer, and waited for the fun to be over. Then Nigel spoke up.

NIGEL: Fuckin' right, mate.

IAN: Yeah, I mean, you know yours is the only country where this sort of business happens on a regular basis, yeah?

Well, I'll be thoroughly and utterly goddamned. I did not see that coming. I mean, now that I think about it, I should have, but at the time I was getting ready for a stern talking-to on how the thing they admired most about America was how *free* it was. That's what I'd come to expect from television

---

5. Sometimes they do though. Anyone wanna go mud wrestle my cousin with me?

pundits of a certain persuasion, at least. I was convinced these men were hard-core conservatives when I first met them, but then I heard this, and the coin was completely flipped. Then it hit me what was really going on: In other parts of the world, belonging to a certain political party doesn't mean you have thrown your common sense out the goddamn window. You can believe something when it comes to policy but still be an otherwise rational human being. It was like I had transported back to the damn nineties, which makes sense 'cause Momma always said the Brits were a little behind us on certain things.

Because these guys, like me, also liked to party, we quickly turned the conversation back to something more lighthearted, which was easy once the bartender came up and said to me, "You know who this fella sounds like? Fookin' Dolly Parton!"

Doing a bit, I informed the bartender to watch his mouth because where I came from, Dolly Parton was as revered as any legitimate patron saint. "As a matter of fact," I said, "Dolly Parton's funeral will probably be the closest we ever get to the Queen's Jubilee!"

Ian laughed. "She's sure as shit accomplished more, hasn't she?"

These guys got it. Cheers to my new friends at the Garrick Inn.

Our interactions with the Brits weren't *exclusively* centered around how insane America is, however. In addition to the positively delightful conversations we got into about sports over there, we did run across a few Brits who were elated to run across a pair of "Yanks." Well, in truth, it was mostly the Scots who responded as such. And based on those interactions, there's something we feel the need to say—something that's honestly a bit difficult for two oft-rejected comedians to express. And that is: thank God for Hollywood.

It's possible that any shred of goodwill we Americans have left in the Western world is due to the silver screen. Those other countries can trash us all they want, but they still line up around the block for our celluloid exports. Evidently, to some foreigners (even while in their own country, they're still foreigners to us, dammit!), the images called to mind by an American accent are *not* entirely guns-and-God themed. No, some of them hear our accents and think of secret agents gone rogue, love affairs gone torrid, family vacations gone madcap. Or, in our case—given the *aw-shucks* nature of our drawl—they thought, specifically, of cowboys.

We were dining at an Inverness restaurant when a bubbly lass of around thirty, who put us in mind of Merida from the movie *Brave*, passed us on her way to the loo. When she overheard a fragment of our animated conversation (probably having something to do with gravy), she stopped in her tracks and pointedly inserted herself: "Aye! Yer fookin' YANKS, are ya?"

When we attempted to politely inform her that, actually, for two men of the Southern states, "Yank" was not the preferred nomenclature, she would have exactly none of it. "Fit ye on aboot! Yer fookin' Yanks!" Then she adopted her best and adorably flawed cowboy voice: "Giddyup, mother-fuckers!" And back to the brogue with "Wha'boot 'at? Zat reit, es et?"

Good luck translating our attempt at phonetic Scottish, but we think you get the idea. She was certifiably *thrilled* with our presence and demanded we join her table, where she continued to imitate our accents fairly terribly to the delight of all involved. It seems that much the same way we Americans may hear a British accent and think, *Ooh! Somebody wants a martini shaken, not stirred!* or *Why isn't he wearing a monocle?* some Brits hear us talk and immediately feel like protecting the homestead from an evil railroad man or riding a motorcycle into a swimming pool from the top of a burning building or putting a woman in her place while wearing a fedora. So that's fun.

ACROSS THE POND
TRAVEL BINGO

Look for an object, and the first one to five in a row/column/diagonal wins literally the best candy bar you've ever eaten in your life.

TOWN NAMED _____ SHIRE	AMERICAN TOURIST BEING LOUDER THAN ANYONE ELSE AROUND	PUB MORE THAN FIVE HUNDRED YEARS OLD	OLDER CHAP CLEARLY DISAPPROVING OF SOMETHING OR EVERYTHING	PEOPLE WEARING SUMMER CLOTHES WHEN IT'S NO MORE THAN SIXTY DEGREES FAHRENHEIT OUTSIDE
TOWN NAMED _____ BURY	SOMEONE DRESSED LIKE A HOBBIT	MOST ORGANIZED QUEUE YOU'VE EVER SEEN	PUB WITH A NAME THAT SOUNDS LIKE A FIVE-YEAR-OLD JUST SAID TWO THINGS HE THINKS ARE COOL	TWEED
TOWN YOU COULDN'T PRONOUNCE FOR A MILLION DOLLARS	MAN SMOKING A PIPE		ROUNDABOUT THAT CANNOT BE SERIOUS RIGHT NOW	GROUP OF TEENS SHOUTING UNINTELLIGIBLY ON A TRAIN
PLACE WHERE THEY USED TO TORTURE PEOPLE PUBLICLY	REGULAR PERSON PASSED OUT IN THE STREET OUTSIDE A PUB	A BRUTALLY SUNBURNED PALE MAN	SOMEONE APOLOGIZING TO YOU FOR A REASON THAT IS UNCLEAR TO YOU	BUNCHA PEOPLE SINGING TOGETHER
MORE THAN ONE CASTLE IN LESS THAN FIVE MINUTES	FULL-KIT WANKER (SOMEONE WEARING AN ENTIRE SOCCER UNIFORM)	BIG OL' TEETH	THE SUN AND THEN DREARY RAIN IN THE SAME AFTERNOON	GUARD IN ONE OF THEM OLD-TIMEY GETUPS

A NOTE ON SCOTLAND

Do you recall how we said we expected to connect more with the Scottish than the English? Well, not only was that exactly what happened, but furthermore, many other people expected that *for us*. Before we got there, multiple different English people we met said some version of "I expect you chaps will feel a certain . . . kinship with the Scots." It was a common sentiment. And because we are the way we are—i.e., just *racked* with nigh-immeasurable amounts of generational insecurities—our impulse was to respond to this defensively: "Oh yeah, because they're *dumb*, right? The type of people to cause a drunken and incomprehensible scene at ten in the morning after someone questions their relationship with livestock—is that it?" And it was. That was it.

No, we're kidding. These people didn't mean anything by it (or, hell, maybe they did but we were just too dumb to realize it). More importantly, they were absolutely right. There are a lot of common sensibilities between Southerners and Scots. Firstly, you know how the South generally views Yankees? If you don't, just take a moment to imagine a truck driver in overalls screaming, *"You ain't no bettern me!"* at a college professor who just mentioned a book. Can you picture that? Now you understand how the South feels about the North. Well, that parallels the sentiment the Scots have toward England.

Also, they would *love* to secede. So there's also that. The English conquered and oppressed them and still tell them how to live, and they ain't for it. The South has that going on too. *However*, and it is vitally important that we make this point: The difference is that Scotland *didn't deserve it*. The American South was in desperate need of a bitch-slapping back in the day, and the Union obliged. It's not the same thing. Still, the resentments

212

are similar. The Scots have a chip on their shoulder; they feel looked down upon, and they don't rightly appreciate it.

But that's not all: Like Southerners, Scots are also loud and proud, with an unmistakable cultural identity. They have a rich literary history and pride themselves on their prowess as writers and storytellers. They're musical and lively and endearingly profane; jokes are just straight-up funnier when they tell them. They know how to have a good time and do so in ways likely to make any stuffed shirt wince. They are what they are, to hell with whether you like it.

That's the way it seemed to us anyway. Maybe we saw what we wanted to see. Or expected to see. Because as we mentioned in the introduction, for anyone who is unaware, the peoples in America who came to be known as "hillbillies" have strong ancestral ties to Scotland. Specifically the border area near the north of England, which you may recall is stereotypically considered the . . . *ahem* . . . less refined region of England. Basically, the part of that lovely island that the other parts generally feel is the most disreputable and slow-witted? Well, Southerners, that's where all of our pappaws' pappaws came from. Explains a lot, right?

A couple of other fun facts regarding the connection between the South and Scotland. To start, the Scottish Highlands and the Appalachian Mountains used to be the same thing back in Pangaea days. You know, when all the continents were living in the house together before going off to do their own thing?[1] Well, back then, the Highlands and the Appalachians were the same range. Pretty wild, right? Wilder still, in our opinion, is that if you're from the Appalachian area and you go visit the Scottish Highlands, you can absolutely tell. We know that sounds like bullshit, but on the train up to Inverness, our first foray into the Highlands, we dozed off for a bit. When we woke up, we were stunned by how much it felt like we were riding the rails in East Tennessee.[2] It was striking and moving.

Another fun fact . . . well, actually maybe *fun* isn't the best term to use here, but an *interesting* fact at least: The Confederate flag is based on the flag of Scotland. So, ya know, sorry about that, Scotland. Our bad. Yours is still cool.

So, yes, we did indeed feel an immediate connection to Scotland. With that in mind, let's get into the experience.

---

1. This is as good as we can do geology.
2. Not that anyone would ever do that since America hates trains.

INVERNESS

WHAT THEIR MOTTO SHOULD BE: Whatever it is, you won't be able to understand it. Oh, excuse us. We meant: Whitevur It Tis, Ye Wilnae Be Able tae Ken It

WHAT TO PACK: Something warmer than you think you're going to need.

WHAT TO EAT AND DRINK AND WHERE: Haggis everywhere.

WHAT NOT TO MISS: There's a castle there you can rent to get drunk in. We didn't, but we wish we would have. Also, Loch Ness and every other part of the area.

We mentioned in the introduction to this Scotland section that we were struck by the resemblance of the Scottish Highlands to the hills of Appalachia (from whence we hail). The cockles of our cold, dead hearts were warmed from the moment we entered the Highlands, and damned if our cockles weren't plumb toasty the entire time we were there. A place of incredible beauty, the Highlands are centered around an enchanting town situated at the mouth of the River Ness called, we suppose appropriately, Inverness.

Inverness is hands down one of the most charming and picturesque cities we've ever visited—on either side of the Atlantic. Bisected by the deep-blue river, the two sides of the town compete for aesthetic supremacy. And it's a hard match to call, as everywhere you look on either side, there's another stunning cathedral or literal castle. Even the damn Best Western we stayed at looked like a castle (or a manor or some such big, pretty, old type of building)!

If we're talking "aesthetic supremacy," though, the architecture may lose out when compared to the surrounding landscape. We took a pleasure cruise (a boat ride) on the famous Loch Ness, and while we didn't see that damn water lizard anywhere (monsters tend to be a bashful sort), we saw plenty enough breathtaking wonders to make up for it. If you think sailing across a dinosaur's lake while in constant awe of the verdant expanses en route to a walking tour of a ruined castle sounds like a good time, then we highly recommend Inverness.

We also were treated to a private driving tour of the local Highlands region during our stay. Our driver, whom we'll call Angus on account of his actual name not sounding Scottish enough for us, was a lovely chap of around sixty who reminded us of nothing so much as a sweet ol' Scottish pappaw. Polite, dapper, and dryly funny, he never tired of talking up his homeland.[1] He drove us through the countryside, extolling the virtues of the land and its history. From him we learned all about the local clans, which had a whole different vibe from the starts-with-a-*K* version we're used to. We learned that the already stunning vistas before us were in other parts of the year blanketed in vibrant purple heather. He explained this in a way that sounded almost apologetic to us. Like, "I know it's kind of disappointing right now, but at the right time of year—" which we found hilarious, given the whole Elysian Fields thing the area already had going on *without* the heather. We learned about the local pursuit of "Munro bagging," which as far as we could tell basically amounted to "walking up big hills." Not that we're knocking it; Scotland has some sweet-ass hills. We also learned about the rich tradition of making drunkwater, aka whisky.

Much of our education on this last point was gained on a tour of the Dalwhinnie Distillery, during which we discovered the professional art of gettin' people silly drunk. These people take their whisky *seriously*, y'all. Upon finding out Trae was from Tennessee, they demanded he proclaim the superior Tennessee whiskey before the tour could continue. He said that

---

1. We're also *pretty* sure he was mildly racist. We did say he was a pappaw, after all.

as a white-trash Tennessee boy, he had a long-standing love affair with Jack Daniel's. This response was evidently not satisfactory, though Trae suspects that in the eyes of these purveyors of fine Scotch (never call it Scotch while in Scotland, in case you didn't know), any whiskey from the Volunteer State would be found wanting. Such is their standard—a standard matched by a pride felt for their product—which they would tell you has notes of everything from vanilla to smoke to apple peels, but which your humble authors found to taste mostly of whisky. Such is *our* standard. Anyway, it was a delightful experience.

Before the end of our time with Angus, he treated us to lunch at a greasy spoon off a country road somewhere outside of Kingussie (a real name of a real place). This spot was noteworthy for—and we suspect was selected by Angus precisely because of—its striking resemblance to a country diner one might encounter on a rural route deep in Dixie. That is, the type of ramshackle, run-down place you expect to have tremendous meatloaf and a lackluster health inspection score. In this little harbinger of homesickness, complete with a matronly lady running the register who had a face that seemed to say, "My name is something close to Ruth, and I am not a known taker of shit," we devoured haggis sandwiches and the hands-down best millionaire shortbread either of us had ever had. So good, in fact, Trae has since given up the practice of making said "homemade Twix bars" confectionery in his own kitchen, as each attempt only reminds him of his own inadequacy in comparison. The whole experience was incredible.

This area of the Scottish Highlands is also home to Culloden, which any history buffs or fans of the historical romance drama *Outlander* will immediately recognize as the site of the final battle of the Jacobite uprising. Now, as you may or may not have ascertained, this is no history book,[2] but these are the broad strokes. A group of Scottish rebels known as the Jacobites led an uprising against the Crown in support of a deposed Catholic prince. This uprising came to an end by virtue of a decisive defeat at Culloden Moor.

We bring all of this up not just because of its relevance to the Inverness leg of our trip, but because we found over the course of our time in Scotland that the issues of the Jacobites—their rebellion, subsequent defeat, and its aftermath—arouse strong feelings in some Scots to this day. The historian

---

2. Some of you might argue that *book* is a generous descriptor.

we met with in Edinburgh actually compared it to the feelings surrounding the Confederacy in (some of) the American South—that is, how many still romanticize the failed rebels and their cause to this day despite the reality being far more . . . *complicated*. A couple of notes here: (a) *We* are not saying that; *the historian* said that; (b) we would argue that the reality of the Confederacy was pretty uncomplicated (read: we ourt notta done all that); and (c) the two of us are admittedly far too ignorant about the Jacobites to draw such conclusions about them or their cause. We just felt it was an interesting point that was made to us. Moving on.

In addition to our driver Angus, we interacted with plenty of other charming, welcoming, and memorable people of the Highlands,[3] all while surrounded by the most stunning vistas one could hope for. Put simply, on a trip whereupon many a lifelong memory was made, Inverness and the Highlands were a highlight.

---

3. And one memorable-for-other-reasons encounter with a slack-jawed lad who threatened to whoop Corey's ass for using hand sanitizer. Turns out, that particular brand of dumbassery is an international concern.

SPORTS YONDER YONDER

E ven though where we come from we are considered artsy-fartsy sissy boys who spin yarns and commit japeries in fancy, form-fitting pantaloons, we are both massive sports fans. Football is our shared favorite pastime, and yes, we mean the American (see: real) version. Just kidding 'bout that "real" part, ya wankers. Don't split your powdered wig! 'Tis only a joke. I mean, of course, we do *prefer* American football, but we ain't the type to sit around and make callin' soccer *queer* our whole personalities like some people who look and sound like us. BTW, Americans deciding to call our sport "football" when football was not only already a thing, but was, in fact, the most popular thing in *the whole world* by, like, *a whole lot* is one of the most American things ever done. We'd like to think that went a little something like this:

> **AMERICAN:** We are gonna call it football!
>
> **EUROPEAN:** Oi, we already got footy ova' 'ere!
>
> **AMERICAN:** I can't understand you. You sound like a pirate.
>
> **EUROPEAN:** Ju'even use yer feet innit?
>
> **AMERICAN:** Uh, yeah. When the first three plays don't go our way.
>
> **EUROPEAN:** Well, then *why* is it called football, aye?
>
> **AMERICAN:** Fuck you. FOOTBALL. *(Farts on a corn dog and gives it to a baby)*

As we said, we were fully aware that football (soccer) was the most popular sport in the entire world before we went to the UK. We've seen *Green Street Hooligans*, and we've seen documentaries about referees being murdered for throwing a yellow card on the team the Argentinian mob had picked to win or some shit. We get it.

At least, we *thought* we got it. A bevy of you folks out there are reading this book right now and saying some iteration of "Oh well, Corey and Trae obviously haven't been to the World's Largest Outdoor Cocktail Party to see the Georgia Bulldogs play the Florida Gators. Ain't no sporting event wilder than that!" But you'd be wrong because, yes, *the hell we have been* to the World's Largest Outdoor Cocktail Party,[1] and we are here to tell you right now that it doesn't hold a candle to a World Cup qualifier. We'd also bet that a regular season *fútbol* game would put the NCAA championship to *shame*. These sons of bitches get wild, y'all!

We were hanging out in Manchester one night, drinkin' and eatin' all sorts of birds and trying unsuccessfully to figure out what puddin' was, when it was brought to our attention that Liverpool was playing a pretty big game against Real Madrid. We were going to be in Liverpool the next day, and as such had a vested interest in the outcome of this match. We can get excited for any competitive event we can put our money on, but this opportunity promised a hometown experience. If Liverpool won, we could get jerseys and celebrate with the villagers in the town square where there was sure to be a feast of suckling pig, barrels of wine, and, for our entertainment, a jester fartin' on a goose! We were pregaming a bit in our rooms before heading out, and though we searched frantically for the game on TV, it was nowhere to be found! *Surely*, we thought, *we must not understand how to use these foreign TVs, what with their buttons on the wrong side of the remote and their channels shown in Celsius!*

None of that is true, of course. When we went to the lobby to ask about the channel, we were told: "It ain't on here 'cause this is Manchester and fuck Liverpool!" Well, shit. We had no idea that Liverpool and Manchester had some sort of beef.[2]

Us bein' degenerate gamblers and all that, we knew how to illegally stream the game on our phones, so we watched it on the tiny screen for a few hours while we drank most of the wine the hotel had. Both of us have tried, multiple times, and failed, multiple times, to get into fútbol. It has never

---

1. "Go Dawgs!"—Corey
2. We'll be honest. It sorta seems like every city over there hates all the other cities. We felt sort of at home.

held our attention for long. As stupid Americans, we have been conditioned not to like anything that can end in a tie. But this match was different because *we were there, man!* We were hootin' and hollerin', cursing the refs, callin' Real Madrid players wankers and cunts (it's OK—apparently you can say it over there). Just really gettin' into the spirit of it all.

And then Liverpool lost. Well, shit. Tomorrow wasn't going to be as fun as we thought.

Much like our fathers were when they thought we'd grow up to be real men, we were wrong. When we got off the train in Liverpool, what awaited us on the streets can only be described as pure, unhinged chaos. A sea of red (Liverpool's color) made waves on every block, spilling along the streets, where the cars they were blocking didn't seem to give even the very first shit. They sang a medley of these old, insane soccer songs at the top of their lungs, both separately and in unison somehow. Everyone had some sort of drink in their hands. Some big plastic cups of beer. Some bottles of champagne and wine. Some carried entire cases of Budweiser on their shoulders and tossed the cans out like candy on Halloween. This, by the way, was the first time we had seen Budweiser across the pond. Turns out that even over there it is the official beer of dipshits rioting over sports. Some of them had bottles, and we know what you're thinking: *I bet they didn't smash them on the ground and against the walls in front of the cops!* Are you a fucking idiot? Of course they did! And guess what? The cops didn't give a shit! We think we saw someone give a baby a cigarette. Not sure that had anything to do with soccer.

Now you're thinking, *OK, Trae and Corey, clearly they had won and you are just stupid and don't even know how to watch soccer properly.* I promise you, that is exactly what we thought too. We got our phones out to recheck the score from the night before, assuming that surely we had watched the wrong game. Perhaps we had seen a rerun? I mean, it *had* to be something, because all of Liverpool was acting like a stepdad the day *Chinese Democracy* finally came out!

Naw. What we had seen was true. They had lost. So we sat there in amazement as we watched the city ravaged in a way that makes the last season of *Game of Thrones* seem even more disappointing than it already was. Perplexed, we asked one of the only half-drunk locals what in the Charles Dickens was going on. What we were told made about as much sense as David Lynch directing an episode of *Blue's Clues*.

So *apparently*, though Liverpool had just lost the Champions League final, they had won . . . some other title a few months back? Oh, and they *also* lost the Premier League title but were still . . . champions of something? They were champions of vomiting in front of a kebab stand—we can tell you that!

To break this down for those of you who only know 'bout American football: Imagine if, after losing the 2022 Super Bowl, Joe Burrow and the Cincinnati Bengals had gone back home to a goddamn ticker-tape parade because they had beaten the Baltimore Ravens in week seven. I mean, we would be all for it because fuck the Ravens (Titan up, baby!), but you get what we are saying. We are huge college football fans. We promise that if the Georgia Bulldogs had lost the national championship to Alabama, Corey wouldn't be gettin' drunk and celebrating how great a season they'd had. He'd be gettin' drunk, sure, but really sadly, the way God intended. Soccer just don't make no goddamn sense far as we can figure.

Later that week, however, we were in Inverness the night Scotland was to play Ukraine for a World Cup play-in. We were having prettttty great luck as far as sports were concerned. One more chance to *root root root* for the home team and see what would happen if the sumbitches actually won!

We went to a sports bar a couple hours before the game to make sure we had some prime seats. It was already startin' to fill up with lunatics singing limericks and telling some pretty offensive jokes about women— jokes I promise we did not laugh at even a little. We definitely didn't do that.[3] When you're an American overseas, it's easy to forget that we have the strictest alcohol laws pertaining to age. You also forget just *how* young eighteen- and nineteen-year-olds look. These hooligans in the pub were but suckling babes swaddled in kilt blankets when we were first in sports bars screaming at televisions. It was nice to see that the next generation is the same as us in that regard.

You may have already guessed where this is going. Since our trip was in 2022, and since Scotland was playing Ukraine, absolutely *no one in the world* was rooting for Scotland except for the people of Scotland—and two American jackasses who really wanted to see a bar get destroyed. Matter of fact, Corey tweeted "Go Scotland" before the match, and like a hundred

---

3. Email us and we will tell you our favorite ones.

people unfollowed him. He might as well have posted "Vote Putin!" We get it. But, hell, we are sports fans way more than we are war fans, ya know?

The game started, and the Scots at the bar were absolutely *killin'* us. Something happened that they didn't particularly care for—someone got a yellow card or Ukraine scored or the coach's tie wasn't tied properly. (Who fuckin' knows with these soccer people?) And the place came unglued. The teenagers started hurling their beer glasses on the ground and against the wall. *Oh shit,* we thought. *These aren't the streets of Liverpool; this is a business. This is about to be a problem.* Well, the only "problem" the owners of the bar seemed to have with it was that they were smashing their glasses in anger instead of celebration. When we tell you they didn't give the first bit of a fuck, we mean it. It was unreal. The waiters just walked around with dustpans cleaning it up and giving us a look like, "Aye, it's footy, you'll have that." And you *will* have that. One of the kids in front of us gave us the biggest laugh of our trip when he stood up and screamed at a Ukrainian player on-screen: "Aye, fuck 'em, they can have their freedom next week!"

Scotland ultimately lost—but not before scoring a goal and causing one of the kids, hopeful for a Scots victory, to pick up a chair, stand up on the bar, and start bashing the tiles of the ceiling one by one as the owners of the pub cheered alongside him.

We can't believe we are saying this, but we are telling y'all . . . college football ain't shit.

EDINBURGH

WHAT THEIR MOTTO SHOULD BE: Come Here 'Cause You'll Get Stabbed in Glasgow!

WHAT TO PACK: Layers of clothes 'cause no matter how good it feels outside, them damn castles are cold.

WHAT TO EAT AND DRINK AND WHERE: You may already be worn out on haggis, but even though it's sort of a trash dish, don't be afraid to try it at a fancy restaurant. They do some wild stuff with it.

WHAT NOT TO MISS: Edinburgh Castle, of course!

We had been told all along our journey throughout the Commonwealth that not only was Scotland (regardless of how some members of Parliament see it) a different country, but that Glasgow and Edinburgh may as well be too.

Where we are from, it isn't odd to conceive of two cities in the same country having two completely different personalities, cultures, and—hell—even words! In America we got cities right smack-dab next to each other that feel this way, and it is usually put on full display at least one Friday night each fall when the two neighboring cities strap on their football helmets and play for the pride of the old men in the stands still squeezing into their letterman jackets somehow.

How it was laid out to us, in no uncertain terms, was that Edinburgh was home to all the high-class, highfalutin, high-nosin' high hatters[1] who were too big for their britches, had more money than sense, were born on third base and claiming they'd hit a triple, just entitled, classist, snobby sumbitches.

Whereas we heard Glasgow was where all the low-class, lowborn, low rent payin', low life expectancy, low-down, good-for-nothin', barefoot heathens lived.

Right. So the North versus the South. Got it.

Please understand, this is not *us* saying any of this. This is what people told us. And if it makes you feel better about us saying all that, just know that we not only fit in with the Glasgow type, but we also thought we would prefer it on most occasions.

We stopped in Edinburgh first, and without question, we were more awestruck than we've ever been by the sight of something. As soon as you exit the train station, you feel like you have stepped out of the DeLorean and are on an adventure with Doc and Marty to save his great-great-great-great-great-great-great (you get it) grandfather from getting beat up and called a medieval butthead. It's magical.

The first thing you see is a castle. Well, it's the first thing *we* saw, on account of our brains and eyes not being used to seeing castles. The grand spectacle made what little hair Corey has stand up on the back of his neck. Once its mystic aura has faded and you realize you are just in a place where people live, it's hard to comprehend. As a tourist, you start looking around at people who are texting, talking on their phones, or arguing with a spouse and think, *How are you not seeing this? How can you walk by a castle and pay it absolutely no mind? What are you, one of those dipshits from Glasgow?* Then you remember that they *live* here and see this every day. That is mind-blowing to us.

We would also like to point out that in addition to its erudite reputation, Edinburgh is actually the first spot in Great Britain where we encountered that little thing we like to call "Southern hospitality." While on the escalator at the train station, Corey's water bottle fell out of his backpack because he's basically a full-grown toddler who makes a damn mess everywhere and can't keep up with anything. It tumbled down the stairs and both he and Trae

---

1. Boy, the word *high* is doin' some work here, ain't it?

thought it gone forever. *Oh well. Guess it's just lost and we look like idiots*, we thought. Until a Scottish man roughly our age made his way through the crowd on the steps and handed it back to Corey. "Ya dropped that there, lad, ye might be needin' it," or whatever he said that we could barely understand. We know this doesn't really seem like a big deal, but to this point on our trip, we had not been treated this way. No one was outright *mean* to us (well, except that guy who tried to fist-fight Corey because Corey deigned to wash his hands in public) but no one had gone out of their way to be nice to us either. We assumed they heard our accents and thought, *Oh God, we've started an exchange program with a corn college. Don't look at them or they'll lick our windows.* If so, we cannot blame them for that. But when our first interaction in Edinburgh reminded us of how we do things back home, we welcomed the change and began to understand why the Scots are our ancestors.

Edinburgh is known in our little comedy circle for Fringe—the mother of all arts and culture festivals. If we hear that a comedian won an Emmy, we might think, *Hell, they must've been part of a good staff of writers.* If we hear they were accepted at Fringe, we have no choice but to kiss their ring and humble ourselves! And when you walk around the city for a bit, you can understand why something of that magnitude could manifest itself there. On just about every corner, you'll find an old-timey pub with men staggering out saying something along the lines of "I cannae believe 'at wench was chargin' 'at fer a pint a whisky! Granted, yer not sposed ta drink whisky by tha pint, boot she ain't met me ole lassy at home, 'as she?" Much to our chagrin, these men were not wearing kilts. Also, if this was how the hoity-toity Edinburgh drunks acted, then what depravity awaited us in Glasgow?

Edinburgh is a charming place that jumps right off the page of the old fables we read as young lads. We don't want you to think for a second we are insinuating that the people there are dumb because of the way they talk and behave; rather, that is part of the reason we feel such a kinship with the Scots. They are a brash sort that don't seem to give nary a damn 'bout how anyone feels about them, and they look and act the part. But perhaps, like us, they want you to underestimate them so they can have an edge on ya. To us, that is the perfect petri dish for great art: a misunderstood bunch who has something to prove but not a fuck to give.

We didn't just pass by castles and take pictures for our Instagram. I mean, we did, but we also fulfilled our tourist obligations and went on a guided walkabout within the walls of Edinburgh Castle.

Edinburgh Castle is, in fact, a damn castle. When we were growing up, we would call big houses castles. We would try to imagine what it would be like if we lived in one of these monstrosities. You'd see the castle on TV and in the picture shows and think you grasped the magnitude of it all, but you truly can't until you've actually seen it in person. People who look and sound like us might say of its size: "You could fit 'bout seventeen of Meemaw's trailer inside of just the goddamn dining room of this sumbitch." Hell, the road you take to get there, the Royal Mile, is a pretty damn good hike on its own. More than we'd walk to get a cold beer on a Saturday night, we can tell you that much. The Royal Mile is filled with old-ass houses that must be pretty damn important, considering the Queen herself used to stay there whenever she hauled it up to Edinburgh for a visit. Walking up the cobblestone roads and along the lantern-laced sidewalks, the coal-faced chimney sweeps begged us for a pence and a pie—OK, that was a joke, but it did seem a place where that would happen.

The castle still had a working cannon called the "One O'Clock Gun" that they would fire off at some point during the day, but no one could say when. The whole walkabout was an immersive experience into a bygone era: when kings sat atop thrones gobbling down turkey legs with red wine flowing down the creases of their chins; when a thumb, up or down, determined the outcome of a man's life; when a woman was meant to lie on a bed atop a pea, squeeze out sixteen children, and pray to the gods above that one of them would be a boy lest she be sent to the torture tower to live her remaining days staring out a window wondering why she had to be born in the past.

All of this was in what's known as the Old Town. You see, Edinburgh is separated into two parts: the Old Town and the New Town. The Old Town is what you see in the postcards and the Instagram pictures. The New Town is what you'd see if *Real Housewives of Scotland* were an actual show. That's not a dig on the area—it is very nice and full of swanky shops and hip restaurants—but it's not what you picture when you think of Scotland, and we only point it out to let you know that Edinburgh isn't just a William Wallace wet dream. But it was ours, and we loved it very much.

A NOTE ON REALLY OLD
SHIT YONDER YONDER

There's an adage regarding Americans and our European cousins: "Europeans think a hundred miles is a long way, and Americans think a hundred years is a long time." As is often the case with maxims, this one is both catchy and true. Briefly a note on the first half: Europeans are so used to being able to take a train to France because they wanted a certain type of fancy bread and still making it home for dinner that they generally fail miserably at understanding bigness. And America is big as all get out. Europeans will visit Hollywood and think they're gonna pop up to the Golden Gate Bridge that afternoon before hitting the tables in Vegas that night. Maybe check out the Grand Canyon while they're at it. And that's just Saturday. Tell a European planning a trip to Disney World how far away the Statue of Liberty is, and they'll be astonished. "Sacrebleu!" they'll say. If they're French anyway. Maybe "Blimey!" if they're British, and some long-ass word that sounds vaguely like it might be a threat if they're German. They just can't handle it. We're being cheeky again here,[1] but the discrepancy is a real thing.

Primarily, though, we'd like to focus on the second part of the afore-mentioned adage, regarding Americans and old shit. Way back in the Charleston chapter, we talked about Americans' low standard for historical impressiveness. To us, anything from before they invented color (you know, how everything used to be in black-and-white?) is certifiably old-timey. And then your mammaw's like, "I went to a black-and-white school!" So you say,

---

1. After all, 'tis a cheeky tome, innit?

"First of all, we both know that school was all white, and second . . . yeah, because you're super old!"

Ask an American what happened during the period preceding photographs, and they'll tell you that's when a bunch of powdered-wig-wearing slave owners invented freedom.[2] Before that? Jesus and stuff. We kid, we kid. Plenty of history buffs reside on our side of the Atlantic, but generally speaking, Americans aren't good with things being old. We're just not used to it. Nothing in our country *can* be much older than four hundred years because four hundred years ago we killed everything that was already here and started over. And we didn't *really* get going in earnest until 1776. And sure, we're somewhat aware of the fact that the rest of the world had all kinds of stuff going on for a long time before all that, but none of it matters all that much to us, due to it not being *about* us. After all, if they're being honest with themselves, wasn't the rest of the world basically just sort of sitting around waiting on America to be invented anyway? How important could any of their shit have really been if we weren't there to interfere with it? *Exactly.*

We're being incorrigible smart-asses, but think about it: Your average historical landmark in America is a bank where John Dillinger once shot the name of his gang onto a wall with a tommy gun or whatever. Meanwhile, every other week in England, some pensioner cleans out his cellar and unearths a medieval well with chain mail at the bottom of it. And that sort of thing is crazy to us, OK? The two of us in particular are complete marks for all that as well. On our trip, if we passed a pub sign illustrated with a donkey reading a scroll and the words "The Ass and Spectacles, Est. 1415," we immediately transformed into wide-eyed schoolboys. "Fourteen fifteen? It was still witches then!" But we'd go inside and "Mr. Brightside" would be playing while some guy in a Nike shirt bitched about the weather. Still, we'd get our pints and sit there, sipping and marveling: "Dude. It's like . . . old as hell."[3]

You've probably heard people gush about the beauty of UK cities before, and they are beautiful. Especially to Americans. Maybe it's 'cause the two of us are hicks, but Edinburgh in particular took our breath away.[4] And

---

2. We're even worse with irony than we are with time.
3. You don't have to be erudite to marvel.
4. That could also be because we're fat Yanks and as such often struggle with our breath.

we think the reason for this aesthetic impression was because of how *old* everything looked. Not literally everything, since they have their shiny high rises too; but around every corner we found something all . . . cathedral-y, staring us right in the face. And it was striking. We all know about the castles, and yes, the Scots are indeed eaten up with castles. Side note: Y'all think countryside youths have castle parties over there, the way we do with barns? Like, are young lads and lasses drinking too many Brit-equivalent-of-Smirnoff-Ices and losing their virginity in dungeons or on battlements or some such? Probably not, but it'd be pretty cool if they did.

Anyway, where were we? Oh right: It's not just the castles. The churches, the universities, the government buildings, and the museums too (the Kelvingrove Art Gallery and Museum in Glasgow beat just about any damn thing we'd ever seen, y'all). The point is, you can walk around any given UK city and see buildings that look like *MTV Cribs* set in the *Bridgerton* universe. It's truly impressive, and again, *especially* if you come from the land of strip malls and McMansions.

But you think to yourself, *Well, yeah, it makes sense that everything there looks so much older than in America . . . everything there* is *so much older than in America.* Totally checks out. But here's the thing: If you go on a few architecture tours in the UK, you discover that the vast majority of those venerable, imposing, seemingly ancient edifices you've been appreciating were built, or at least took their current form, in the 1800s! Now, we don't know how up on American history y'all are, but *we were totally a thing then*. And a very busy and industrious thing at that. In the 1800s, America was laying down railroads and revolutionizing industrially and oppressing various peoples and fighting a war with ourselves and just expanding and building *like it was our job*. And we've pretty much kept that same job ever since, come to think of it. The point is, while they were throwing up and finalizing grand structures that would impart a sense of majesty and magnificence for generations to come, we were over here just . . . panning for gold and building whorehouses in Kansas, we guess?

No, there's obviously more to it than that. While it did blow our minds when we first found all this out, there are legitimate explanations for it. Ultimately, it still comes down to our country's relatively young age. During the Victorian era, when many of these structures took shape, the UK was a firmly established global power with a long and proud history, and we were naught but a suckling babe of an empire, with a laser focus on expansion and trail-blazing. Ain't got time to work on a damn necropolis when you're busy manifesting destiny, baby! They had a past to care about; we were all about the future. It was a grand new era, and by God we were gonna dominate it—the American way. Well, part of that happens to be tearing down old shit so you can replace it with new, fancier shit. And doing that again. And again. Until eventually you got a bunch of overly modern cities with buildings whose defining characteristics are "glass" and "square." And look, skyscrapers are cool too. But we do wish we had held on to at least a *little bit* more of our humble, old-world beginnings. At least as far as the architecture goes. The humble, old-world beliefs and ideas can stay in the damn past.

GLASGOW

So now we've been with the Scottish "Yanks" as we'd call 'em. We've seen what passes for high-class livin' with the Gaels. We ate fancifully plated haggis and root vegetables and drank the warmest beer the country had to offer. But now it's time for us to tell you about where the rednecks are.

To illustrate what Glasgow folk think about Edinburgh folk, we were told by the first person we met that "a Glasgow stabbing is more fun than an Edinburgh wedding!" If that ain't just 'bout the most red-ass-Southern-United-States shit we done ever heard! Taking your region's less than glamorous reputation and turning it into a point of pride is a type of art we know well, and support fully.

Because we are taking this book serious and wanted to get straight to work, the first thing we did was go get drunk at a pub and eat—what else— more haggis! The first thing we noticed was that, sure enough, prices were a touch lower in Glasgow than in Edinburgh. We guess you can chalk it up to Edinburgh bein' the capital and all, and since it's a more popular tourist spot, they know they can get our dumb asses to buy anything there. But Glasgow is a bigger city. By a lot. And if one thing is true where we come from, the big city is always more expensive. "They must be real proud of this goddamn cheeseburger!" our pappaws would say.

Glasgow also has more of a "punk" feel, if that makes sense. Both Edinburgh and Glasgow were stunning visually, but walking around Glasgow was like walking around a rock hall, whereas Edinburgh was like a garden where you drink beer. Glasgow has murals everywhere—it's colorful in that way—but it also has a rustic look to it from years of port industry. I hope you understand, in this case, that *rust* is meant as a compliment. When it's the bumper of your truck, rust is bad. When it's the vibe of your city, rust is badass as hell.

A contradiction to this vibe was the *ton* of restaurants that were either outright vegan or had a bountiful selection of vegan options. We aren't saying that's a bad thing. I mean, it ain't for us, but having that option is great. We did not expect as much from a place we were told was a Gaelic honky-tonk, ya feel?

During our barhopping, aka "work," we came across a bar with a sweet little patio. We thought we'd stop there for drinks so we could do as the trash do and vape our fruity-flavored space cigarettes without fear of being thrown out. As soon as we sat down and ordered, a gaggle of bridesmaids surrounding a sash-covered bride-to-be approached us. *Oh goody, they have stupid bachelorette parties here too!* They all spoke to us at the same time and all with different pitches of the same indiscernible accent. It was like a Panama City Beach quartet singing about their favorite seltzers in harmony, only in a different, equally as redneck voice. After doing to them what so many do to us and asking them to repeat themselves about five times so we could (a) understand them, and (b) laugh, we finally figured out that they were asking us for a cigarette. As we do with most women we talk to, we let them down. Instead of being sane and saying, "Oi, at's all right, there's four of us on a literal bachelorette party and we don't have any either!" they opted to laugh and point at us and call us what we can only assume were homophobic slurs. We may not speak their language, but we are multilingual when it comes to being called queers. We didn't mind though. Made us miss our uncles.

Once the sun started to go down, we had a downright brilliant idea: Let's keep drinking! We stumbled into another dimly lit bar that had two designated cold taps, which had become a requirement for us by this point because it was unseasonably warm and we are trash who require a "cold drank."[1]

We sat down at a corner table and noticed a guitar and a fiddle behind a tip jar sitting onstage. So they *did* take tips for something . . . huzzah! A burly man approached the microphone and picked up the guitar. We normally refrain from commenting on people's weight (unless it's our fat asses) but we only point it out here so you can get the visual that his belly was such a shelf for the guitar that it almost made a strap pointless. He could just kind of smush it in there. This provided him a unique positioning for plucking the strings like you would a piano. And boy, did he ever pluck them. He played a medley of Gaelic folk songs that we'd give anything to remember right now, but we were so emotionally moved that our phones (which we were using to take notes) remained firmly in our pockets because, boys and girls and friends beyond the binary, you don't pull your phone out in church!

After a few hymns, he started to strum the very familiar Oasis smash hit "Wonderwall." Now in America, a man playing "Wonderwall" on an acoustic guitar is such a cliché that you will get shit on if you try it, but perhaps, we thought, that's not how it was for them? I mean, Glasgow is famously where Oasis was first signed—so maybe it was like their "Free Bird," and you don't dare make fun of those playing "Free Bird" (or at least you don't in front of us, by God!).

As we sat there, prepared to hear a Scottish man's version of the song we grew up loving, he approached the first verse, stopped abruptly, and said, "Just kiddin'. I ain't playin' that shite!" The crowd burst with laughter, most of all from the two drunk American comedians who appreciate a well-timed joke, no matter the setting.

---

1. A drank that is cold.

After that, it was time to shift gears, and he picked up the violin—or the fiddle, as we call it. Again, we would kill to know what he was playing, but he sounded like what them sumbitches on the *Titanic* were playin' when that bastard finally broke in half and was never seen again, until by Bill Paxton (RIP).

He was singing no words, but the fiddle said them all as it cried out across the bar. The crowd sat in silence, some with their eyes closed as if praying or remembering the loss of a loved one. Or they were drunk and passed out. Who's to know?

About that time, a chubby little bald man who looked like he'd be the day manager at a Home Depot approached the stage, turned to the crowd, crossed his arms, and transformed from man to angel. It was unbelievable— much like the first time one of our buddies put a Flowmaster on his Ford Ranger. That little thing ain't s'posed to sound like that, but damn, it sounded good.

He was singing in Celtic or Gaelic—we're not sure which one or if there was a difference—but it didn't matter. You could tell what he meant by his inflection and mannerisms. It was one of the most emotional things we have ever been a part of. The crowd swayed slightly with their eyes either closed or full of tears, ours included.

You could tell he was a working man, and this song was of his people. In that moment, no matter the differences between the patrons in the bar, we were all one—people who had more in common than we did otherwise. If we had to say, it was sorta like bein' back home in North Georgia and East Tennessee. This is where our people got it from, and thank God for that.

CONCLUSION

ONE MORE THING BEFORE
WE MOSEY ON OUT!

Well, we sure hope you enjoyed reading about our various dalliances in vagabondery[1] as much as we enjoyed living them! It has always been our dream to travel around the world, and to get paid for it beats 'bout all we've ever seen. We sure appreciate all of you who make our silly little careers possible.

Nuance is vital in life, so let us be frank: We also very much enjoy doing *nothing*, and both of us love the comforts of our homes more than just about anything you can't melt over chips. But something about this trip across the pond stirred within us something that no other trip ever has. That's not to say we weren't blown away the first time we saw Yellowstone National Park or weren't filled to the brim with extreme (if undeserved) patriotism the first time we walked the cobbled streets of historic Boston. We love this country, we love history, and we love having friends from all over the place so we can better see things from a wide array of perspectives. OK, it's mainly for the different foods, but still! That said, over the past six years of touring, we revisited some cities so many times that traveling in the States had become a rote part of the job instead of a thrilling new endeavor.

This all changed when we got to Great Britain and experienced *new* for the first time in quite a while! Something about being somewhere you've never been will force your head to swivel more. Your surroundings won't

---

1. If that ain't a word, it is now, by God.

blur into your subconscious. We were alive and enthralled in every moment, and we daresay it awoke the travel bug we had sorta kept at bay for years. How stupid were we to have never stepped outside our own country before?[2] Oh, wait, we forgot about Canada. So stepping out of North America, that is. But you can get drunk and wake up in Canada or Mexico, so that's hardly the same. What else is out there waiting to be cast upon by these hillbilly eyes?

We have so many unanswered questions to get to the bottom of! How do the French stay so skinny when they put butter on damn near everything? Do Italians have some secret pasta they aren't telling us about? Do German preschool teachers also sound like Bond villains when they are passing out juice? Is it true that in Japan one out of every eight dogs is actually a robot? We don't know! But we sure as hell want to find out.

We want to go to Spain and watch pretty men in Mickey Mouse hats narrowly escape being gored by bulls . . . We want to go to the Netherlands and let a grandma with pigtails fit us for wooden shoes . . . We want to go to Australia and have a knife fight with a gigantic spider.

Some experiences along our journeys we could have done without (places with warm beer, places with low-alcohol beer, places with no beer), but just as frequently, we found things we wish we could have at home all the time (taco trucks, titty bars, the Perpendicular Gothic architecture of England). And at the end of the day, ain't that what makes the world great?

Take it from us. The next time someone invites you somewhere you ain't ever been, go. You may just find out that the key to your happiness lies in a faraway land you had previously considered out of reach. You might discover that your new favorite food is something you didn't even know existed! Hell, you may mess around and find that the love of your life has been working at the Buckingham Palace gift shop all along, waiting for you to come in and buy your niece a teddy bear. Or you may be miserable and have diarrhea the whole time. It's a toss-up. At least you have something to talk about when you get back home.

Take care, y'all!

---

2. Except on a cruise, but, hell, they don't count 'cause you're still with people who sound like you in matching Martina McBride cutoffs.

ACKNOWLEDGMENTS

FROM TRAE

The great philosopher Winnie-the-Pooh once said, "How lucky I am to have something that makes saying goodbye so hard." To Katie, Bishop, and Benton: Thank you for that, and, more so, for being there when I return.

To my dad (RIP): Thank you for putting the notion of travel in my head. You used to talk about how one day we'd see the South together. The universe, cold bastard that it is, had other notions. But this book is for you.

To Paige: Thanks for always being there and making me laugh. To Mema and Uncle Tim, thanks for always believin'. To Mama, who honestly was the first believer on the list, thank you too.

And lastly, of course, I have to thank my partner in wanderlust, my hetero road and life mate, the Man with Wine in His Room, the Cho himself, Corey Ryan Forrester. Hell of a thing we get to do, ain't it?

FROM COREY

To my dad, who instilled in me a lifelong love of the road trip; to my mom, who made sure we never got lost; and to my sister, who kept me company in the back seat.

To my wife, for always riding shotgun no matter the destination.

To my son, Bain, and my nieces, LJ and Sadie, and my nephew, Barrett: I don't actually know if I want you to read this book, but I hope its existence encourages you to follow your dreams as wildly as I did mine. You are much brighter than me anyhow. ☺

ACKNOWLEDGMENTS

To my Granny Bain, who I still miss every day. You'd be mad at what the English call biscuits.

And to Trae, who my wife calls my soulmate. On my Granny Bain's porch we used to get drunk and dream of this. We said we'd wait to go to Europe until we tricked someone into paying for it, and look at us now, baby! How do you like them apples?

In terms of the book itself, first and foremost the single most important person in the entire process of this tome's authorship was Bessie Gantt. Turning our hayseed, half-English musings into an actual book fit for consumption by actual people is the very definition of a Herculean effort, and Bessie, for the second time, you did it with the patience and grace of a saint. Thank you.

Also, thanks and big ups to Amy Hughes and Nat Goldberg, a bit of a dream team when it comes to convincing people that we can do this. On that note, thanks to Andrea Nisbet and thanks to HarperCollins, in particular Meaghan Porter, Matt Baugher, Kara Brammer, and Kevin Smith, for coming to believe as much as well. And for the trip of a lifetime. It's been a blast.

ABOUT THE AUTHORS

TRAE CROWDER grew up in Celina, Tennessee, a town sometimes described as having "more liquor stores than traffic lights" (2–0 as of last count). Trae first gained national attention for his "Liberal Redneck" series of viral videos. He has been performing his particular brand of gravy-covered intellectual comedy for over a decade and touring nationally with Corey and their comedy and drinking partner, Drew.

COREY RYAN FORRESTER grew up in Chickamauga, Georgia, where he fell in love with comedy watching Carson and then Leno from a blanket on the floor next to his daddy, Dale. At sixteen, lying about his age, he worked up the nerve to do his first open mic. He spent the next decade hawking jokes at night, then waking up to do random day jobs. He also ran the family bakery with his mom, where he was known as "Head Quiche Chef." These days he tours with Trae and Drew on the wellRED stand-up tour, making all his comedy dreams come true.

The Liberal Redneck Manifesto: Draggin' Dixie Outta the Dark, Trae and Corey's first book, written along with their buddy Drew, was published by Atria in 2016.